AL-JAZEERA AND US WAR COVERAGE

PETER LANG
New York • Washington, D.C./Baltimore • Bern
Frankfurt • Berlin • Brussels • Vienna • Oxford

TAL SAMUEL-AZRAN

AL-JAZEERA AND US WAR COVERAGE

PETER LANG
New York • Washington, D.C./Baltimore • Bern
Frankfurt • Berlin • Brussels • Vienna • Oxford

Library of Congress Cataloging-in-Publication Data

Samuel-Azran, Tal.
Al-Jazeera and US war coverage / Tal Samuel-Azran.
p. cm.
Includes bibliographical references and index.
1. Al Jazeera (Television network)
2. Television broadcasting of news—Objectivity—Qatar.
3. Television broadcasting of news—Objectivity—United States.
4. Afghan War, 2001-—Mass media and the war.
5. Iraq War, 2003-—Mass media and the war. 6. Mass media and war—Qatar.
7. Mass media and war—United States. I. Title.
PN1992.92.A39.S36 070.4'3335670443—dc22 2009039369
ISBN 978-1-4331-0865-5 (hardcover)
ISBN 978-1-4331-0864-8 (paperback)

Bibliographic information published by **Die Deutsche Nationalbibliothek**.
Die Deutsche Nationalbibliothek lists this publication in the "Deutsche Nationalbibliografie"; detailed bibliographic data is available on the Internet at http://dnb.d-nb.de/.

The paper in this book meets the guidelines for permanence and durability of the Committee on Production Guidelines for Book Longevity of the Council of Library Resources.

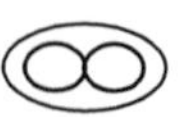

29 Broadway, 18th floor, New York, NY 10006
www.peterlang.com

Printed in the United States of America

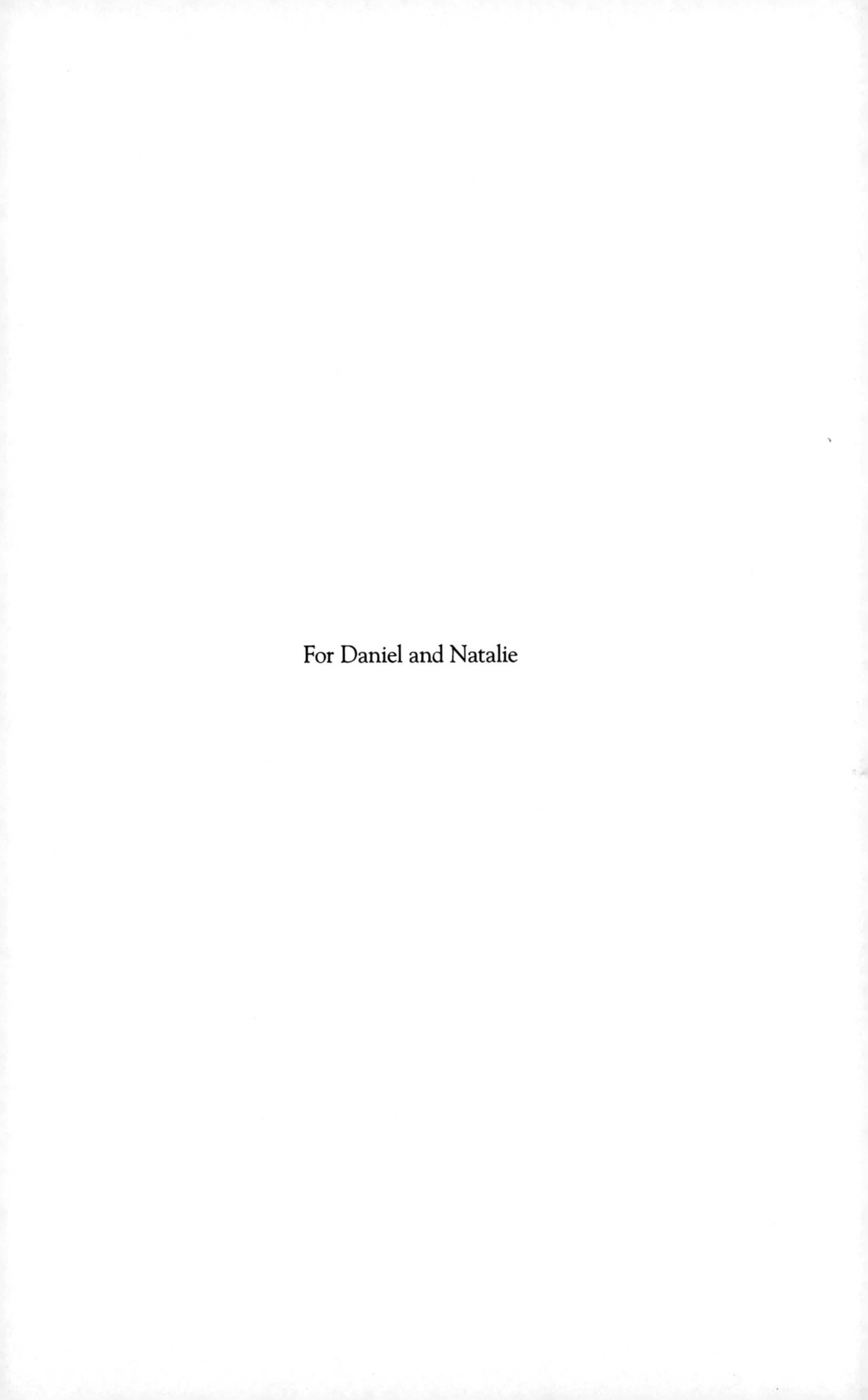

For Daniel and Natalie

TABLE OF CONTENTS

FOREWORD – PROFESSOR SIMON COTTLE ix

INTRODUCTION 1

CHAPTER ONE AL-JAZEERA AND THE MEDIA GLOBALIZATION ARGUMENT 7

CHAPTER TWO AL-JAZEERA RE-SHUFFLES THE GLOBAL INFORMATION ORDER 13
The Western media and "cultural imperialism" 14
Counter-hegemonic global news and the subsequent "information war" 17

CHAPTER THREE ANTI-HEGEMONIC IMAGES IN US WAR REPORTING 23
War images and the development of censorship 23

CHAPTER FOUR IS AL-JAZEERA A LEGITIMATE NETWORK? 31
Al-Jazeera: An advocate of Qatar's interests? 31
Al-Jazeera: A religious network? 33
Al-Jazeera: Cross-cultural understanding? 35

CHAPTER FIVE DISREGARDING THE PAIN OF OTHERS: THE WAR IN AFGHANISTAN 41
The military frame 43
How the networks self-censored the biggest war story 47

CHAPTER SIX THE ENEMY'S VOICE 53
The Administration's position on Al-Qaeda Messages 54
The Bin Laden videos and the debate re Al-Jazeera's credibility 56
CNN's exposé of Bin Laden's Al-Jazeera interview 67

CHAPTER SEVEN THE WAR IN IRAQ 73
Discrediting the message: The double standard in image censoring 77
Discrediting the messenger: Building the "Al-Jazeera is biased" frame 80
The Battle of Fallujah: "Why Show Civilian Casualties?" 86
The Abu Ghraib photos and the "Information War" 89

CHAPTER EIGHT THE DARLING OF THE ALTERNATIVE MEDIA WEB SITES: english.aljazeera.net 93
Re-presentation of english.aljazeera.net reports 94
What did Western internet users derive from Al-Jazeera reports? 96
Implications 99

CHAPTER NINE AL-JAZEERA ENGLISH IN THE US 101

CHAPTER TEN CONCLUSIONS 113

APPENDIX A METHODOLOGY 117

APPENDIX B DISCOURSES OF THE GLOBAL PUBLIC SPHERE 121

APPENDIX C POLITICAL COMMUNICATION THEORIES OF WAR REPORTING 125

APPENDIX D THE RELATIONS BETWEEN QATAR, ISRAEL AND THE US 133

APPENDIX E THE IMPACT OF WARTIME IMAGES ON PUBLIC OPINION 137

REFERENCES 141

INDEX 153

FOREWORD

Al-Jazeera, the pan-Arabic satellite television channel, was first set up with financial backing from the Emir of Qatar in 1996 following the demise of the London-based BBC and Saudi Arabian Arabic television network. Since then it has become catapulted around the world as a major source of non-Western news – a startling feat given the hitherto and seemingly entrenched Western monopoly of the international news marketplace. Its contribution to the transformation of broadcasting and journalism practices in many Arab states would be hard to over-estimate. In the West, however, Al-Jazeera appears to have principally become known for its confronting style of journalism and regional perspectives on the world post 9/11. In particular, controversies surrounding its reporting of the invasions of Afghanistan in 2001 and Iraq in 2004, its circulation of video messages from Osama Bin Laden, transmission of graphic scenes of Iraqi civilian casualties and images of US military dead and injured as well as US prisoners of war.

Predictably, perhaps, it has incurred considerable 'flak' from the US Government as well as other mainstream broadcasters. In the context of invasion and insurgency, 'flak' should not be assumed to be discursive in nature only but can also assume deadly form. The Al-Jazeera Baghdad bureau was shelled by an American missile on April 8, 2003, killing Tariq Ayoub one of its correspondents, and this despite the news organization having previously informed the Pentagon about the bureau's exact location. The Al-Jazeera office in Kabul in the Afghanistan invasion in 2001 was also deliberately targeted by an American missile. Like the messenger of old it seems, bringing unfavorable news to the Emperor is fraught with risk.

Al-Jazeera today for many has come to symbolize the democratizing promise of new global communication flows and the expanded range of views and voices, images and ideas, discourses and dialogue emanating from different vantage points and perspectives around the world and now increasingly infused into an encompassing global communications and media environment. Here contra-flows of news, images and commentary are often thought to productively enter into the Western mainstream news media, revealing as they do so something of the geo-politics of international power, entrenched cultural differences and outlooks and also the dissonance of different styles and professional norms of journalism. At least that's the often heard claims and promise of Al-Jazeera and other emergent non-Western news organizations. But how realistic are these claims about the pluralization of views and the democratizing impacts of 'counter-hegemonic' contra-flows of news entering Western mainstream news media discourse? In times of crisis, times of war, what has been the distinctive contribution of Al-Jazeera's journalism and how exactly has it influenced and been represented in the Western news media? Much hangs on the answers to these questions, both politically and theoretically.

Tal Samuel-Azran's *Al-Jazeera and US War Coverage* sets out to tackle these important questions head on. Based on detailed PhD scholarship, his book provides a timely and necessary contribution to wider debates about, and the theorization of, contemporary global news flows and how new regional news players either help to pluralize and democratize the traditional Western dominance of news and contribute to an emergent global news sphere or, alternatively, become effectively co-opted and politically neutered when 're-presented' within and through the Western news prism. Going against the grain of much current thinking in the field of international and global media scholarship, Samuel-Azran argues that the spectacular rise of Al-Jazeera should not be simply taken as evidence for an emergent and democratizing global public sphere. On the basis of his detailed empirical analysis such *globalist* pretensions, he argues, are premature and a far cry from Al-Jazeera's actual contribution to US news media discourse that has remained in times of crisis stubbornly nationalistic and wedded to US political interests.

His thesis, then, is that the US media's use of Al-Jazeera news reporting has in fact eroded, not enhanced, the counter-hegemonic debate in US war reporting and this is principally because the US Administration managed to persuade US networks to see themselves pitted against Al-Jazeera in an 'information war'. Notwithstanding the heavy use of news and film reports originated by the Qatar-based news service, and documented in this study, the US networks are found to have systematically self-censored newsworthy war images and crucial events such as accidental bombings of innocent civilians, reformatted 'counter-hegemonic' material, and labeled the news provider as a 'deviant' network. Paradoxically it is the global rise and stature of Al-Jazeera, argues Samuel-Azran, that may actually have strengthened the bond between the US Administration and the US media and inadvertently led to the minimization of media dissent against the US Government and its policies in Afghanistan and Iraq.

This analysis is not confined to the major US TV news network alone, nor should it be given the complex flows, formations and different mediums of today's world news ecology. Samuel-Azran's study also attends to Al-Jazeera's English language website and the Al-Jazeera English channel and their reception, respectively, by news bloggers and cable and satellite carriers. Only on rare occasions does he find 'counter-publics' represented that oppose the anti-Al-Jazerra lobby, and rarer still are examples of Al-Jazeera's news reports being used in their original, integral, form or without preceding 'health warnings'. This further points, says Samuel-Azran, to the success of the US Administration's capacity to influence media and communication networks and limit public discourse.

The era of media globalization, concludes the author, is all too easily asserted by media and communication theorists today but on closer inspection things are far less clear cut. Communication flows in fact continue to exhibit, and communication controls continue to exert, a heavy Western-centric and ethnocentric bias, especially in times of war. In this 'global' context, talk of transnational news discourse, an emergent global public sphere and alternative news contra-flows too often remain blinkered to the continuing operation of US hegemonic power and the general subservience of the news media. Whatever one's preferred views and thinking on such matters, this book offers an important opportunity to move beyond generalizing statements about media globalization and democratizing communication flows and to reappraise how infusions and insertions from outside the heartland of Western new media actually become channeled in practice and conditioned in the encounter with the US mainstream news media. This, it seems to me, represents an important advance in our understanding of the complexities of the operations of power in today's global communications environment.

Professor Simon Cottle

INTRODUCTION

In the wake of the horrific September 11, 2001 events and the ensuing "war on terror", Al-Jazeera has become a major player on the global news scene and a global household name due to its exclusive positioning behind enemy lines in Afghanistan and Iraq. Throughout the war, news networks worldwide including the United States (henceforth US) media empires CBS, NBC, ABC, CNN and even the conservative Fox News added Al-Jazeera - a network that was often referred to as an entity that "speaks the enemy's language" - as a regular source for images of civilian and military casualties from the battlefield. The astonishing fact is that between the horrific events of September 11, 2001, and September 4, 2004, the day the US-installed Iraqi interim government shut Al-Jazeera in Iraq indefinitely, the five major US stations mentioned above re-presented 2732 news items from Al-Jazeera (*Lexis-Nexis* news archive , 2009). The unprecedented use of information from the warzone provided by Al-Jazeera is significant since it marks a transformation in the way war is being reported in the US. Whereas US reporters traditionally struggled with the Pentagon's censorship of events in the battlefield, Al-Jazeera has bypassed these restrictions, disrupting the power-balance between the Administration and journalists by securing access to events traditionally kept away from the camera's eye.

Already on October 6, 2001, the eve of the war on the Taliban forces, the then anonymous Al-Jazeera was the only source that had secured a place behind enemy lines due to its exclusive positioning in Kabul and Kandahar. This was not only a matter of luck; while the US networks maintained no bureaus in Afghanistan (due to local viewers' lack of interest in the Afghan civil war) and the Taliban expelled the few Western journalists who remained in Afghanistan before the war began, Al-Jazeera was allowed to stay in the battlefield due to its strong ties with the Taliban. While the US Administration argued that these ties involved links to terrorists and tried to brand the channel a mouthpiece for the Taliban and Al-Qaeda, Al-Jazeera insisted that they are a legitimate source that formed these links throughout years of coverage of the Afghan civil war. In light of Al-Jazeera's strong presence in Afghanistan, on the eve of the war two of America's leading channels - CNN and ABC - signed content exchange agreements with the channel.

As the war on terror progressed, it became obvious that Al-Jazeera's arrival onto the global news scene with its exclusive access to events was not coincidental. On the fourth day of the war in Iraq (February 22, 2003), Al-Jazeera distributed graphic images of dead US soldiers and prisoners of war which reached audiences worldwide, including the news media in Australia and the United Kingdom, the US's closest allies. The global spread of these non-traditional images was one of the reasons that US networks CNN and CBS decided to show glimpses of the brutal deaths despite the US Administration's protests.

A year later, in April 2004, Al-Jazeera again frustrated the Pentagon when it aired exclusive "controversial" images of Iraqi victims in the US army battle against Muqtada Al-Sadr's militia in Fallujah.

As a result of these journalistic scoops and their resonance, Al-Jazeera has become a brandname in the US. In 2004 Al-Jazeera was nominated by the *Webby* Awards team (the "Oscar" equivalent of website design) as one of the five finalists for the "best news Web sites" award, along with BBC News, and *National Geographic*. That year it was also voted by the annual Manhattan-based Brandchannel.com Readers' Choice Award survey as one of the top five global brands, after Apple, Google, IKEA and Starbucks and before Coca-Cola, Nokia, *Nike* and *Toyota*. In 2006 the same audience survey selected it as "the most impactful news channel in the world". That Al-Jazeera has become a topic of interest in the US can also be illustrated by the success of the 2004 documentary film *Control Room* (which followed the Al-Jazeera team throughout the early days of the war Iraq). In its opening weekend at the prestigious Film Forum Cinema in New York, every performance was sold out (Usher, 2004).

Al-Jazeera's ambition to expand its presence in the West is ever-growing. Not content with reaching Western audiences solely through re-presentation on Western media, Al-Jazeera has pushed to foster *direct* contact with Western viewers. Already in November 2001 it added English subtitles to its broadcasting 12 hours a day in the United States and Europe. In February 2003, during the early days of the Iraq War, it launched an English news website, which allowed surfers worldwide to access Al-Jazeera directly without the mediation of Western media. According to *Alexa* 2009 global statistics (Alexa, 2009), Al-Jazeera's Arabic website is one of the most popular 1000 websites on the web, with 15.7% of its traffic coming from the US (significantly more than any other country on the list). A further move to win a Western audience took place on November 15, 2006, when it launched a 24/7 television channel in English. The channel proudly declared its aim as "emphasizing news from the developing world, without an Anglo-American worldview" as well as "revers[ing] the [North to South] flow of information" (Al Jazeera, 2009).

What is the significance of this unprecedented rise of an Arab news channel into US consciousness? Nine years into the war on terror, most globalization scholars are certain that the arrival of Al-Jazeera's images into the heart of the American news scene signify an "information revolution", where the Arab perspective penetrates Western discourse. They assert that Al-Jazeera's popularity in the West marks the weakening of the US hegemony on information in favor of a more cross-cultural, transnational discourse. They also claim that Al-Jazeera's success proves that under globalization the boundaries between center and periphery become blurred as even a network originating in the peripheral Qatari Emirate can influence the politics of "the dominating center". The result: A world where cultural differences between nations gradually melt and understanding of the other side's perspective increases as cultures become relativized to each other.

More specifically, the *Al-Jazeera effect* is described as a gradual weakening of the "old system" of the nation-state in the West in favour of cross-cultural dialogue. It is argued that thanks to the wide distribution of Al-Jazeera's images, US discourse has finally opened up to a non-Western perspective and that the Qatari stations' footage can "enforce political pressure on national politics and provide a communication realm, which would otherwise not be possible on a national level." (Volkmer, 2002, p. 243). Books published on Al-Jazeera in the last few years illustrate the argument: From *Al-Jazeera: How the Free Arab News Network Scooped the World and Changed the Middle East* (El-Nawawy and Iskandar, 2003), through *Al-Jazeera: The Inside Story of the Arab News Channel That is Challenging the West* (Miles, 2005) to *Mission Al-Jazeera: Build a Bridge, Seek the Truth, Change the World* (Rushing, 2007), and until the recent *The Al-Jazeera Effect: How the New Global Media Are Reshaping World Politics* (Seib, 2009) where the Al-Jazeera effect argument is summed as follows:

> ...Al-Jazeera is a paradigm of new media's influence. Ten years ago, there was much talk about "the CNN effect," the theory that news coverage—especially gripping visual storytelling—was influencing foreign policy throughout the world. Today, "the Al-Jazeera effect" takes that a significant step further ... "The media" are no longer just the media. They have a larger popular base than ever before and, as a result, have unprecedented impact on international politics. The media can be tools of conflict and

> instruments of peace; they can make traditional borders irrelevant and unify peoples scattered across the globe. This phenomenon, the Al-Jazeera effect, is reshaping the world. (Seib, 2009)

However, based on a comprehensive empirical analysis, this book calls for a paradigm shift in the perception of the Al-Jazeera effect. The analysis presented in this book reveals that the global clout of the Qatari station actually makes it an agent that strengthens the bond between the US media and the Administration and minimizes media dissent against the US Government actions during wartime. This is a result of the US Government's success in persuading the US networks that they are fighting an "information war" against Al-Jazeera, and that the Arab network is a deviant source (without substantial proof). The book reveals how, as a result of this perceived information war, the US media has developed new tactics of sovereignty protection such as the systematic self-censorship of legitimate and newsworthy war images from Al-Jazeera without regard to basic principles of professionalism. This includes the self-censorship of events considered newsworthy throughout former conflicts, such as the accidental bombings of innocent citizens. These newsworthy images have been considered "contaminated" throughout the war on terror due to their Arab source and as a result the overall criticism of war has been significantly reduced. The analysis also reveals that in the rare cases that Al-Jazeera did manage to enforce images on the US networks, the US media reformatted the counter-hegemonic material from Al-Jazeera in a manner that demonized both the message and its messenger.

The book argues that the media globalization idea in general and the Al-Jazeera effect in particular is a myth that blinds us from seeing the true direction war coverage is taking in an interconnected world. Through the case study of Al-Jazeera's interplay with US media it reveals that when mainstream society feels threatened by [counter-hegemonic] globalization processes, local debate becomes even more *centralized* and *ethnocentric*.

This two-part book consists of 10 chapters. The first part provides the historical and theoretical context for the analysis. The second part consists of an empirical analysis of Al-Jazeera report transmission by US media. Chapter 1 reviews the media globalization argument, particularly the assertion that the Al-Jazeera effect is similar to the (perceived) overwhelming influence of the BBC World News and CNN International cross-border broadcasting on international discourse. Chapter 2 presents the argument that the emergent global news order in light of Al-Jazeera's dominance resmbles an information war between the West and the non-West. Chapter 3 further contextualize the Al-Jazeera-US media interplay by examining the traditional media-Administration nexus in the US during wartime and the treatment of non-Wesern news sources before September 11. Chapter 4 examines the various discourses regarding Al-Jazeera's credibility.

Through empirical analysis, Chapter 5 examines the re-broadcasting and framing of Al-Jazeera's material throughout the war in Afghanistan. The chapter is divided into two parts: The first examines the representation of Al-Jazeera's images of US military actions (military frame), the second the representation of Al-Jazeera's images of Afghani civilian casualties (humanitarian frame). The analysis reveals that although Al-Jazeera was the only news source behind the enemy lines in Afghanistan, the US networks mostly aired consensual images of precision bombing, rejecting graphic images and reports on civilian casualties. Chapter 6 examines the US media's framing and treatment of Al-Jazeera's videos of messages from Osama Bin Laden and the Al-Qaeda leaders. Chapter 7 examines the re-broadcasting of Al-Jazeera material throughout the war in Iraq. Illustrating Al-Jazeera's ability to *enforce* images on the US networks, it tracks how the US stations "explained" these images to their viewers by distracting their attention from the content of the images and building a whole new media frame to attack Al-Jazeera's credibility. Chapter 8 extends the analysis into the virtual world. On September 1, 2003 Al-Jazeera launched an official English-language website designed "to fill a niche for English speakers who want to get the other side of the story, the Arab perspective" (Associated Press, 2003). This chapter explores the resonance of three randomly selected reports from English. Al-Jazeera.Net throughout the US occupation of Iraq on Western websites. It illustrates the potential of the web to promote a genuine cross-cultural dialogue, albeit on a small-scale. Chapter 9 examines the reaction to the newly-launched Al-Jazeera English channel in the US. It focuses on the unwillingness of US cable and satellite carriers to provide Al-Jazeera English to their viewers and the pressure of the anti Al-Jazeera lobby. Based on the above analysis, Chapter 10 draws a new map of practices in US wartime reporting post September 11.

CHAPTER ONE

AL-JAZEERA AND THE MEDIA GLOBALIZATION ARGUMENT

According to the media globalization theorists, the Al-Jazeera effect is the ability of Al-Jazeera to reverse the traditional global news flow by exporting Arab images and perspective into Western discourse (in stark contrast to the traditional one-way flow of images from Western media to the non-West). This perception of an information revolution created by Al-Jazeera and able to influence politics in the West is derived from the popular notion that international news networks have the power to influence debate in the receiving countries. This chapter tracks the roots of the argument regarding the impact of CNN and BBC World News, and how it was mistakenly applied to Al-Jazeera in the wake of the September 11 events.

The argument regarding the power of global news was crystalized with the fall of the Soviet Union and the rise of the global era, which was characterized by the parallel rise of transnational news networks (particularly CNN during the 1991 Gulf War). Media globalization scholars argued that global reporting increased tensions between the national and the transnational. They asserted that the *supra-national* perspective of stations such as CNN, BBC World News, MSNBC, and Sky News weakens the dominance of the patriotic perspective of local stations and leads to the extension of both political accountability and the public debate from a national to a global level (Anderson, 2004; Held, 1995, p. 126; Robertson, 1992, p. 183; Habermas, 1992, p. 444; Garnham, 1990, p. 18). They therefore claim that international news networks contribute to the *pluralization* of ideas and the decrease of nationalism, patriotism and ethnocentrism.

Media globalization scholars believe that the international media holds such power over nations as their transnational reports affect them in three ways: First, they can force a change in *local* policy on countries that break principles that are valuable for most nations and cultures. This creates international pressure on governments to reconsider local policy even at the price of a loss of sovereignty over internal affairs. Second, they argue that international news networks can affect *foreign* policy and promote humanitarian interventions by global aid forces in troubled regions thanks to pressure on local governments engendered by repeated 24/7 broadcasting of images of human suffering. Third, they claim that these networks can contribute to *conflict mediation* and understanding between nations and cultures thanks to their perceived ability to show the "full picture" and not to take sides due to their commitment to a global perspective. This supra-national perspective of events presents to each of the conflict sides the other party's perspective and allegedly promotes cross-cultural understanding.

The ability to interfere in local policy refers to the various events that international media brings to the forefront of global consciousness, compelling nations to change their policies. These include environmental matters such as Greenpeace's success at stopping Shell UK's plan to dump the Brent Spar oil platform in the North Sea in 1995, the successful attempts to stop French and Chinese underground nuclear tests in 1996 (after adopting the *Comprehensive Test Ban Treaty*), the current pressure on Canada to enforce its policy regarding the hunting of baby seals (Humane Society International, 2009; Woods, 2008) and the international campaign to stop global warming. In all these cases, pressure was created to stop the atrocities after international news networks distributed the reports around the world. In addition, the international airing of reports can also affect internal policy regarding civil rights. Serra's (1999) study on the influence of international media pressure in halting Brazilian internal policy concerning the murder of street children found a link between transnational media pressure and the Brazilian National Congress's establishment of a Commission of Inquiry to investigate the killing. According to Serra, articles in *Newsweek*, *Time* and on CNN were among the leading factors in the international pressure that led to the launching of a national plan to combat violence against children and the enactment of a new law that radically changed the legal framework in Brazil (Serra, 2000, p. 156).

That international networks can also influence *foreign* policy refers to the perceived ability of international networks to trigger the decisions made on humanitarian interventions in crisis regions. This phenomenon, it is argued, occurs as global networks air images of war, famine, civil war and other atrocities taking place in various parts of the world (usually in developing countries) 24 hours a day, 7 days a week to a global audience, thus forcing the issue into the global news agenda. It is therefore claimed that it was CNN and its sister networks and not the Clinton Administration that brought various atrocities in the 1990s onto the daily agenda and served as the chief driving force in the decision to send an intervention force to the crisis-striken countries. Globalists argue that while throughout the Cold War such incidents remained underreported and left outside the public eye (for example, the self-censorship of the massacre in 1975 East Timor on US media, see Herman and Chomsky, 1988, pp. 253–296), the international news networks ensure that the world will not be able to turn a blind eye to such horrors ever again. Livingston (1997) assigned three consequences to CNN's 24/7 images, which when combined create such an impact that policy-makers are forced to intervene in crisis zones. They are seen as 1) an *accelerant* to decision-making mechanisms, as the repeated airing of the images demand immediate response; 2) an *impediment* to the achievement of desired policy goals, as real-time images can hurt the morale of citizens and soldiers and threaten the security of military operations and 3) an *agenda-setting agency*, as emotional, compelling coverage of atrocities or humanitarian crises reorder foreign policy priorities.

The first event where it is widely argued that transnational media affected foreign policy took place in July 1991, as images of the plight of Kurdish refugees fleeing Iraq after an unsuccessful rebellion attempt were broadcast repeatedly on CNN. These images (arguably) forced the US Administration to protect the Kurds and thus prevent a public relations crisis. Veteran CBS correspondent Daniel Schorr argued: "Within a two-week period, the President had been *forced*, under the impact of what Americans and Europeans were seeing on television, to reconsider his hasty withdrawal of troops from Iraq" (1991, p. 23; see also Shaw, 1996, p. 156; Ammon 2001). Another example where a global media campaign affected foreign policy was in 1992 when the United Nations Security Council decided to authorize an operation to assist starving Somalis rather than other areas in Africa where comparable atrocities were taking place at the same time (such as Angola and Sudan) as a result of a specific media campaign on Somalia (Cohen, 1994; Gibbs, 1994). In this case, the media interest arguably also ended the crisis, as images of a dead US soldier dragged in the streets of the Somali capital Mogadishu by Muslim militants opposing the US presence in the region allegedly forced the pullout of US troops in 1993. BBC World News presenter Nik Gowing summed up his feelings about the media's effect on the decision to intervene: "television got the US into Somalia...and got the US out" (1994, p. 68).

That global networks have mobilized foreign policy has also been voiced with regard to US interventions in Haiti 1994 and Rwanda 1994 (Strobel, 1997), Bosnia 1995 (Robinson, 2002) and Kosovo 1999 (Babak, 2007; Livingston, 1997). In the case of Bosnia, Robinson (2002) argued that a combination of media pressure and weak policy of the Clinton Administration regarding the crisis motivated the NATO intervention despite the lack of political interest in the region. In the Kosovo case, Babak (2007) argued that the media determined the entire political stance of the government, including a reversal of policy. Babak perceived that the media pushed the US to form an alliance with the *Kosovo Liberation Army* (KLA) against the *Federal Republic of Yogulavia* (FRY) although the US initially supported the FRY, in light of the "excessive" TV coverage of three massacres performed by the FRY.

Surprisingly, several policy makers confirmed that there is some truth in these arguments. President George H. W. Bush admitted that during the 1991 Gulf War he learned more from CNN than the Pentagon. On the opposing side, both Saddam Hussein and his government also reportedly watched the war on CNN: Apparently, when Iraqi foreign minister Tariq Aziz was asked if he was familiar with a pronouncement by President Bush, he sarcastically answered that he also watched CNN (Andreson & Carpignano, 1991). In his memoirs, former Secretary of State (1989–1992) James Baker III wrote: "In Iraq, Bosnia, Somalia, Rwanda and Chechnya, among others, the real time coverage of conflict by the electronic media has served to create a powerful new imperartive for prompt action that was not present in less frenetic times" (1995, p. 103). The former UN Secretary-General Boutrus Ghali also proclaimed that throughout his appointment (1992–1997) CNN served as "the 16th member of the Security Council" (cf. Shechter, 2003, 47).

The third and final effect that scholars refer to, which is most relevant to the Al-Jazeera case, is the ability of global networks to replace the traditional local-patriotic angle that local media take during crisis with a transnational angle, thus promoting conflict resolution. Media globalization scholars believe that when policy-makers, local media producers and viewers from conflicting sides watch the same televised representation of a conflict in which their country is involved in on a transnational channel they are in a better position to understand the other side's argument. CNN's popular program *World Report*, that allows producers from various countries to present a local perspective of events, has repeatedly been used to illustrate this point. Flournoy (1992; see also Flournoy and Stewart, 1997, p. 162) found that the show is used in crisis regions (e.g. Cyprus-Greece-Turkey, Bulgaria-Turkey) as a two-way communication channel between conflicting nations. For example, throughout a dispute regarding the treatment of Turkish minorities by the Bulgarian government, Bulgarian producers placed emphasis on Turkish minorities who were not interested in the Turkish heritage, while on the same show Turkish producers stressed that Bulgaria was trying to wipe out the culture of the Turkish minorities. After watching CNN *World Report*, viewers on both sides testified that they understood the other side's perspective better. Fluorney argued: 'If Ted Turner [CNN's founder] has his way, international conflict will be less and international understanding will be greater (Fluorney, 1992, p. 21). In light of these findings and based on her own research Volkmer argued that the formation of international broadcasting "...results in a construction of a global public sphere. On the macrosphere this...implies international co-operation, affiliation and syndication structures as well as news exchange systems (such as globally operating news agencies), on the microframe... news language and presentation routines (avoidance of stereotypes, placing of news events in a larger regional, continental, multinational or global context" (Volkmer, 1999, pp. 4–5).

Where does Al-Jazeera fall within this rosy view of cross-cultural cooperation in the age of international news reporting? In the wake of September 11 and the war on terror, Volkmer applied the same traits to the Qatari station, asserting that it has extended the formation of a global public sphere (see Appendix B for a further explanation of the global public sphere notion), as the global spread of its counter-hegemonic news reports refine the patriotic news perspective of Western news networks and communicate the Arab perspective of events to US viewers (Volkmer, 2002, pp. 241–243). Under this new communication realm, she argues, the traditional media-Administration relationship is reshaped, and US journalists gain a new role as "reflectors" and "mediators" between the national and the global (Volkmer, 2002, pp. 243–5). She asserts that eventually, Al-Jazeera's images, which counter the traditional one-way flow of information from West to non-West, contribute towards a horizontal global news flow, where all nations are exposed to multiple perspectives on news events. This, in turn, promotes a cross-cultural dialogue between the West and the Arab world.

The argument that Al-Jazeera affects global public opinion and flattens the world of information has since been repeated in numerous forums by a variety of professionals, including journalists (i.e. Friedman, 2005; Zednik, 2002; Gowing, 2002), media and communication scholars (Reese, 2009; Miles, 2005; El-Nawawy and Iskandar, 2003; Cassara and Lengel, 2004 see http://www.tbsjournal.com/Archives/Spring04/cassara_lengel.htm) and international relations circles (Aysha, 2005). These accounts draw a direct line between the power of the Western-based CNN and BBC World News to that of Al-Jazeera to influence global public opinion: "From the early days of satellite television to the CNN age, what really existed was a 'US Village' of global reach. In contrast, regional informational umbrellas can now collect and disseminate information quite independently on a local basis, while increasingly being able to broadcast their version of events globally... ...People now talk of the Al-Jazeera effect as they once did of the CNN effect" (Aysha, 2005, p. 198).

Specifically, Al-Jazeera's global reach and the *speed* by which it disseminates images around the world are considered the major reasons behind its perceived power to force Western governments to respond to counter-hegemonic images. In "The Emerging Chaos of the Global News Culture", McNair assigns Al-Jazeera and its comparable popular Arab station Al-Arabiya immense power "The global availability of real-time satellite news, from Al-Jazeera and Al-Arabiya as well as BBC World News, Sky News and CNN, alongside a sprawling virtual universe of online media, means that political elites in democratic societies ... must respond to events at speeds that might conflict with the demands of good government" (2008, p. 158).

Al-Jazeera's power presumably extends to provide a whole new global perspective to Western media that did not exist before the arrival of counter-hegemonic news sources. Jasperson and El-Kikhia (2002 and 2003) argued that CNN's content-exchange agreement with Al-Jazeera throughout the war in Afghanistan promoted humanitarian and military aspects that embarrased and challenged the Pentagon: "... the prominent role of Al-Jazeera provided a new perspective and generated new questions not asked during the 1991 Persian Gulf War" (Jasperson and El-Kikhia, 2002, p. 6; see also Jasperson and El-Kikhia, 2003, p. 129).

The realistic approach in political science (which states that military intervention only takes place in order to pursue power or other interests) in particular has widely attacked the "naivity" of the media globalization argument. It argues that humanitarian interventions are driven by pure political interests and not by media pressure. In the case of the intervention in Somalia, for example, it claims that the US had economic interests (specifically the proximity of the Somali civil war to the strategic Ban-el-Mandeb straits, where the US Company *Conco* heavily invested in oil explorations) which dictated the intervention (Gibbs, 2000).

The next chapter reveals the media globalization paradigm's blind eye to the effect that the advent of Al-Jazeera has had on the international news map. It draws an alternative map of an emergent information war between the West and the non-West in the wake of September 11.

CHAPTER TWO

AL-JAZEERA RE-SHUFFLES THE GLOBAL INFORMATION ORDER

Since the horrific events of September 11, 2001, a new phenomenon has evolved in global news that has received very little attention: The inception of a genuine "counter-hegemonic contra-flow" in the form of Al-Jazeera and other pan-Arab networks that threatens the traditional Western news hegemony.

Counter-hegemonic news flows did not reach the West until the war on terror began. Reports from anti-hemgemonic stations and news agencies normally remained within the borders of their own regions and did not gain global resonance. The Cold War was characterized by a lack of interaction between the official news agency of the Soviet bloc (ITAR-TASS) and the West, as Western viewers were not interested in its content (in contrast to their interest in Al-Jazeera). Independent news agencies originating in developing countries, such as Inter Press Service (IPS), that emphasized the anti-hegemonic perspective, also failed to export their content to the West.

Al-Jazeera's images, however, pose the greatest challenge to Western news hegemony in the history of global media, as it is capable of challenging the Western perspective on a global level and sometimes even of forcing images on Western stations that portray a non-Western point of view. In other words, Al-Jazeera fulfills Robertson's (1992) prediction that under globalization no one can feel "at home" anymore, not even the "dominating center." The global spread of Al-Jazeera's reports marks the advent of *oppositional* counter-hegemonic material on Western computer and television screens. In the new media environment, Al-Jazeera broadcasts an alternative outlook on events aimed at viewers worldwide. While there is no doubt that Al-Jazeera vastly alters the way that anti-hegemonic voices interact with the West, this chapter argues that this interaction is actually perceived by the US Administration as the advent of an information war rather than an extension to the other international news networks. To underscore the significance of this phenomenon, this chapter opens with a historical review of the global information news flow debate which illustrates the Western dominance of global information flow. It then proceeds to explain why non-Western information flows before Al-Jazeera actually reinforced Western values. The chapter concludes with insights regarding the emergent global news order in the Al-Jazeera era.

The Western Media and "Cultural Imperialism"

From the late 1960s to the mid-1980s, international communication discourse revolved around the unilateral media flow from the West to the non-West and its perceived effects of "media imperialism". The media imperialism theory suggests an international "hypodermic needle" media effect, wherein capitalist consumption values are injected into the Third World's "hearts and minds" through advertising and television programs, thus threatening cultural identity. Examining US global dominance of news agencies, magazines, films, radio and television, Boyd-Barrett (1977) argued that US-based transnational networks specifically affect the production of local media organizations in non-Western countries. He defined "media imperialism" as "... the process whereby the ownership, structure, distribution, or content of the media in any country are singly or together subject to substantial external pressures from the media interests of any other country or countries, without proportionate reciprocation of influence by the country so affected" (Boyd-Barrett 1977, p. 117). The media imperialism theory gained massive popularity after several studies established the prominent role of the US advertising industry in promoting consumerism worldwide at the expense of socialist values (Wells, 1972; Ewan, 1976; Mattelart, 1991). One particular study even illustrated how capitalist values are injected into Chilean kids through Donald Duck's comic books (Dorrfman and Mattelart, 1975).

This lack of information exchange was taking place mainly (but not only) in the news industry. In the 1970's over 80% of the global news flow was controlled by four major Western-based news agencies - Associated Press International (API – USA), United Press International (UPI – USA), Reuters (UK) and Agence France-Presse (AFP – France) . They transmitted the Western perspective of news events to the non-West. In 1964, Wilbur Schram identified that as a result of the Western hegemony on global news important events in the non-West are either ignored or represented in a distorted manner (Schrumm, 1964, p. 5).

The media imperialism theory provided a major conceptual thrust for the movement for a fairer information exchange between nations. In 1979, the International Commision for the Study of Communication problems was set up by the United Nations Educational, Scientific, and Cultural Organization (UNESCO) under the chairmanship of Nobel Peace Prize Laureate Sean MacBride. In 1980, the commission submitted a special report to UNESCO with the aim to take immediate action to replace media imperialism with a *New World Information and Communication Order* (NWICO). The NWICO's resolution proposed "respect . . . for the rights of each nation to inform the world public about its interests, its aspirations and its social and cultural values" (cf. Thussu, 2000, p. 47). To eliminate of the global media flow imbalance, the resolution proposed providing assistance to non-Western stations to improve their media infrastructure and equipment as well as an assurance that the training of non-Western journalists will take place in their own countries (Thussu, 2000, pp. 34–35).

The West vehemently opposed the NWICO resolution, perceiving it as fundamentally contrary to the liberal Western values of free flow of information. Western news organizations argued that the media imperialism paradigm was designed to impose censorship and keep away foreign journalists. The news networks contended that they were only reporting the realities of life in the Third World, i.e. economic backwardness and political instability. In the early 1980s, the Reagan Administration (with the support of the Thatcher Government) imposed significant restrictions on aid programs to developing countries under the slogan *Trade not Aid*. It also pressed developing countries to grant more freedom to US-based private media and telecommunication initiatives, rather than government monopolies, in the construction of communication infrastructures as part of its privatization policy (Preston, 2001; McPhail, 1987 ;Hamelink, 1983). In response to the NWICO resolution, the US and UK terminated their membership in UNESCO, as the resolution was seen to conflict with the principle of free market competition.

Following application of NWICO in the mid-1980s, a revisionist argument was put forth, claiming that the approach perceiving international communication as a unilateral cultural flow that injects Western values to non-Western countries is too deterministic. Several audience reception studies of non-Western viewing of the popular American soap opera *Dallas* which was aired in over 120 countries found that non-Western audiences were "culturally decoding" the series, noting their ability to filter and resist capitalist messages in Western text (Ang, 1985; Katz and Liebes, 1990).

The revisionist view also identified the equally important inception of global flow of information from non-Western countries. The emergence of non-Western transnationals is perceived as an aspect of three phenomena: (a) copying the

US model of professional and commercial television in countries exposed to US broadcasting; (b) the availability of satellite technologies, that encouraged international broadcasting to maximize profits; and (c) cross-border trade deregulation thanks to the neo-liberalist global free international trade environment of the post-Cold War era. Under these conditions, private media broadcasters from non-Western countries expanded their operations globally, aiming at their diasporic communities in lucrative Western markets – and (in the case of Al-Jazeera) even beyond. From a media globalization perspective, the significance of these networks is the emergence of *counter-flow* in global media, in which "countries once thought of as major 'clients' of media imperialism . . . have successfully exported their programs and personnel into the metropolis – the empire strikes back" (Sinclair et al., 1996, p. 23). The first and most notable example of counter-flow came from so-called culturally-imperialized Latin America in the form of the *telenovela* – the Latin American version of the daily soap opera. Scholars saw telenovelas growing into an illustration of the potential of Third World cultural industries for resistance, alternatives and contra-flow, thus weakening Western global media hegemony and contributing to a fairer form of horizontal, diversified and heterogeneous global media flows (Tomlinson, 1991, pp. 56–57; Sinclair et al., 1996, p. 13). Some even argued that the non-West reconquered "culturally occupied territory" from the West, maintaining that the export of telenovelas to the respective geolinguistic Spanish-speaking countries (i.e. Spain, Portugal) and other Third World countries contributed to "reverse colonization" (Antola and Rogers, 1984, p. 33; Lopez, 1995).

While the concept of contra-flow has undoubtedly complicated the argument for "cultural imperialism", some consider that it tends to put too much weight on marginal contra-movements, so that the real power structures in global communication are disguised (Schiller, 1991, p. 22; Roach, 1990, pp. 295–296). For example, Disney alone surpassed the revenues of the entire Indian (*Bollywood*) film industry in 2006 (Hoovers online, 2009). The idea of contra-flow is also undermined when we examine the content of telenovelas and Bollywood films that have "gone global". Usually, producers have to compromise authentic angles and *Westernize* broadcast content to cater to the global palate. Both Bollywood and telenovelas had to portray near-Western values in their globally exported content: Latin American broadcasting networks have effectively adopted the US commercial system, implanting American commercial values at the core of their broadcasting. Thus, Telenovelas are inspired by the US soap opera genre and are deeply permeated by Western capitalist values such as consumerism (Oliviera, 1993; Tufte, 2000; Martin-Barbero, 1993). Similarly, recent

Indian movies compromise Indian values and are gradually losing their cultural distinctiveness, as illustrated in the new trend of baring skin and showing explicit love scenes (as contrasted with traditional expression of love fantasies through song and dance). In addition, Bollywood is welcoming Western actors and scripts more than ever (for example, in 2009, Kylie Minogue starred in the Bollywood film *Blue*, which is inspired by the Hollywood production *The Deep*). Thus, instead of challenging Western values these programs actually play an instrumental role in "legitimizing consumerist values" and in providing "*complementary* rather than oppositional [contra-flows] to the US-based media transnationals" (Thussu, 2006, p. 199; emphasis mine).

While the non-Western entertainment industry has somewhat surrendered to Western values when exporting TV shows and films, non-Western news stations such as Al-Jazeera refuse to align with Western demands and insist on distributing globally graphic images that challenge the Western perspective of events. These counter-hegemonic images lead to an information war between the former Western media empires and the global non-Western news outlets.

Counter-Hegemonic Global News and the Subsequent "Information War"

In the 1980s and early 1990s, an official UNESCO study found no evidence that the advent of regional non-Western news agencies, that emerged as a result of NWICO, affected the dominance of the Western ones in any way (Boyd-Barrett and Thussu, 1992, p. 141). The gap between non-Western news agencies and Western news agencies actually *increased significantly* in the post-Cold War era. In the late 1980s, the global dominance of Western news agencies was augmented with the emergence of transnational networks, such as Star TV, Sky News, BBC World News and the "global news leader," the US-based CNN. The political economy tradition believes that these transnational media lead to the emergence of a 'global elite' conversation taking place mostly in English (Sparks, 1998; Schlesinger, 1999; Thussu, 2000, p. 196): A pan-Asian study found that CNN, Discovery and Music Television (MTV) were the most popular channels among the affluent sections of society in Asia (Madden, 1999, p. 36).

Furthermore, the 1990s saw the strengthening of the already hegemonic Western stations at the expense of non-Western news agencies. The British news agency *Reuters* became one of the top five global media corporations, with nearly 200 news bureaus, while the major non-Western news agency Gemini (that focuses on news from the developing world) collapsed and others such as the Pan-African News Agency (PANA) and the Caribbean News Agency (CANA) "dissolved... [and] have been reborn in smaller, mostly commercial, guises" (Sreberny-Mohammadi, 2003, p. 16).

Therefore, Al-Jazeera's arrival onto the global news scene in the wake of September 11 and its ability to challenge Western news domination in terms of values and scope is nothing short of a *revolution* in the global information order. Since the Al-Qaeda attacks on the US, the global spread of Al-Jazeera reports has gradually been eroding Western dominance and promoting a counter-hegemonic news perspective among audiences worldwide on a variety of platforms. As noted in the Introduction, shortly after the attacks European and American audiences who wanted to watch an alternative viewpoint to the one presented on local stations, have been able to watch Al-Jazeera with English subtitles since the beginning of the war in Afghanistan (Al-Jazeera added English subtitles to its broadcasting 12 hours a day in the United States and Europe due to high demand from English-speaking viewers). In 2003, Al-Jazeera also launched an English-only website (http://english.aljazeera.net) and on November 15, 2006, it launched a 24/7 English television channel to compete with leading global news stations CNN and BBC World News, offering a global perspective to a potential world audience of over one billion English speakers.

Al-Jazeera poses a challenge to Western channels not only in terms of its [pro-Arab] content but also in its global spread. According to its website, the Al-Jazeera English television channel is available to over 160 million viewers in 80 countries, including Australia, Germany, Denmark, France, Japan, the US and Israel. Despite the US Administration's ambition to block access to this channel (see chapter 9), technology renders it nearly impossible to do so for viewers who are poactively interested in the channel and willing to watch it online or set their satellite dishes to Al-Jazeera (Schiesel, 2001). Although most American cable providers have agreed not to carry the channel, viewers with broadband connections can easily view the channel online on YouTube or directly on Al-Jazeera's website. DishTV and Globecast satellite system subscribers, as well as cable subscribers in Ohio, Virginia and Washington, are able to receive the English-language Al-Jazeera for an extra fee. In an age of media concentration, in which the US media environment is controlled by five major corporations (Time Warner, Disney/ABC, Viacom/CBS, News Corporation and Bertelsman, in comparison to 50 corporations in 1983 – see Bagdikian, 2004) to the dissatisfaction of many critical viewers, Al-Jazeera has become a news source for Westerners seeking an alternative point of view (see chapters 8 and 9).

Al-Jazeera is thus refining the global news map rapidly by inspiring the emergence of regional and global counter-hegemonic news networks in developing regions. In 2005, Hugo Chavez launched La Nueva Televisora del Sur (Spanish: The New Television Station of the South), known as teleSUR, in Latin America to offset the Western-centered Spanish-speaking CNN and Univision. TeleSUR, whose slogan is "Our North is the South," is co-owned by Venezuela, Argentina, Uruguay, Cuba, Bolivia, Ecuador, Chile and Nicaragua and broadcasts to most of the South American continent. On its inception, both Chavez and teleSUR President Andres Izarra said that the birth of the channel was inspired by the success of Al-Jazeera. In fact, Latin Americans often call the channel "the Latin Al-Jazeera." In early 2006, teleSUR established its link to Al-Jazeera by signing a content-exchange agreement with the Qatari network.

The trend to counterbalance CNN *a*nd BBC World News spread to other non-Western regions as well. In July 2007, both Iran and Pakistan joined the ranks of countries with news networks established to offset Western-centered global news stations. The Iranian-run *Press TV* (http://www.presstv.ir) aims at countering accusations concerning the country's participation in the nuclear arms race and at showing the world the Iranian side of the story. The station, based in Tehran, broadcasts in English around the clock. Pakistan's former president Pervez Musharraf launched Dawn News (http://www.dawn.com) as part of Pakistan Herald Publications Limited (PHPL), Pakistan's largest English-language media group. In Africa, Africans Together Vision (ATV) launched, in September 2008, a Pan-African news agency named A24 broadcasting in English which is modelled on Al-Jazeera (http://www.a24media.com). The South African Broadcasting Corporation (SABC) has also announced its plan to launch SABC International, a CNN-competitor with 13 news bureaux planned around the world, in 2010. Competition to counterbalance the influence of CNN and BBC World News is also taking place in the G8 countries: Russia, Germany and France have all launched their own English-channel news networks recently, namely Russia Today, Deutsche Welle and France 24, respectively. In the case of the summer 2008 crisis in South Ossetia, for example, Russia Today was able to provide a Russian perspective on events to a potential global audience.

Another layer in the gradual weakening of the global Western hegemony is the ability of Al-Jazeera to supersede in popularity and sometimes even replace major Western stations in non-Western regions, including Latin America, Southeast Asia and Africa. For example, SABC discontinued its CNN service in 2004 and BBC World News in 2006, offering Al-Jazeera instead.

In the eyes of the US Administration, Al-Jazeera's global reach is seen as a declaration of war on the global information hegemony of the US. In response to Al-Jazeera's growing clout in the Arab world, the US Administration's counter-propaganda efforts have included the establishment of the *Office of Global Communications* (OGC), aimed at reversing what the Administration sees as a misunderstanding of the US and its policies in the Middle East due to Arab media propaganda. The mission statement of the OGC declares that the organization's purpose is "to prevent misunderstanding and conflict, build support for and among United States coalition partners, and better inform international audiences" (http://www.whitehouse.gov/ogc/). One means of accomplishing this goal is to improve the US's image by publicizing its own assessment of Al-Jazeera. The OGC's long-term strategy reads:

> *OGC coordinates government-wide efforts to convey America's message to the world by improving communications about US humanitarian and pro-democracy efforts. Drawing on the President's outreach to Arab and Muslim audiences, OGC is working closely with the State Department to increase our interaction with existing pan-Arab news media. Also, the Office is encouraging efforts to reach Muslim audiences directly via US-supported broadcasting, exchanges, and new products.* (White House Office of Global Communications memo, 2003. Retrieved from: http://georgewbush-whitehowwuse.archives.gov/ogc/aboutogc.html)

To reach Muslim listeners and viewers, the OGC launched a US-sponsored radio station (Radio Sawa) and two TV stations (Al-Hurra and Al-Iraqiya) with the aim of "winning Arab hearts and minds" and minimizing what they saw as Al-Jazeera incitement.

Besides the US efforts, the French, British, Russian and Chinese governments have also attempted to join the battle over Arab public opinion, thus complicating and adding to the web of global propaganda. In 2006, France 24 added an Arabic version to its programming. Russia launched an Arabic version of Russia Today in 2008 and in July 2009 China lanched an Arabic version of China Central Television (CCTV). In 2008, BBC relaunched an Arabic channel (after the orginal BBC Arabic was shut in 1996). In addition to governmental efforts, the Qatari station's success also prompted the January 2002 launch of CNN Arabic.

These attempts are perceived hostile by many Arab viewers as these networks do not endorse Arab lingo and insist on Western terminology to describe news events in the region (for example, they refuse to call suicide bombers "martyrs" (Barkho, 2006). Arab viewers, in turn, rate CNN and BBC low on credibility in comparison to Al-Jazeera (Johnson and Fahmy, 2008).

All these recent developments - the initiation of counter-hegemonic international and regional news networks, the Western ambition to reverse the impact of these stations and return its news hegemony, and the subsequent resistance of Arab viewers to these attempts - can be seen as the emergence of an information war between nations over the dominance of the global and regional news realm. Under this environment, instead of providing a genuine global perspective of news events, government-sponsored channels are spreading propaganda and culturally-tilted information in order to enforce their nation's own interests.

With this in mind, the next chapter moves to examine the extent to which anti-hegemonic voices such as Al-Jazeera were allowed in US war reporting in the era preceeding the information war. This will allow us to later asses the real change that the advent of Qatari images bought to US wartime reporting.

CHAPTER THREE

ANTI-HEGEMONIC IMAGES IN US WAR REPORTING

Throughout the war in Iraq and Afghanistan, Al-Jazeera repeatedly aired gory images of dead Iraqi and Afghani civilians and dead and wounded US soldiers. To better understand what determined the US media decision-making regarding what images to present and what to filter, this chapter examines the evolution of US wartime censorship mechanisms in the last 150 years.

War Images and the Development of Censorship

The history of war coverage began with the 1854 Crimean War, when William Howard Russell's criticism of the British Light Brigade was published in *The Times*. (Knightley ,2000; Hallin, 1997; Carruthers, 2000), Before that time, editors "either stole war news from foreign newspapers or employed junior officers to send letters from the battlefront" (Knightley, 2000, p. 2). Between the end of the American Civil War (1865) until the First World War (1914), there was no concept of censorship and the popular press had the means to use telegraphy for unlimited reporting of distant events. The military establishment was slow to realize the power of newly aroused public opinion (Knightley, 2000, pp. 43–44) and graphic images aroused public opinion throughout the American Civil War (Zelizer, 2002, p. 52). Moreover, as the outcomes of most wars during this period (the Franco-Prussian and Russo-Turkish Wars, for example) did not directly concern the US and the British Empire, journalists from these countries could describe atrocities without interference. Knightley (2000) called the period between the Crimea War and the First World War *The Golden Age of War Correspondents*.

The First World War marked a turning point in the history of war reporting and the emergence of media censorship. After reports of British defeat in *The Times* and the *Daily Mail*, the British Parliament feared it would lose the propaganda war to Germany and subsequently denounced those newspapers for their oppositional coverage (Knightley, 2000 pp. 97–103). The British Cabinet wanted stories of British heroism and imposed censorship accordingly, requiring reporters to comply with the new system. Similarly, when the US entered the war on April 6, 1917, war correspondents took an oath before the Secretary of War, vowing to serve American public interests and refrain from unfavorable reporting. Previously censored photos of heavy combat, released only after the war was over, revealed the scope of the tragedy and the extent to which the news had been manipulated (Goldberg, 1991, p. 196).

During the Second World War, the Western media management system was ambivalent in its relations with the media as they understood its potential to promote support on one hand and protest on the other. Consider that during the Invasion of Normandy (D-Day), whose coverage demanded total military cooperation, the US army exterted great efforts to allow reporters to cover the landings while at the same time they tried to stop graphic images sent from the battlefront (Knightley, 2001, p. 353). This ambivalent media-government nexus is further illustrated by the appointment of radio broadcaster Elmer Davis as Director of the US Office of War Information, blurring lines between the state and the press (Hallin, 1997, p. 209).

During the Cold War and particulary the Vietnam War, however, there was no formal censorship (Hallin, 1997, p. 209) –control over media output was loosened and reporters only had to agree to protect military security before entering the battle zone. As such, they covered the war from the *field* and not from their hotel rooms. Throughout the war, the values of objectivity in reporting and detachment were born as part of a larger process of media professionalization. In light of their first-hand access to war zone and war atrocities, reporters "began to question again the ethics of their business" (Knightley, 2000, p. 448; Hallin, 1997; Carruthers, 2000; Knightley, 2000). Thanks to the development of sound cameras and transportation and communication technologies, television brought daily photos of death and destruction, focusing primarily on the devastation of American soldiers. Most importantly, journalists covered the war from a *critical* rather than a *supportive* perspective, terming it "*the* war" rather than "our war" (Hallin, 1986, pp. 127–131). Specifically, three shots of the savagery of war that appeared after the Tet Offensive (the simultaneous attack of North Vietnamese and Vietcong forces on major US and Allied military bases on January 30–31, 1968, in which 243 servicemen died) were considered to be major contributors to the escalation of antiwar protests in the US. The first is the photo of the South Vietnam Police Chief executing a Vietcong suspect during the Tet Offensive, the second is the 1969 My Lai massacre and the third is the 1972 shot of a young girl (Phan Ti Kim Phuc) fleeing a napalm attack.

From a political point of view, it was widely held that the media caused the defeat by exposing its audience to the atrocities of the war and by (allegedly) practicing misrepresentation and providing biased coverage that reflected the "adversary culture" of the 1960s. The *New York Times* television critic John Corry blamed American television for being an "accomplice of the left" (Herman and Chomsky, 1988, pp. 169–171). In the late 1960s, based on public opinion polls, various political science studies displayed a rise in public cynicism and a decline in trust of the American government (e.g. Miller, 1974; Lipset and Schneider, 1983). For Huntington, the media have become "the most notable national power" of the 1970s (Huntington, 1975, pp. 98–99). Miller, Erbring and Goldenberg's (1974) empirical study of the impact of newspapers on public opinion concluded that the media's style of reporting had a significant impact on their audiences and that readers of the more critical newspapers were more distrustful toward the government (Miller et al., 1974, pp. 80–81).

In 1979, the US media were again perceived adversarial by the Administration as images of the 50 Americans taken hostage by the Iranians during the Iranian revolution were widely aired a few months before the 1980 elections. These images are seen by political analysts as the primary reason for incumbent US President Jimmy Carter's defeat.

In another incident, in 1983, pictures of two truck bombs that killed 241 US Marines in Beirut and of the wreckage of their barracks prompted the eventual US pullout.

As a response to the perceived adversarial coverage of the above events, the US Administration enacted a new censorship method to ensure maximum control over media output known as the "pool system", which it adopted from the British military's control-mechanism over media output developed during the 1982 Falklands/Malvinas War. After Argentina invaded and took control of the islands in April 1982, British journalists had to rely on the military for transportation to the islands (situated 8,000 miles from Britain) to cover the war and were thus largely dependent on the British government. As the war was short and successful, it was easy for the military to assume tight control over the media. The British Ministry of Defence individually selected a "pool" of 29 preferred journalists (such as Max Hastings, an avid proponent of the British Army) and rejected "controversial" ones (such as war photographer Donald McCullin, famous for his hard-hitting coverage of the Vietnam War and the Northern Ireland conflict; Glasgow University Media Group, 1985; Foster, 1992, pp. 158–159; cf. Carruthers, 2000, p. 123). Most of the chosen reporters were not only physically unfit and ignorant of military protocol (Carruthers, 2000, p. 123) but also had to contend with "minders" that acted as censors and were responsible for transmission of all journalistic reports to London for review by press officers. After the Argentinian attack on a British troopship, the *Sir Galahad*, the BBC's radio correspondent recalled being told "we only want you to print good news" (Carruthers, 2000, p. 125). Journalists only received reports that strengthened British morale and faced various obstacles when trying to transmit their own stories. In one instance, reporters found that none of the three vessels on which they were detained had communication capabilities. In other cases, transmission depended on the captain's goodwill towards the reporters (Carruthers, 2000, pp. 125–126). British correspondents, in turn, relied overwhelmingly on British rather than Argentinian sources for information about casualties, including statistics; moreover, no pictures from the battlezone were supplied (Morrison and Tumber, 1988, pp. 280–282).

The British pool system was adopted in the US in the 1980s with some modification: To prevent surprises, the Pentagon only allows a small, manageable number of approved journalists to accompany the troops. Public Affairs officers select and brief soldiers to be interviewed and are present when the interviews take place. Before sending footage to their US headquarters for editing, US officials are required to submit it to Public Affairs personnel for examination. These officials then edit the reports submitted and often censor them or delay their release, deleting all information considered sensitive (Neuman, 1996, pp. 207–209; Mattelart, 2000, p. 93).

These pool system methods were adopted and used by the US Government for the first time a year after the Falklands/Malvinas War: In the 1983 invasion of Grenada reporters were barred from the island in the first and crucial days of the operation. Similarly, in 1989, the journalist pool only arrived in Panama a few hours after the war began; reporters were detained at command headquarters and shown films comparing Noriega to Hitler. The US army also used the same tactics in El Salvador. Pedelty (1995), who joined the troops in order to learn first-hand about the media-military interplay in the warzone revealed that war reporters "rarely went into the actual battlefield" and thus played a relatively small role in the process of discovery, analysis and representation. He maintains that journalists served as "conduits to official state sources," who effectively "framed" the events for them (Pedelty, 1995, pp. 23–25).

The pool system's efficacy reached its peak in the 1991 Gulf War. In Iraq, field censorship was applied for the first time since Vietnam, as the army restricted the media's access to battle zones. In accordance with the pool system's principles, Vietnam veteran and media savvy General Norman Schwarzkopf kept the number of reporters "to a manageable 192". Reporters were confined to headquarters, away from the airstrike zone (Neuman, 1996, pp. 207–209). Unilaterals (a common term for journalists who chose not to join the pool but rather report independently) also failed to reach the battle zone, as illustrated in the case of CBS's Bob Simon, who was captured by Iraqi forces during the opening days of the Gulf War in January 1991. As the war was being fought primarily from the air, journalists were provided with recordings of successful airstrikes only after they were reviewed by the Pentagon. At the same time, the Administration adopted new tactics to maintain control over the technological advanacement of real-time satellite feed (the Gulf War set a precedent as the first war in which live images were broadcast to international audiences through modern satellite-feed technology, primarily by CNN). In the new environment, the Pentagon encouraged journalists to broadcst live the direct hits of US "smart bombs" which were aimed at hitting a single building without causing a lot of "collateral damage". Unlike Vietnam War broadcasts, Gulf War television presented the "accoutrements" of war, the "light and talk" but thanks to the Pentagon's control of information without the atrocities... Interspersed with the patriots in the sky, CNN's reporters conveyed a sense of being there, even when there was a bed in a hotel room nine stories up from the action (Neuman, 1996, pp. 212–213). As a result, the 1991 Gulf War was perceived "the most information-controlled war in the new media age" (Hallin, 1997).

Despite military control and attempts at using technology and spectacle to cover the 1991 Gulf War, a tragic wartime event demonstrated that even within the atmosphere of tight military control under the pool system, it was still possible for *counter-hegemonic* images of atrocities to penetrate the agenda and challenge Administration policies. On February 13, 1991, US forces dropped two electro-optical "smart bombs," each weighing 2,000 pounds. The bombs smashed through the steel-reinforced roof of a large concrete building in the middle-class Baghdad suburb of Al-Amiriya that was being used as a bomb shelter by many women and children. 288 people died in the bombing (Facts on File, 1991). The sources that led Western reporters to the site seven hours after the incident were Iraqi "minders" acting on behalf of Saddam Hussein, who hoped that the footage of civilian casualties would destroy support for the war in the US and ordered his minders to uncover civilian casualties while preventing access to strategic targets successfully hit (Thomson, 1992, p. 234). After the minders "prepared the scene", Western reporters and film crews were allowed to witness the disaster and began covering it extensively. This event will be discussed in further detail in Chapter 5.

The potential of counter-hegemonic material to challenge US policy can also be illustrated by a famous incident two years later. In 1993, the wide distribution of the Somali militia's interview with captured Black Hawk pilot Michael Durant in US media mobilized public opinion against Administration policy in Somalia. The interview was released after 18 US soldiers were killed, 65 were wounded and two Blackhawk helicopters were shot down on October 4, 1993 as a result of an ambush on US soldiers. The ambush was part of a war between the army of the anti-US warlord Muhammad Aidid and the US military. CNN aired a videotape, provided by Aidid's faction (recorded by a Somali freelance cameraman), of the interview with the captured pilot, who appeared frightened and severely beaten. Although clearly produced for propaganda purposes, the US television stations also aired the video around the clock until Durant's release ten days later, on October 14. Following the airing of the video, thousands of Americans called Capitol Hill to demand that US troops be withdrawn. The US pulled out of Somalia a few months later and the UN withdrew its forces in March 1995. Despite President George H. W. Bush's famous declaration that the apparent success of the 1991 Gulf War finally cured the Vietnam Syndrome, the Somalia withdrawal showed that the syndrome had returned. Reporting on the impact of these images in the US, the *Guardian's* Simon Tisdall (1993) wrote: "Ever since the [1979–80] Iranian crisis, hostage-taking has had the potential to outrage and mobilize the American public like no other foreign issue. No American has forgotten the yellow ribbons which were displayed throughout the country during the captivity of US hostages…".

The impact of the Somalia events and their place in US collective memory can be illustrated by the cultural artifacts documenting the events in the following decade. In 1999, the Somalia incident was the topic of a book that chronicles the events (Black *Hawk Down: A Story of Modern War*, 1999. The book was made into a successful Hollywood film in 2001 as well as a successful video-game in 2003).

To conclude, even with the strict hold on information between the post Vietnam era and the September 11 events, there was still room for oppositional counter-hegemonic images during war. Some of the non-consensual images – such as the 1979–80 images of US hostages in Iran, the images of the bombing of marine barracks in Beirut in 1983, the bombing of the Al-A'amiriya bunker in 1991 and the 1993 images of dead soldier dragged in Somalia - challenged the Administration and even forced a change of policy. In all these cases the graphic images came from enemy sources. In 1979–80, the images came from the *Iran Times* newspaper. In 1983, the images came from Lebanese forces. In 1991, Saddam Hussein's minders provided footage of the bunker in Al-A'amiriya and in 1993, it was Somali militants who supplied images of injured US prisoners of war. This shows that the US media did not hesitate to present images from much less credible enemy sources than Al-Jazeera in the past. Judging on past experience, allegations regarding Al-Jazeera's credibility need not interfere with the airing of its images.

Having said that, the next chapter evaluates the question of Al-Jazeera's credibility, in light of repeated allegations that the channel is a terror entity.

CHAPTER FOUR

IS AL-JAZEERA A LEGITIMATE NETWORK?

In order to ascertain if the US media has been fair in its interplay with Al-Jazeera, this chapter discusses the Qatari station's credibility through the prism of three perspectives. The political economy perspective argues that Al-Jazeera is a political tool of the Qatari Emir. The conservative perspective sees Al-Jazeera as a pro-Islam station that promotes incitement against the Christian and Jewish world. Finally, the liberal perspective argues that Al-Jazeera is a legitimate network that adheres to Western norms of objectivity.

Al-Jazeera: An Advocate of Qatar's Interests?

The first prism sees Al-Jazeera as a puppet of its sponsor, the Qatari Emir Sheikh Hamad Bin Khalifa Al Thani. In 1996, the Emir started Al-Jazeera with a 150 million dollar grant. Although on its launch date, Al-Jazeera executives declared that they aspired to become independent in five years, Al-Jazeera still failed to see revenues in 2001. Consequently, the Qatari Emir secured an annual subsidy of US$30 million to the station. All in all, by 2009, the government of Qatar had invested more than $1 billion in Al-Jazeera English and covered more than $100 million a year in losses from Al-Jazeera Arabic and Al-Jazeera English (Helman, 2009). It is argued that the Emir continues sponsorship of the channel since it serves as excellent public relations to the country (in fact, Al-Jazeera is the only news station that is more famous than its country of origin). In return for the sponsorship, Al-Jazeera allegedly regularly criticizes "everybody" but the Qatari government. For example, in October 2004, Al-Jazeera failed to report that the Emir collectively stripped of their citizenship 6,000 people belonging to the Al Ghafran clan, who took part in a failed coup against the Emir in 1995.

Da Lage, (2005) and El Oifi (2005) allege that Al-Jazeera specifically serves two political aims of the Emir: The first is his desire to achieve greater power against rival Gulf countries, particularly its mighty neighbor Saudi Arabia. The second aim is to allow Qatar to serve two masters at the same time to ensure its prosperity: The West and the Arab world.

It is widely believed in the Arab world that Al-Jazeera's inception was a response to the threat the Emir perceived from the Saudi-run Middle East Broadcasting Center (MBC). MBC was launched in 1991 as the first privately owned and independent Arabic satellite TV station and its daily news show gained immediate popularity in the region. The Qatari necessity to counter MBC was emphasized following the 1992 Al-Khofous border dispute (the dispute erupted after Qatar refused to allow the Saudis to set up a frontier post at Al Khfous during Iraq's invasion of Kuwait in 1990. In 1992, Qatar accused Saudi forces of attacking the Qatari border post, killing two guards and capturing a third in the process). Since this incident, the Emir's chief aim has been to position the politics of Qatar in opposition to those of Saudi Arabia. This led to him resuming diplomatic ties with Iran and Iraq against Saudi interests, initiating diplomatic relations with Israel (a country whose existence Saudi Arabia refuses to acknowledge) and adopting a constitution that guarantees civil liberties and religious freedom in stark contrast to the Saudi conservatism.

The second aim that Al-Jazeera allegedly fulfills for the Emir is to distract attention to the diplomatic ties that Qatar has with the US and Israel by attacking these countries on air. Qatar is the main host of US troops in the Middle East since the September 11 attacks and the ensuing prepations for the war in Afghanistan. US forces occupy both the Al Udeid base, the world's most important base for the US outside its national boundaries (excluding the Philippines) (Da Lage, 2005, p. 59) and the Al Sayliyah base, the world's largest prepositioning base for the US. The Al Sayliyah base is used by the army component of the US Central Command (US CENTCOM) and the international media teams covering the war. At the same time, Qatar maintains businss ties with Israel. The ties started during the 1994 Oslo Accord and continued throughout the Al-Aqsa Intifada and the 2006 Lebanon War, when Qatar kept the Israeli chamber of commerce operating even when most Arab countries pulled their representatives from Israel (see Appendix C). To distract the Arab public opinion and dismantle criticism that Qatar betrays Arab interests, Al-Jazeera allegedly "compensates" for these ties with the US and Israel by fiercely attacking these regimes.

Al-Jazeera: A Religious Network?

According to the conservative perspective, Al-Jazeera promotes Islam by focusing on topics such as the Intifada and the war on terror from an Islamic point of view. For example, this view asserts that during the Al Aqsa Intifada, Al-Jazeera acted as a fund-raising body for terror organizations by organizing telethons to raise money for families of militants committing suicide attacks, thus crossing all boundaries of professionalism. Al-Jazeera also frequently displayed images constituting Muslim symbols, including the Al Aqsa Mosque and the Dome of the Rock, accompanying songs about the Intifada with sporadic photos of civilian casualties, which it is asserted promoted hatred towards Israel and motivation to participate in the violent battle. Militants committing suicide attacks were presented on the network as "martyrs" (*shahids*). Zayani argued that the graphic war images that were repeatedly broadcast on Al-Jazeera during the Intifada served as an excuse for Arab governments to spend more money on armaments (2005, p. 176), adding fuel to the fires of this already war-torn region. In addition, he asserts that Al-Jazeera interviewed Israelis during the Intifada not to portray the other side's perspective but rather to display their weakness: "[Al-Jazeera] has made Israelis more human and, in fact, more vulnerable in the eyes of the public. They have been denuded of the aura that surrounds the myth of their invincibility" (quoted in interview with Christopher Ayad, For Al-Jazeera, Bin Laden sells, *Liberation*, October 12, 2001).

Examining Al-Jazeera's representation of the ban on women's veils in French schools, Cherribi (2006) argued that Al-Jazeera acted as a *religious* rather than a professional network in covering the issue. Cherribi found that the veil was the subject of 282 current affairs shows and news items as well as dozens of short news pieces. In one show, a news analyst explicitly stated "If you touch one finger, the whole body will react as one" (Al-Jazeera News, December 23, 2002), alluding to the reaction from the transnational Muslim community around the world. In addition, soon after the ban was imposed, anchorwoman Khadija Ben Gana "suddenly" started wearing a fashionable veil, illustrating that it can be worn in a modern environment. Ben Gana demonstratively wore the veil when questioning then French Minister of Foreign Affairs Dominque de Villepin about the ban. Cherribi concluded:

> *The image that Al-Jazeera tries to inculcate in the public mind of offering "the opinion and the other opinion" is really trompe l'oeil or a cover-up for the larger religious message. If CNN had an extremely popular Christian minister each week in a one-hour program live during prime time, who offered his judgment, his prohibitions, and his permissions on what those in*

> *the audience might or might not do, then we would be approaching a Christian version of what we find with Al Qaradawi's program. Al-Jazeera is not a "liberal" or "neutral" channel; it is a religious channel that allows other programs that are liberal or neutral to be shown occasionally.* (Cherribi, 2006, pp. 13–14)

El-Nawawy and Iskandar (2002, p. 60; see also Hosenball, 2002 and Chafetz, 2001) note Al-Jazeera's tendency to support Arab conspiracy theories. In November 2002, for example, Al-Jazeera aired an interview with former *Ku Klux Klan* leader David Duke (whom Al-Jazeera has labeled as an ex-GOP representative from Louisiana, as Duke once served in the Louisiana House of Representatives), who said that Israel had prior knowledge of the events of September 11 and subsequently warned its citizens to evacuate the Twin Towers before the attacks.

In addition, Israeli officials claim that Al-Jazeera persistently cooperates with Islamic "terrorist organizations" Hamas and Hezbollah. In March 2008, Israel contended that Al-Jazeera aired images of members of the Palestinian Parliament and others lighting candles, supposedly in response to Israel's threat to stop electricity in Gaza (which came in response to rockets fired at Israel by Palestinian militants), even though it was actually still light outside. Israel also claims that on July 19, 2008, the Al-Jazeera bureau chief in Beirut, Ghassan Bin Jeddo, organized and broadcast a party for terrorist Samir Kuntar and called him a pan-Arab hero (Kuntar was convicted by an Israeli court of killing three Israelis, including a four-year old girl) after he was released from Israeli prison as part of an Israel-Hezbollah prisoner swap. In response, the Israel Prime Minister's Office announced that ties with Al-Jazeera would be severed. In this particular case, Al-Jazeera admitted the the airing of Kuntar's party was a mistake, and a few days later after the broadcast an official letter was issued by Al-Jazeera's director general, Khanfar Wadah, in which he admitted that the programme violated the station's Code of Ethics (The Code of Ethics was published by Al-Jazeera on July 13, 2004. It promises to "distinguish between news material, opinion and analysis" and to "avoid the snares of speculation and propaganda" (Reuters, 2004)).

Finally, US officials blamed Al-Jazeera for supporting Saddam Hussein's regime and Al-Qaeda due to their Islamic nature at the expense of journalistic professionalism. On August 6, 2004, US Defense Secretary Donald Rumsfeld alleged that Al-Jazeera reporters in Baghdad had been on the payroll of Saddam Hussein's regime, basing their allegation on documents obtained by *The Times*, apparently showing that three Iraqi agents worked at Al-Jazeera from August 1999 to November 2002 to secure favorable coverage by the network for the Saddam Hussein regime. Al-Jazeera's General Manager, Mohammed Jassim al-Ali, who helped set up and run the network since its inception and promoted its alleged hawkish style, was said to have been in touch with these agents. Jassim was sacked in June 2003, around the time the affair was exposed, although Al-Jazeera denies that he was dismissed for that reason. In another case, Al-Jazeera's cameramen Sami Al Hajj and reporter Tayseer Allouni were arrested on charges of terrorism activity. Al Hajj was detained on charges of being a "security threat" on his way to Afghanistan in December 2001 at Guantánamo Bay (until his release without charge in May 2008). Allouni, who was one of the two journalists reporting from Afghanistan throughout the 2001 war, was convicted on September 2005 by a Spanish court to seven years in jail for serving as a financial courier to Al-Qaeda "terrorists" in return for an interview with Bin Laden.

However, in the last few years, scholars have identified a weakening of Al-Jazeera's religious stance based on dramatic changes in the senior management personnel (Boyd-Barrett & Xie, 2008; Sakr, 2007). They argue that the removal of hardliners such as former Managing Director Muhammed Jassem al-Ali in 2003 and Director General Wadah Khanfar in 2007 and the appointment of pro-US personnel (former Qatari Ambassador to the US Hamad Al-Kuwari and pro-US Ahmed Kholeifi) signify that the US has managed to moderate Al-Jazeera's "antagonistic" style. In addition, Boyd-Barrett and Xie(2008) argue that Al-Jazeera English's ambition to acquire widespread distribution in the US further illustrates that commercial considerations have persuaded the Emir that Al-Jazeera should retreat from its hard-line reporting style.

Al-Jazeera: Cross-Cultural Understanding?

The third perspective regarding Al-Jazeera asserts that the network adheres to values of journalistic professionalism and that the only difference between Al-Jazeera and Western networks is the pro-Arab rather than pro-Western stance. This view sees that in order to better understand Al-Jazeera and the context under which it operates, we need to consider the media atmosphere of the Middle East before and after the advent of Al-Jazeera. Before Al-Jazeera's inception, Arab television had been controlled by the governments in the region for four decades (1956–1996). These governments took note of the potential of television as a tool to maintain control over its citizens, and, in turn, stations were funded from the national budget, reporters were considered "public sector employees" and the station's goals were seen as a tool to form public opinion, even with the price of lying to its audience (Ayish, 2002). Arabs viewers, in accordance, stopped paying attention to their media, particularly after they caught the lies of Arab media during the 1967 Six day War with Israel: When Arab radio gave false reports of Arab victory, despite Israel having crushed the Egyptian army at the turn of the war, Arabs became aware of this deception, riots broke in Algiers and Tunis and the Egyptian cultural centre was set on fire (Oren, 2002). Consequently, until the advent of Al-Jazeera, Arabs did not pay much attention to the media in their own countries. They considered this information as little more than an extension of the views of their own governments and in turn, many Arabs turned to the Western media for more objective analysis. In the 1991 Gulf War, the majority of Arab viewers turned to CNN and BBC rather than their own media. However, these Western stations were still considered foreign sources and were easy targets of attack by anti-Western individuals and groups and Arab viewers were waiting for free media of their own.

In the 1990s, 2 new models of Arab media evolved alongside the government-controlled media model. The first was the *reformist government-controlled* model, a hybrid between state and private media (for example, Abu Dhabi Satellite Channel, a government-operated service that broadcasts from the United Arab Emirates). This system was developed as a consequence of the opening up of some Arab media systems to national and global development, as Arab officials concluded that they needed to develop new methods in order to remain relevant. Reformist government-controlled networks are, by definition, tied to national interests. Although the margins of "red lines" remarkably extended comparisons to the government-controlled model, there are still many limits to the freedom of broadcasters. The second model, to which Al-Jazeera and the Saudi-sponsored Al-Arabiya belong, is the revolutionary *private commercial* model. These networks declare professional and commercial rather than national considerations, and an ambition to bring a critical as well as pluralistic view of Arab society. Since most of the staff of these networks are Western-educated, they tend to adhere to norms of impartiality and objectivity (Lynch, 2005; Ayish, 2002).

These new critical reporting methods have promoted the emergence of a new Arab public sphere and enraged the autocratic regimes in the region. Al-Jazeera's critical broadcasting led many Arab countries who did not like what they saw as too much freedom of expression to enact sanctions on the network as well as on its host country Qatar. Amongst the countries that have shut Al-Jazeera offices are Algeria, Kuwait, Saudi Arabia, Bahrain, Jordan and even the Palestinian territories. The show that causes most of the stirs is *Al Ittijah Al Mo'akis* (*The Opposite Direction*) which is built on the concept of CNN's *Crossfire*. Throughout the show, two guests from different worldviews debate controversial matters, including issues previously considered taboo in the Arab world. For example, in a show about polygamy, one of the guests called the practice "anachronistic", possibly contradicting the Quran. In another, a Professor of philosophy at the University of Damascus claimed that Islam is a "backward" religion. Most notably, on February 21, 2006, Syrian psychiatrist Wafa Sultan bashed Muslims (from a Los Angeles studio) in a manner that would have been censored on most other stations. Sultan recognized the accomplishments of Jewish and other members of non-Muslim society versus the alleged backwardness of Muslims. Not only did Al-Jazeera not censor Sultan, but it also invited her to appear again on the same show. Similarly, on June 12, 2008, Sami Haddad, the anchor of Al-Jazera's other talkshow, *More than One Opinion*, allowed a 5-minute interview with Israeli Professor Mordekhai Kedar, who emphasized that Jerusalem has belonged to the Jews for 3000 years "and will forever" and that Jerusalem was never mentioned in the Quran as a holy city.

Al-Jazeera's objective stance is also illustrated by its choice to interview Israeli officials. During the Al Aqsa Intifada, Al-Jazeera aired interviews with Israeli officials - including Shimon Peres, Ehud Barak and former Deputy Director of Israel's National Security Institute Gideon Ezra - despite Palestinian allegations that their leaders are not accorded similar treatment on Israeli television. Furthermore, throughout the 2005 Israeli disengagement from Gaza, many Arabs felt that Al-Jazeera was taking the Israeli narrative and focuses too much on the pain of Israeli settlers. After Al-Jazera showed images of Jewish mothers wailing when they had to leave their homes, Director of the Institute of Modern Media at Al Quds University in Ramallah Daoud Kuttab, stated his belief that Al-Jazeera caused Arabs to emphasize with the Israelis: "Israeli settlers and Jewish extremists appeared human on Arab TV. This is not to say that Arabs have suddenly become soft on their historical enemies. But hours and hours of watching - on all stations, including Al-Jazeera - close-ups of mothers and babies, of young women and older men, visibly in anguish as they were forced out of their homes, had an emotional effect" (Nahmias, 2005). Abd Al-Bari Atwan, editor-in-chief of the London-based al-Quds al-Arabi, also criticized the "pro-Israeli" coverage of the disengagement, saying, "we understand the international media falls into the traps set by the settlers, and they voiced their opposition to the move by showing these live images. But we can't understand how the Arab media fell into the same trap" (Ibid.). Even during the controversial 2009 Operation Cast Lead, Al-Jazeera interviewed Israeli officials and scholars including Foreign minister Zipi Livni. These interviews were assumedly an attempt at facilitating the normalization of Arab-Israeli relations and a demonstration that Israelis are "human beings" rather than "pigs and monkeys" (their description in audiocassettes distributed in the Palestinian territories and in several Islamic textbooks, see Solnick, 2002).

In addition, Al-Jazeera routinely broadcasts speeches and press briefings by US officials. After September 11, Al-Jazeera conducted interviews with US officials Collin Powell, Condoleeza Rice and Donald Rumsfeld.

Muhammad El-Nawawy and Adel Iskandar (2003) assert that Al-Jazeera is as objective as Western stations, and that the West's expectations from Al-Jazeera for objectivity is unrealistic since it serves the Arab and not the Western audience. They termed the Al-Jazeera tendency to look at events with a local pan-Arab eye "contextual objectivity", based on the presumption that reporting angle of networks "comes with the audience". The argument goes that while Fox News looks at global events from a Republican-conservative perspective and Sky News looks at events from a British perspective, Al-Jazeera sees at the same events with Arab lenses. Indeed, a comparative study has found that when Al-Jazeera aims at Western viewers with channels such as Al-Jazeera English, its content is softer and more balanced towards Israel than the Arabic version (Abdul-Magid, 2008). Other scholars illustrated that "contextual objectivity" takes place in the West as well: After September 11, CNN US and CNN International intentionally presented a different agenda in order to satisfy their significantly different target audience (McChesney, 2002).

To emphasize the contextual objectivity argument, it is important to present Al-Jazeera's response to the allegations against it. Regarding the airing of graphic war images, Al-Jazeera argues that the Arab world is used to seeing such images not only on the screen but also in everyday life owing to both the culture and endless conflicts in the region. A survey conducted by Fahmy and Johnson (2007) found that 87 percent of Al-Jazeera's viewers want to see graphic images. Regarding the Bin Laden videos, Al-Jazeera executives assert that they do edit and sometimes even self-censor the messages. They claim that the videos are always broadcast in context and with commentary by Al-Jazeera's anchors. They also argue that this criticism comes from jealousy, as most other networks would have gladly "put their hands" on the newsworthy videos of terrorist leaders (for example, CNN interviewed Saddam Hussein in 1991). Regarding the allegation that Al-Jazeera was showing beheadings in Iraq (which was made by Rumsfeld and repeated by various other sources), the network denied that it aired such images since it is against its Code of Ethics and asked the media that aired Rumsfelds allegation to retract. Some outlets, including the *Gurdian* newspaper (http://www.guardian.co.uk/world/2005/nov/24/usa.terrorism), answered the call and published a correction. In response to the allegation of ties with the Taliban, the network argues that the ties stem from their long stay in Afghanistan as they maintaied a bureau there when most of the Western stations left. During this period, they claim, they gained the Taliban's trust. However, they deny any liking between them and the Taliban and argue that the Taliban still looks at the Al-Jazeera reporter with a suspicious eye. After Allouni's arrest in Spain on suspicion of cooperation with the Taliban, Al-Jazeera complained about the "double standard" and wrote to then Spanish Prime Minister Jose Maria Aznar: "On several occasions Western journalists met secretly with secret organizations and they were not subjected to any legal action because they were doing their job, so why is Allouni being excluded?" (Roman, 2003).

From an empirical perspective, the allegations against Al-Jazeera's reporting norms were not established. On the contrary, a cross-cultural analysis of 1820 articles published on ABC, CBS, NBC, CNN and Fox News versus Al-Jazeera throughout the war in Iraq found that the overwhelming number of stories published on Al-Jazeera and the American networks were "balanced". 89.2% of the Al-Jazeera articles were coded as "neutral", which is very similar to the number of "balanced" stories on the other channels. The odd one out in the study was actually Fox News, with only 62.1% of articles coded "neutral" (Aday, Livingston and Herbert, 2005).

To conclude, despite Al-Jazeera's strong stance toward Arab and Muslim values, there is no conclusive empirical evidence to substantiate that it is a terror entity or that it promotes terrorism. In addition, when considering that the US media rebroadcast newsworthy messages originating from terror groups throughout former crisis (see chapter 3), we can sum up that the US networks have had no substantial reason to censor Al-Jazeera's images at any point during the war on terror.

With this in mind, we now move to the empirical analysis.

CHAPTER FIVE

DISREGARDING THE PAIN OF OTHERS: THE WAR IN AFGHANISTAN

The war in Afghanistan put the US media in a unique position. For the first time in the history of war reporting, US networks had to rely on a network that "speaks the enemy's language" to report on a war that its own forces started. On October 7, 2001, the day the US and British troops launched the so-called war on terror by attacking the Taliban forces, the only two reporters allowed to remain in the country were Al-Jazeera's Youssef Al-Shouli in Qandahar and Tayseer Allouni in Kabul. The US networks had no bureaus inside Afghanistan, primarily because there had been little interest in the region among Western viewers. The Taliban allowed CNN and the BBC to open bureaus in Kabul during the civil war of the 1990s, but CNN declined for lack of viewer interest. The BBC bureau operated for a few years until it was closed, shortly before the war, because of Taliban resistance to the network's presence in Afghanistan. The Taliban also ejected the few Western journalists that remained in Afghanistan before the war began. The so-called "unilaterals" – journalists who tried to bypass these restrictions and cover the war from neighboring Pakistan – were in grave danger, as demonstrated in the case of *Wall Street Journal* reporter Daniel Pearl, who was kidnapped in the war zone on January 23, 2002 by a militant group and beheaded 6 days later.

US media had no access to the battle zones themselves, as is evident in a conversation between Howard Kurtz and Walt Rodgers of CNN:

> Rodgers: . . . *The worst of times, plainly and simply, the Navy locked us down and we could not file live. We just could not file live. And it was 20 hours before we could get our story out . . . The television operations had the worst of all worlds there. We couldn't file live from the ship, we had to package our material, put it on a cod, fly it three hours to Behring and then have it edited here. It was actually 12 to 20 hours after we completed a story that it ever made air. It was like ancient television. Howard.*
>
> Kurtz: *Very frustrating. You also were a bit of a captive audience, as you've made clear . . . And there's not much that journalists can do about it in this environment. I mean, the Pentagon*

> *controls the information, decides where journalists go. Right now, they've put people like Walt Rodgers out on the aircraft carriers, but they haven't put them on any ground troops.* (CNN Reliable Sources, October 13, 2001)

In addition, journalists reported that the pool system (see Chapter 3) was tighter under Rumsfeld than under previous Defense Secretaries. The military revealed far less information than it did during past crises and tried to conceal as much as it could. Veteran CNN reporter Tom Defrank described the information control applied in the Afghanistan War as follows:

> Defrank: *Well, we're getting, we're getting more face time with the Secretary of Defense than we did ten years ago, but the information flow is much, much less. I mean, there was a lot more information handed out by the Pentagon in 1991 than now. And that's a reflection of a couple of things. One, it reflects Don Rumsfeld's personality... I was an Army public affairs officer for 22 years: Two in active duty, 20 in the reserves, all of the Pentagon, I think, I have a pretty good sense of what you should never talk about and what it is OK to talk about, and all I'm saying is there is that... this Pentagon, and especially this White House, is not interested in going into that area of where you could talk about things without compromising operational security.* (CNN Reliable Sources, October 13, 2001)

Because of restrictions on media access, during the first few days of the war, CNN and ABC signed (separately) content exchange agreements with Al-Jazeera (El-Nawawy and Iskandar, 2002, pp. 164–166).

As all this indicates, Al-Jazeera's news reports gave US networks unprecedented access to information from behind enemy lines such as the killing of civilians and access to military casualties that the traditional Pentagon's ban on access to information prevented them from seeing. Poitical communication scholar Lanmce Bennett (1990) recalls that when NBC's legendary news anchor Tom Brokaw was asked at a press conference why the media stopped questioning the integrity of civilian leaders in El Salvador after the 1984 election victory of the Christian Democrats, the "frustrated Brokaw" replied that the media could not report on the issue after the government "fell silent" on it. Brokaw then admitted he could not even imagine how to cover a conflict without the support of government officials. In Afghanistan, Brokaw and his colleagues were able to bypass this censorship and gain unprecedented access to events behind enemy lines thanks to Al-Jazeera's reach.

However, this chapter will show that in reality the US stations persistently self-censored all counter-hegemonic news material from Al-Jazeera, without regard to the principles of objectivity and impartiality. The unprecedented opportunity to provide a supra-national perspective of events was missed as US

networks refused to challenge the Administration with images from a c
hegemonic source.

The chapter examines re-presentation of two types of Al-Jazeera images: US military actions (military frame) and Afghani civilian casualties (humanitarian frame).

The Military Frame

In her acclaimed book *Regarding the Pain of Others*, Susan Sontag points out that images of air bombings are traditionally screened in the US to illustrate American "air superiority" over its enemy and to present an image of a sterile "techno war" (Sontag, 2003, p. 68). According to Baudrillard (1995), such images create a sense of hyperreality, in which the viewer finds it difficult to differentiate between reality and the representation of reality in the form of something similar to a video game. In turn, viewers are left with the feeling that they were watching some virtual reality show and the war never happened.

In Afghanistan, US stations proactively sought Al-Jazeera's images of air bombings. News anchors' commentary emphasized that the bombings mean air superiority, as they did in the 1991 Gulf War. To illustrate the language used to frame these "air superiority" images, consider the following airstrike report:

> ... *Got some pictures to show you that are sort of signs of the times. These are off that Middle Eastern television network, Al-Jazeera and it is a picture of ... planes in the air right over Kabul flying not only now at night, as they did when the attacks began, but during the daytime, as well, with air superiority established now*... (ABC, *Good Morning America*, October 11, 2001)

In fact, the networks fought over the right to air the bombing images. By displaying these images, CBS, Fox News and NBC were actually breaching the exclusivity agreement that Al-Jazeera signed during the early days of the war with CNN and ABC, often failing to credit Al-Jazeera as the source of the material (Michalsky & Preston, 2002, p. 16). In response, the networks criticized CNN's exclusive deal with Al-Jazeera, citing the principle of "fair use," that allows widespread use of broadcast material during times of national emergency. Fox News' Vice President for Legal Affairs, Dianne Brandi, said: "These were the only pictures where the United States was beginning a war. There was no question we would use them" (El-Nawawy and Iskandar, 2002, pp. 163–5). CBS and NBC executives asked for permission to use the images, but after they were told CNN was enforcing its agreement with Al-Jazeera, both networks used the footage anyway. CBS's spokeswoman Sandra Genelius claimed: "The American public interest was served today [October 7, 2001] by putting its right to be informed above petty competitive issues" (Ibid.).

Besides the airstrike images, that strengthened the military superiority frame, Al-Jazeera also provided the US networks with the first footage proving that the air operations successfully hit Taliban targets. On the second day of the war, CNN broadcast first-hand eyewitness reports from Al-Jazeera's Tayseer Allouni, confirming that the hits were accurate:

> Kahn: Mr. *Allouni, you've just described some of the military targets that were hit in Kabul. Based on what you are seeing yourself, do you believe that the air defense system of the Taliban has been seriously compromised by the attacks?*
>
> Allouni (through translator): *Yes, I think so because the last attack which took place just before dawn was very intense – intensive and the air defenses were very intensive – sorry, they were actually low. In the first attack, air defenses were very heavy indeed. So I believe, yes, the attacks have affected air defenses – Afghani air defenses around the capital, Kabul.* (CNN *Live This Morning*, October 8, 2001)

In another incident, on October 23, 2001, the networks re-presented Al-Jazeera's exclusive footage of the precise bombing of a moving Taliban fuel convoy (CNN Sunday Morning, 23 October, 2001; CBS Evening News, October 27, 2001), a further indication of the efficiency of precision bombing technology and of the ability to hit moving targets. However, these were the only Al-Jazeera images selected for this report, as images of civilian casualties were self-censored.

In contrast to the supply of sterile images of precision air bombings from the Pentagon, the original Al-Jazeera reports also included military failings, such as lost warplanes, as well as graphic images of the results of these bombings: The killing of innocent civilians. The US networks, however, filtered these images out.

As early as October 6, 2001, the eve of the outbreak of war in Afghanistan, Al-Jazeera emerged as a news source that could challenge the Pentagon on an event that would have otherwise possibly remained unreported. On that day, Al-Jazeera showed authentic images of a US spy plane shot down by Taliban antiaircraft fire. The availability of these images reinforced the report's authenticity against the Pentagon's denial of having lost a spy plane. CNN, that had just signed an exclusive content exchange agreement with Al-Jazeera, even challenged Pentagon officials over the downing of the plane:

> John King, CNN's Senior White House Correspondent: *We will ask the Pentagon and the White House, although we should tell you, the Pentagon and the White House both have been very reluctant to discuss any details of any of the military activities. At first, the Pentagon did*

not even acknowledge at all that one of its spy planes was missing about two weeks ago, finally the Defense Secretary, Donald Rumsfeld, did acknowledge it was missing. They have yet to acknowledge at the Pentagon that it has been shot down, as the Taliban claims – Kyra.

Kyra Phillips, host: *And John, we're seeing that video. You just saw the video that we ran moments ago. Do you think, because we did bring pictures about that the Pentagon will have to respond? And what do you think about those pictures? Is this something that we definitely should believe in?*

King: *Well, the Pentagon will have to respond to our questions. Just what they will say, we will find out in the minutes ahead, I am sure. Very reluctant to discuss any operational details.* (CNN Breaking News, October 6, 2001)

The report on an aircraft shot down at such an early stage of the war was counterproductive to the US Administration's efforts to present the war as smooth and to its well-touted air superiority frame. Jasperson and El-Kikhia (2002, p. 9) used this report to support their claim regarding Al-Jazeera's influence on US reporting, noting that such a report probably would not have been revealed to US viewers without Al-Jazeera. This is true, but one important aspect of assessing the Al-Jazeera Effect is *frame magnitude*, which is missing from Jasperson and El-Kikhia's study. Gitlin defined media frames as "*persistent* patterns of cognition, interpretation, and presentation, of selection, emphasis and exclusion, by which symbol-handlers *routinely* organize discourse, whether verbal or visual" (Gitlin, 1980, p. 7; emphasis mine). Consequently, when studying the re-presentation of Al-Jazeera images, we need to measure the *level* of exposure to the news item in question, providing a vantage point and perspective for examination of the case. In an age of 24/7 news channels, one brief report of an event is guaranteed to create near-zero impact on the daily agenda. Indeed, ABC, CBS, NBC and Fox News did not pick up this report and CNN did not follow up on the downed aircraft and investigate the accident further on other programs, despite the availability of images and the Pentagon's admission that it lost an aircraft. The report virtually disappeared after one airing, possibly as a result of "flak" or a patriotic stance during the war.

The low magnitude pattern for images portraying US military vulnerability also persists in other, similar reports: On October 23, 2001, CNN learned about another military accident through an Al-Jazeera news report that showed Afghanis holding the wheel of what was perceived as the remains of a US helicopter that the Pentagon denied losing (October 23, 2001, CNN *Tonight*). In the report, Jamie McIntyre, CNN military affairs correspondent, notes that there is no way for reporters to really know what is going on inside Afghanistan because there is no access to soldiers, even after missions are completed and that in turn "it took Al-Jazeera to tell Americans that a helicopter had a problem" (CNN *Tonight*, October 23, 2001). Again, however, CNN did not follow this report up, nor was it aired on other networks.

Another event that the US networks ignored was the November 12, 2001 US bombing of Al-Jazeera's offices in Kabul. Various commentators saw the attack as targeted. The BBC's Nic Gowing, who investigated the bombing, concluded: "The US military makes no effort to distinguish between legitimate satellite uplinks for broadcast news communications and the identifiable radio or satellite communications belonging to 'the enemy'." (BBC World News, April 8, 2002; cf. Hoskins, 2004, p. 72). The feeling that the attack was targeted is also buttressed by a "top secret" document from the British Prime Minister's Office, leaked to a *Daily Mirror* reporter in November 2005. The document revealed that US president George W. Bush had discussed bombing Al-Jazeera's offices in various places, including in Qatar. According to the report, British Prime Minister Tony Blair opposed Bush's plan, arguing that such action would cause "a worldwide backlash." Blair's resistance apparently tarnished Bush's plan. According to the report, while one government official dismissed the President's suggestion as "humorous, not serious," another source told the *Daily Mirror*: "Bush was deadly serious, as was Blair. That much is absolutely clear from the language used by both men" (AKI, 2005).

Other signs that the bombing was not coincidental could be found in the fact that the bombing of Al-Jazeera's offices took place about two weeks after Rumsfeld blamed Al-Jazeera for manufacturing images of Afghani civilian casualties (see below) and less than a month after Al-Jazeera's Youssef Al-Shouli reported on a previous bombing attempt:

> *Actually right now we are passing through quite a calm [unintelligible] yesterday [unintelligible] there was one bomb that fell 10 centimeters out of our office. The bombs and rockets were blasting here last night starting from seven o'clock until 12 in Kandahar's time and rocketing from four o'clock up till seven or eight o'clock in the morning. It was very severe shelling targeting all areas.* (CNN *Live Event/Special*, October 19, 2001)

Subsequently, Al-Jazeera stopped broadcasting from Afghanistan and was not able to report the entry of the Northern Alliance forces into Kabul, which according to some accounts was accompanied by massacres of women and children (Hudson, 2005).

The US networks, including Al-Jazeera's content partners CNN and ABC, ignored the report of the strike on Al-Jazeera's offices. None of the US networks criticized the attack or provided any detailed coverage of it. Fox News presented the bombing of the Al-Jazeera offices somewhat sarcastically as "tough luck": "It's been a tough couple of days for the Arabic Al-Jazeera satellite news service, which is Osama Bin Laden's network of choice. First its office in Kabul was hit by American bombs Monday night. American military officials say they had information that the building was being used by the Al-Qaeda terrorist network" (*Fox Special Report with Brit Hume*, November 14, 2001). In another show, Fox News host Bill O'Reilly indicated his support for such tactics as bombing the offices of hostile news networks: "All right, so this is just a fanatical fringe television station, but unfortunately has a tremendous amount of influence in the Arab world. Nothing we can do about it. We bombed them in Afghanistan, we can't take them out in Qatar, that wouldn't be nice" (Fox News, *The O'Reilly Factor*, November 17, 2001).

The self-censorship of reports on US military vulnerability pales, however, to the avoidance of Al-Jazeera reports on Afghani casualties.

How the Networks Self-Censored the Biggest War Story

The Bush Administration was careful to frame the war in Afghanistan as a *targeted* attack on the Taliban terrorist regime and emphasized that it was not a war against Afghanistan or a total war against Islam. In his pre-war speech, Bush stressed that attacks would be targeted against the Taliban regime only:

> *On my orders, the United States military has begun strikes against the Al-Qaeda terrorist training camps and military installations of the Taliban regime in Afghanistan. These carefully targeted actions are designed to disrupt the uses of Afghanistan as a terrorist base of operations and to attack the military capability of the Taliban regime.* (Speech of George W. Bush, as reported on CNN, October 7, 2001)

The tactic of "carefully targeted" airstrikes aimed to frame the war as a "techno war," a sanitized war, in which the Taliban regime would be destroyed with minimal damage to civilians. This is similar to the framing of the humanitarian interventions of the 1990s, in which the technology of "precision bombing" was emphasized to frame US military operations as humanitarian.

Undoubtedly, frequent airing of such reports on the killing of helpless casualties in Afghanistan, one of the poorest countries of the world that was still trying to recover from a civil war, would have undermined moral justification of the war. For a short period, the CNN – Al-Jazeera news-exchange agreement demonstrated the potential inherent in collaboration between Western and non-Western networks for creation of a global (rather than local-patriotic) perspective of news events. The CNN reports illustrated to their viewers that ordinary Afghani citizens and not militants were the main victims of the US bombings. On October 9, two days after the war began, CNN aired Al-Jazeera images of civilian casualties with the following commentary:

> CNN's Paula Zahn: *As you have seen, the American missiles have actually hit a humanitarian aid building and a poor populated area was completely destroyed. But it seems that the fighting concentrates on airports and the air defense installations... There were pictures from the hospital inside Kabul, which showed some injuries, showed some children, women and men who the Taliban claim have been injured in the previous night's attack. Reports of fear from ordinary civilians...* (CNN Live, October 13, 2001)

CNN then gave Al-Jazeera's reporters Tayseer Allouni and Youssef Al-Shouli a platform from which to provide its "global viewers" with the Arab perspective of the suffering of civilians remaining in Afghanistan. The Al-Jazeera reporters revealed to the audience that the civilians left to suffer the US bombings were only the poor who could not afford to flee the bombing sites, casting doubt on the war's moral justification:

> Paula Zahn: *You mentioned that a number of Afghan refugees were trying to flee Kabul, going to nearby villages. And yet behind you it appears as though there are children playing in the street with a ball.*
>
> Tayseer *Allouni, Al-Jazeera correspondent (through translator): The number of – we are unable to count the number or know exactly what the number is. But it's worth mentioning that the people who are leaving at the moment are leaving with difficulty. It's very difficult for them. And the reason why many families have remained in Kabul is that they are too poor to travel. They don't have enough money to rent a car or take taxis to move them outside the capital or to other countries, Pakistan or Iran, for example.*
>
> *Secondly, most of the people, if asked – and we've asked them – why they haven't left the capital under that stage of circumstances, they said first the – a large number of them told us that, that they don't have enough money to travel and they don't have somewhere to go to.*
>
> Zahn: *So poverty has prevented many people from leaving the capital.*
>
> Allouni: *A lot of the people of Kabul have moved out. They've tried leaving the city, the capital, but most of the people who stayed on are the very poor and desperate, who have no – who have – they can't actually go elsewhere. As they told us, they don't have anywhere to go to. The only possible way would be for them is to go out in the open. They are very depressed and very desperate. This is a very painful – ironic.*
>
> *This man is actually looking through the rubble, trying to find any bodies underneath. We saw a lot of families who actually live on bread and tea. They can't go elsewhere; they don't have the money and they don't have the resources.* (CNN, *Sunday Morning*, October 28, 2001)

As the transcript shows, Allouni's interpretation revealed the gloomy fate of the poor Afghanis – a perspective of which both Zahn and US viewers were unaware. The other networks (including Al-Jazeera's content partner ABC) completely ignored these Al-Jazeera eyewitness reports. Altogether, the five networks re-presented Al-Jazeera's reports on civilian casualties only on 17 news shows over the course of the war in Afghanistan (October 7 to November 13, 2001, the day Al-Jazeera's office in Kabul was bombed), 12 of which were on CNN. Considering that Al-Jazeera had exclusive presence in many incidents of bombing of casualties, this is undoubtedly a very low usage of Al-Jazeera's footage of civilian casualties.

Overall, it is safe to say that the networks fell silent in Afghanistan on civilian attacks that were presented on Al-Jazeera. One powerful explanation may be the Administration's success in framing Al-Jazeera as a network that serves terrorist interests. An NBC report of bombed villages and civilian casualties contextualized the Al-Jazeera report in line with Defense Secretary Rumsfeld's unsubstantiated allegation that Al-Jazeera had manufactured the images. In an interview on NBC on October 28, 2001, Rumsfeld accused Al-Jazeera of propaganda and described its coverage as "propagandistic and inflammatory," claiming that they were manufacturing images: "What they do is when a bomb goes down they grab some children and some women and pretend that the bomb hit the women and the children" (NBC Evening News, October 28, 2001).

Most important, in Afghanistan the US networks chose to self-censor what could have been under different circumstances the biggest news story of the war arguably because its source was Al-Jazeera: The images from the accidental massacre of 122 civilians on October 23, 2001. On that day, the US military bombing of a village near Kandahar killed 93 civilians and another bombing in the village of Quetta killed another 29 civilians. The Pentagon has acknowledged that on at least two occasions on that day, its bombs mistakenly hit civilian areas (ABC World News Now, October 23, 2001). The Pentagon and Al-Jazeera were the only sources of footage of the attack. To report the incidents, CNN, NBC and ABC used the Pentagon footage, that showed injured civilians in a hospital in Baghdad, mostly in good condition compared to those featured in Al-Jazeera's images. The original Al-Jazeera reports, however, included very graphic images, ranging from young children bruised and bandaged in hospitals (including one famous image that showed severely bruised dead children) through mothers wailing and lamenting the loss of families, to bodies laid out on stretchers and people digging graves for civilians. CNN chose to show the relatively "sterile" and after-the-fact images of houses reduced to rubble and of covered bodies and wounded citizens (CNN Live, October 8, 2001). While the US networks self-censored the killing of Afghani civilians before, such as the October 8, 2001, bombing that destroyed a military hospital around Kabul and the October 9 report of a US missile attack that hit a mine-clearing humanitarian organization and reportedly killed four of its Afghani employees, this time the massacre was of such a scale that the US media could not ignore it according to the basic professional standards of impartiality, especially in comparison to the presentation of similar events during the previous crisis.

To seek perspective on the reporting of this tragedy, we can recall that in the 1991 Gulf War, a tragedy of similar scale became one of the most memorable events of the war. On February 13, 1991, US forces dropped two electro-optical smart bombs, each 2,000 pounds in weight, on a civilian center. They smashed through the steel-reinforced roof of a large concrete building in the middle-class Baghdad suburb of Al-Amiriya that was being used as a bomb shelter by a large number of women and children. According to official sources, 288 people died in that bombing. While the massacre in Afghanistan was mostly ignored by the US networks, Western reporters and film crews were taken to the scene of the Al-Amiriya disaster around seven hours after the event and began to cover it widely. Brent McGregor, who studied television coverage of the bombing, described the reporting as "overdrive reporting [of] what promised to be *the single most important story of the air war*" (McGregor, 1994, p. 242; emphasis mine). The reporting involved "... the unprecedented issue of large numbers of reporters working from an enemy capital under fire, filing reports that the enemy might use for propaganda purposes to reach over the heads of governments and their persuasion machines to speak directly to Western public opinion" (McGregor, 1994, p. 242).

In 1991, CNN was the first international network to report the event. Peter Arnett –one of America's most experienced reporters and the winner of a Pulitzer Prize for his coverage of the Vietnam War – spoke of seeing bodies "charred almost beyond recognition" (cf. McGregor, 1994, p. 242). He mentioned that there was no military target within miles of this carnage, adding: "This is the worst of the civilian incidents we have seen in Baghdad so far" (Ibid.). In a subsequent interview with the CNN anchor, scenes of Al-Amiriya were shown. One shot displayed a clearly visible sign reading "Shelter" in Arabic and English – a sign that cast blame on the US for bombing the site. Other photos showed three wide shots of blanket-covered bodies lying outside on the ground. Even the battle-hardened Arnett described them as "one of the most grisly scenes I have ever seen" (McGregor, 1994, p. 243).

In contrast to their 2001 Afghanistan war reporting patterns, the free-to-air networks – ABC, CBS and NBC –covered the 1991 massacre extensively. On ABC, studio anchor Peter Jennings said: "What we all agree is a tragic loss of civilian life" (ABC *World News Tonight with Peter Jennings*, February 13, 1991). Viewers saw images of grieving Iraqis and a local man who said to Americans: "This is the product of your democracy" (Ibid.). Dr. Boghos Boghossian, a doctor tending to the injured, spoke directly to the camera: "Is this in conformity with international regulations? Just have a look, won't you [pointing to bodies]? Would you call this mercy and justice? This is the most horrible, the most cruel thing I have ever witnessed" (ABC *World News Tonight With Peter Jennings*, February 13, 1991).

CBS went even farther. It accepted the original Iraqi tally of five hundred bodies (later reports gave, as we have seen, the more cautious total of 288). Dan Rather presented the massacre as a result of the failure of the "precision bombing technology," saying: "Today that same high technology may have led to the worst civilian losses of the war" (CBS *Evening News*, February 13, 1991), confirming that there were "many, many women and children among the casualties" (Ibid.). Before pictures of the bombing damage were aired, Dan Rather cautioned his audience that they included "some graphic scenes of the reality of war." The report showed a grief-stricken man looking at the wounded and bodies and asking: "Is this a military target? Our families were killed. I can't find my daughter" (Ibid.). NBC adopted a similar policy. It presented graphic images taken from BBC coverage of Baghdad and broadcast interviews with the grieving father of one of the victims, who said: "I only hope that those responsible for this can be forgiven by God" (NBC *Evening News*, February 13, 1991).

Clearly, no media blackout was imposed on US television networks. On the contrary, the media covered the massacre extensively, used graphic images of the dead and raised no objection when their own anchors, such as Dan Rather, deplored "precision bombing" technology as such. There is an apparent contrast between the case of precision bombing gone wrong, erroneously killing civilians in 1991, when Western news sources were brought to the bunker by Saddam Hussein's minders and the self-censorship of Al-Jazeera's images in Afghanistan.

CHAPTER SIX

THE ENEMY'S VOICE

This chapter examines the US media's re-presentation of messages aired on Al-Jazeera from "the enemy" – Bin Laden and his terror group Al-Qaeda. Counterinsurgency theorists (Laqueur, 1976; Clutterbuck, 1981; Wright, 1984) maintain that by reporting on terrorist acts, the media creates a platform for terrorist organizations and thereby encourages the terrorists to carry out more attacks. In the wake of the September 11 attacks, Liebes and Kampf (2004) argued that the US media has given more airtime then ever to the messages of terrorists, listening to their explanations despite the format in which the messages were brought; unmediated video or audio messages in which there was no room for questioning of the message. Liebes and Kampf (2004) argue that one of the reasons behind the rise of terrorist voices in the US is the advent of "CNN-like" Al-Jazeera to the news scene: "... 'quoting' from channels such as Al-Arabia, Abu-Dhabi or Al-Jazeera, whose more empathic stance toward terrorism offers an address for terrorists to send tapes and grant interviews, softens the criticism against Western channels as giving legitimacy to terrorists" (Liebes & Kampf, 2004, p. 81).

By contrast, Sontag argues that terrorist messages should not be censored if they contain an important message. She argues that the Daniel Pearl video, for example, was censored before Americans had a chance to see that the kidnappers had a list of demands and that they linked the kidnapping with the US's pro-Israel policy (Sontag, 2004, p. 69).

This chapter takes a third view: If and when the US networks decide to present such messages, they ought not apply a double standard. They should not filter information in accordance with the Administration's interests.

The second assumption that this chapter makes is that a fair representation of Al-Qaeda videos is important in light of Americans demand in the wake of September 11 to address the question: "Why do they [Arab world] hate us so much?"

This chapter shows, through an analysis of the re-presentation of the Al-Qaeda terrorist video delivered by Al-Jazeera, that in light of the 'flak' (negative response) received from the Bush Administration, the US networks backed off and addressed the Administration's requests to downplay any "explanation" for the attacks . The analysis reveals that while Al-Qaeda messages that support US allegations regarding Bin Laden's responsibility for the September 11 attacks were emphasized, those that challenge the US Administration's stance, such as denying such responsibility and messages that refer to US failure to capture Al-Qaeda operatives, were self-censored. At the same time, the US media argued for a strong link between Al-Qaeda and Al-Jazeera as a response to the demonization of Al-Jazeera by the Bush Administration.

The Administration's Position on Al-Qaeda Messages

After the September 11 attacks, the US Administration viewed Al-Jazeera's broadcasts as detrimental to the US policy of winning the "hearts and minds" of Arabs in what they saw as the emergent "propaganda war." In particular, the Administration feared that Al-Jazeera's broadcasting of Bin Laden's messages depicted US military activities in the Middle East as a war on Islam rather than a war on terror. The direct broadcast of these images to Al-Jazeera's 50 million viewers worldwide led the Administration to believe that the US is engaged in an information war with Al-Jazeera over Arab public opinion.

Initially, neoconservatives and liberals disagreed regarding the best way to combat Al-Jazeera's clout in the Arab world, as did several high-ranking civilian and military officials (Hudson, 2005). The State Department in particular, headed by Secretary Colin Powell, thought that the US should take advantage of Al-Jazeera and other Arabic channels, with their huge Arab audience, seizing every opportunity to appear on Middle East satellite television. By contrast, the neoconservatives and Pentagon hardliners saw Al-Jazeera as an enemy that needs to be brought to submission. Consequently, policies concerning Al-Jazeera were rather ambiguous: As early as October 3, 2001, Powell took the first step towards stopping Al-Jazeera's broadcasting and urged the visiting Emir of Qatar to rein in the network for being unbalanced and airing vitriolic and irresponsible anti-American statements. The US also launched numerous public attacks on the integrity, quality, and credibility of Al-Jazeera. At the same time, it sought to convey its own message through that same network: Powell,

Condoleezza Rice, Donald Rumsfeld and other high ranking US officials allowed themselves to be interviewed by Al-Jazeera (Saeed, 2003, p. 2). In addition, the US Administration's counter-propaganda efforts included the establishment of the Office of Global Communications (OGC), an important tool in the fight over Arab "hearts and minds". (The attempts at reversing the Al-Jazeera clout on Arab psyche are documents in chapter 2).

This chapter traces the manipulation in the presentation of Bin Laden's messages, in line with the Administration's information war declaration. It begins with the less well known first message from Bin Laden, in which he denies his responsibility for the September 11, 2001 attacks.

Although many are familiar with Bin Laden's famous October 7, 2001 message, arguably demonstrating his involvement in the September 11 attacks – the first post-September 11 Bin Laden message actually came as early as five days after the attacks. On September 16, Bin Laden faxed a message to Al-Jazeera, denying any role in the deadly attacks: "I stress that I have not carried out this act, which appears to have been carried out by individuals with their own motivation." The fax came as a response to the Bush Administration's allegations that Bin Laden was behind the attacks.

However, none of the networks aired this denial of responsibility from the main suspect in the terrorist attacks. The message was only mentioned in retrospect, after Bin Laden's guilt was established. For example, in its report on a December 13, 2001 Pentagon message indicting Bin Laden, ABC reported that "[the] message was different from the one previously delivered to the world by the Saudi millionaire" (ABC *Evening News*, December 13, 2001).

In addition to the denial of his responsibility for the attacks, Al-Jazeera aired a re-run of an exclusive interview with Osama Bin Laden taken after the 1998 US Embassy bombings in Kenya and Tanzania (which killed 12 Americans and hundreds of local citizens (Bin Laden and his vice Al-Zawahiri were the masterminds behind the attacks). As a result, on October 3, US Secretary of State Colin Powell met with the emir of Qatar Sheikh Hamad bin Khalifa al-Thani, asking him to use his influence to "tone down" Al-Jazeera's coverage.

When Al-Jazeera continued to air messages from Bin-Laden, the Administration declared an information war with Al-Jazeera. This started a debate about the attitude towards Al-Jazeera: The US channels that had business ties in Afghanistan argued for Al-Jazeera's credibility, while the other channels argued that Al-Jazeera is an enemy in the emergent information war. This debate was the beginning of the framing of Al-Jazeera as a deviant source.

The Bin Laden Videos and the Debate re Al-Jazeera's Credibility

On October 7, 2001, Al-Jazeera aired the video message arguably indicting Bin Laden, allegedly filmed a few hours after the US-led coalition commenced its attack on Afghanistan. Over the next three days, it was discussed on 12 different news shows on the five networks. In the video, Bin Laden states that "America will never taste security and safety unless we feel security and safety in our land and in Palestine" and justifies the attacks in the name of Muslim revenge. Bin Laden then called Bush "the head of the infidels" and blamed him for starting a war on Islam in the name of a "war on terrorism". Bin Laden also mentioned what he described as past US "war crimes," such as the nuclear bombing of Japan during the Second World War. In his message, Bin Laden addressed some notes from Bush's speeches after September 11, 2001: In response to Bush's call for countries to take sides either for or against the terrorists, Bin Laden called Muslims to take sides either in the "camp of belief" or with the infidels.

The US Administration did not respond immediately to this message and in turn the networks continued to screen large segments of the message and discuss its contents. CBS (*60 Minutes*, October 7) rebroadcast the message in its entirety and then discussed some of Bin Laden's allegations. ABC's Peter Jennings specifically asked reporter John Miller to "take us through what he [Bin Laden] had to say" (ABC *World News Tonight*, October 7, 2001). Miller repeated Bin Laden's message that Americans will never be safe until Israel is out of Palestine and that the attacks on the World Trade Center were "God's work." He also repeated Bin Laden's three "explanations" for the attacks (as presented in the tape): (a) US sanctions in the bombing of Iraq, (b) US support of Israel against the Palestinians, and (c) the continued presence of US forces in his homeland of Saudi Arabia. Furthermore, Miller reported that Bin Laden was "taking a page" from President Bush's speech when he called on Muslims to take a position and unite against the West (Bush, as noted, called for nations to decide whether they are with "us" (the free world) or with "them" (the terrorists). CNN and NBC also aired the message in its entirety and CNN's terrorism expert Peter Bergen (CNN *Live at Daybreak*, October 8, 2001) and NBC's reporter Andrea Mitchell (Today, October 8, 2001) analyzed the contents of the entire video message during its airing. The networks reported that Bin Laden did not admit responsibility for the attacks in the message, although some accounts mentioned that it has been Bin Laden's strategy in the past to not admit responsibility immediately for terrorist attacks that he was behind.

Airing the message served the US Administration's interest of linking Bin Laden with the attacks but also presented a counterargument to Bush's allegations, showing that the enemy "has a name and a face" and even countering Bush's accusations regarding Al-Qaeda. Moreover, it contributed to a more inclusive perspective of events that illustrates the enemy's point of view

The Administration responded immediately following the networks' engagement with the contents of the message, criticizing the "lack of context" under which it was aired (Moran, 2001). On October 9, Secretary of National Security Condoleezza Rice called the networks' managers and asked that they censor the Bin Laden message because it might contain hidden codes to terrorists regarding plans for future attacks. A day later (on October 10, 2001), White House press secretary Ari Fleischer also blamed Al-Jazeera for airing the messages unedited, thus playing into the hands of terrorists, stating the Administration's position as follows: "At best, this is a forum for prerecorded, pre-taped propaganda inciting people to kill Americans. At worst, the broadcasts could contain signals to "sleeper" agents. The concern here is not allowing terrorists to receive what might be a message from Osama Bin Laden calling on them to take any actions" (Agencies, 2001. http://eveningsun.com/headlines/censorbin.htm).

In response to the Administration's suspicion that the messages might contain orders to terrorists, the five major US networks agreed to self-censor the messages unilaterally, although there was no clear proof of the allegation. In an official statement, Fox News said: "We believe a free press must and can bear responsibility not to be used by those who want to destroy America and endanger the lives of its citizens" (Agencies, 2001).

This unity behind the consent to censor the images should raise a few concerns as to whether the networks complied with the Administration's request at the expense of free public debate, for three reasons: First, the allegations that the messages carry codes to terrorists were never proven; second, as Al-Qaeda did not depend on messages on national television networks to plan the attacks of September 11, 2001, but had already used other methods of international communication (i.e. electronic mail), it is difficult to claim that they depended on national television as a communication method; third, the networks did not consider alternative broadcasting methods – such as dubbing the messages into English – that would minimize the chances of Al-Qaeda's depending on them for future attack planning.

Furthermore, the networks' apparent acceptance of this unsubstantiated allegation, that clearly discredits Al-Jazeera as a (free) news source, is somewhat surprising, as they had praised Al-Jazeera as "free and independent" only a couple of months before the September 11, 2001 attacks (CBS, 60 *Minutes*, August 26, 2001). Before September 11, the Al-Jazeera network was relatively anonymous in the West, even if it was the most popular station in the Arab world. The few times the Al-Jazeera name appeared on Western screens were after its exclusive images of US bombings in Iraq during the 1998 Desert Fox operation and in early 2001, after Al-Jazeera aired exclusive images of Taliban fighters destroying historically valuable statues of Buddha in Kabul, showing the world the organization's brutality. CBS then dedicated an item to Al-Jazeera on its flagship current events show 60 *Minutes*, calling it "the news network that might bring democracy to the Middle-East." CBS lauded Al-Jazeera for challenging the autocratic regimes in the Middle East by airing stories on topics formerly considered taboo in the Arab world, such as human rights, women's right to vote and privatization of the public educational system, thus promoting freedom of speech and mobilizing public opinion in the region towards democracy.

While all networks agreed to edit and censor the messages before airing, an analysis reveals disagreement between the networks that signed content-exchange agreement with Al-Jazeera (CNN and ABC) and those that did not (CBS, NBC and Fox News) regarding Al-Jazeera's link to Bin Laden. While all the five networks agreed that an "information war," aimed at persuading Arabs that the war is on terrorism and not on Islam, emerged in the wake of September 11, they disagreed on how to fight it. CBS, Fox News and NBC saw Al-Jazeera as a "problem" for US propaganda efforts because of its alleged "anti-American stance" and links to Bin Laden, while CNN and ABC saw it as more of a "solution" and a conduit through which the US could fight the propaganda war and win the "hearts and minds" battle. CNN and ABC encouraged interviews of US officials on Al-Jazeera's airwaves to explain US policy to Al-Jazeera's viewers directly.

To illustrate the framing of the Al-Jazeera–Al-Qaeda link by NBC, who saw Al-Jazeera as a problem to US foreign policy, consider the following statement by NBC's Tom Brokaw:

> *As we were reminded once again tonight by the latest chilling words from an al-Qaeda spokesman, one of Osama Bin Laden's most potent weapons is propaganda. And to get his anti-American messages out to the world he often relies on a controversial 24-hour television network that the US State Department criticized just today for its role in this propaganda war.* (NBC *Nightly News*, October 9, 2001)

The interview that followed this statement was hostile from the start, particularly because of the repeated use of "accusatory questions" (see Clayman and Heritage, 2002, pp. 221–226):

> Dawn Fratangelo [NBC]: ... *But why give air time to the most wanted man in the world?*
>
> Sami Haddad (Al-Jazeera correspondent): *We have people who criticize, somebody who is defending what's on. And we deal with the taboos in our world which other stations don't, and that is why we have become famous.*
>
> Fratangelo: ... *But Al-Jazeera is also famous for seeming to steer clear of the Western view and thereby gaining the trust of some extremists and leaders like Saddam Hussein.* (NBC *Nightly News*, October 9, 2001)

Fratangelo then reminded the audience that Secretary of State Colin Powell asked Al-Jazeera to "tone down" what he called its "anti-American sentiments." In conclusion, Fratangelo repeated Tom Brokaw's earlier accusation that Al-Jazeera was a conduit for Bin Laden: "Al-Jazeera has been controversial from the start and never more so than now as Osama Bin Laden uses its airwaves to declare a holy war on the United States." (NBC *Nightly News*, October 9, 2001). Traditionally, reporters/anchors would present both sides of an argument during the closing segment of a story; in this instance, however, Fratangelo notably failed to echo those who defend Al-Jazeera's credibility in favor of emphasizing the accusations leveled against the network.

Next, on October 22, 2001, NBC *Today* anchor Matt Lauer interviewed Al-Jazeera reporter Ghida Fakhri. During the opening segment, Lauer noted that Al-Jazeera recently came to the attention of Americans "for broadcasting statements made by Osama Bin Laden and others linked to Al-Qaeda." Lauer failed to mention that Al-Jazeera was also famous for its exclusive combat footage from Kabul, that was being used by all of the American networks at that time. During the interview, Lauer accused Al-Jazeera of inciting hatred: "People here in this country who have now come to know ... Al-Jazeera in the last six weeks, think it is just an outlet for American hatred" (NBC, *Today*, October 22, 2001). When Fakhri commented that she was surprised that the US was attempting to limit freedom of speech, Lauer dismissed her response and asserted that Fakhri was "only a reporter" and therefore ill-equipped to answer his question: "Well, let me ... You don't run the network ... you're a reporter, you're a correspondent." Lauer consistently employed a coercive and hostile questioning technique known as negative formulation, that projects a "yes" response to rhetorical questions (see Clayman and Heritage, 2002, pp. 217–221): "... But when you see videotapes of Osama Bin Laden or his associates calling for a holy war against Israel and the United States, is it not fair to say that Al-Jazeera is being used to stir up hatred of America throughout the world?" (NBC, *Today*, October 22, 2001)

CBS took a similar stance. On October 7, 2001, anchor Ed Bradley reported that President George W. Bush and Secretary of State Colin Powell had asked the Emir of Qatar "to tone Al-Jazeera's reporting down" and repeated their allegations that Al-Jazeera was being used by Osama Bin Laden as a "conduit" to the Arab world. Reaffirming the Administration's complaints, he stated: "When he [Bin Laden] has something to say, you will see it on Al-Jazeera and there's been increasing criticism that the network has become his mouthpiece and is not reporting the news." (CBS, *60 Minutes*, October 7, 2001). Bradley then cited an anonymous "Cairo source" who speculated that the message's improved recording quality suggests that Al-Jazeera provided Osama Bin Laden with a new camera. This, of course, strengthened the viewers' conception of a relationship between Bin Laden and Al-Jazeera; Bradley reaffirmed: "Dan, it's clear that if Al-Jazeera doesn't know how to reach Osama Bin Laden, he sure knows how to reach them" (CBS, *60 Minutes*, October 7, 2001). Dan Rather also questioned the source of Al-Jazeera's funding, alleging that it is terrorists rather than the Emir of Qatar that back the network financially: "Any indication that Osama Bin Laden, through some shell game, has helped finance this operation?" (CBS, *60 Minutes*, October 7, 2001). Notably, Rather refers to Al-Jazeera as an "operation" rather than a network, possibly implying a sinister nature or purpose and a specific agenda.

On October 11, 2001, CBS *Early Show* co-host Jane Clayson accused Al-Jazeera's Washington Bureau Chief Yosri Fouda of acting as a conduit for Bin Laden: "Fouda, you've faced a lot of criticism for airing such inflammatory rhetoric. Do you feel like you're a mouthpiece for ... for a world terrorist? ... Is there an understanding or an agreement between Al-Jazeera and Bin Laden and his associates about airing this videotape? Why are ... you the only ones to receive it?" (CBS, *Early Show*, October 11, 2001)

Similarly, Dan Rather opened the October 12 CBS *Evening News* with an acknowledgement that the "rules of the game" for broadcasting had changed with the emergence of Al-Jazeera. He stated that Osama Bin Laden took advantage of this new Arab news channel and benefited from it directly: "The world's most wanted terrorist reaches millions, including thousands in this country, thanks to a network that speaks his own language." (CBS *Evening News*, October 12, 2001). By comparison, consider the text of the August 26, 2001 broadcast of CBS's *60 Minutes* that explored the emergence of Al-Jazeera as a force for positive change in the Middle East, with Ed Bradley describing Al-Jazeera as a "free network," referring to it as follows:

> *Until recently, what people in the Arab world watched was strictly controlled by the hereditary rulers and the authoritarian leaders who held power in the region for decades. Now, as we saw last spring, for the first time, their control is being challenged ... The challenge is coming from, of all places, one of the smallest countries in the world, an upstart desert kingdom on the Persian Gulf called Qatar and, from of all things, a tiny television network with a big mouth ... It's called Al-Jazeera Satellite Channel, and it's the first 24-hour television news network in the Arab world. It is also the first Arab news organization that is independent and uncensored.* (CBS, 60 *Minutes*, May 6, 2001; second broadcast on August 26, 2001)

Obviously, the post September 11 transcripts demonstrate a clear shift in perception of Al-Jazeera from a network that plays a major role in democratizing the Middle East – much lauded by the networks and the US Government – to a mouthpiece for terrorists.

Perhaps predictably, of the five major news networks, it was Fox News that consistently took the strongest stance against Al-Jazeera. During a panel interview on October 10, the *Fox Special Report with Brit Hume* show raised the question of whether the US media should air Osama Bin Laden's messages. While the panel interview format usually brings "people together who are worlds apart" (Clayman and Heritage, 2002, p. 300) to debate conflicting viewpoints, in this instance, all panel members (selected *a priori* by Fox News' producers) shared the same oppositional perspective of Al-Jazeera, typified by their commonly held belief that Al-Jazeera actively cooperated with Bin Laden. During a discussion about the US Administration's ability to intercept electronic transmissions (e.g., cellular phones), *Roll Call* magazine editor Mort Kondracke and National Public Radio reporter Mara Liasson suggested that Osama Bin Laden used Al-Jazeera's website to communicate with other terrorists, thereby bypassing the threat of interception. Kondracke then commented: "... anybody who buys a satellite that gets Al-Jazeera, check him out" (*Fox Special Report with Brit Hume*, October 10, 2001). None of the other participants opposed this idea.

On October 18, 2001, another *Fox Special Report with Brit Hume* panel discussed a proposed joint Al-Jazeera/CNN interview with Osama Bin Laden. The panel argued that Al-Jazeera was attempting to use CNN's credibility and resources to spread Bin Laden's message. Guest panelist Mara Liasson saw that Al-Jazeera was "tricking" CNN and warned that should CNN choose not to air the interview, Al-Jazeera would still be able to broadcast the piece using CNN's logo: "All of a sudden, Osama Bin Laden is broadcast to millions of people in the Middle East, and here, to people who get it off the dish network, with CNN on it, which makes it much more legitimate and an even bigger figure than he is today." (*Fox Special Report With Brit Hume*, October 18, 2001). Fred Barnes, Executive Editor of *The Weekly Standard*, also insinuated that the joint interview was an Al-Jazeera – Bin Laden plot: "Yes, look where this came from. It wasn't CNN's idea. It came from Al-Jazeera, who said they'd been approached by somebody who would get these questions dealt with by Osama Bin Laden. I think this is a further propaganda effort by Osama Bin Laden." (*Fox Special Report With Brit Hume*, October 18, 2001). In another instance, Fox News anchor John Gibson and guests discussed why America was having such difficulty conveying its point of view about the war on terror to the Muslim world. Gibson blamed both Bin Laden and Al-Jazeera for the failure of US "propaganda efforts," claiming that Al-Jazeera was responsible for persuading Muslims to fight against America: " … and it seems like there's a billion Muslims around the world who are quickly becoming very radicalized by Al-Jazeera and Osama Bin Laden and the rest. What are we supposed to do about this?" (Fox, *The Big Story*, November 2, 2001).

On Fox News *The Unresolved Problem* (November 26), anchor Bill O'Reilly explored the role of Al-Jazeera "which reaches 35 million Arabs, and has been unrelentingly anti-American" in the information war between the West and the Muslim world. O'Reilly introduced his guest, Dr Walid Phares, a senior research fellow at the Foundation for the Defense of Democracies (FDD), as a scholar who was "monitoring" Al-Jazeera. Phares referred to Al-Jazeera as a "mouthpiece" for Islamic Jihad, and noted that its influence over Arabs was extensive: "There are millions and millions around the Arab world who watch them, because what they did was to present themselves as the TV which is independent. Indeed, they are independent from the regimes in the region, but they're not independent from the ideology that they are promoting, which is jihad, after all." (Fox News, *The O'Reilly Factor*, November 26, 2001)

As noted, both CNN and ABC, the two networks that signed content agreements with Al-Jazeera, did not accept the allegations that Al-Jazeera cooperates with Bin Laden, perhaps because doing so could mean that they also assisted Al-Qaeda indirectly through their cooperation. It is reasonable to argue that CNN – whose founder Ted Turner emphasizes its "international" stance and banned its reporters from relating to global news items as "foreign" news – aimed at gaining a competitive advantage over the other networks thanks to its relationship with Al-Jazeera, similar to the edge that CNN gained over its competitors through Peter Arnett's access to reports from behind enemy lines in the 1991 Gulf War.

In turn, it should not come as a great surprise that CNN – and to a lesser extent ABC – did not initially support the attack on the credibility of their new content partner. Both networks adopted a more ambivalent stance regarding the alleged link between Al-Jazeera and Al-Qaeda. While CNN and ABC agreed to censor Bin Laden's messages, they adopted a far more measured tone than Fox News, CBS and NBC: ABC has never conclusively refuted or confirmed the allegation but only implied once that some connection between Al-Jazeera and Bin Laden might exist, using the somewhat ambiguous term "mysterious" to describe it: "When Osama Bin Laden wants to speak, a tape mysteriously arrives at Al-Jazeera's offices in Kabul" (*World News Tonight*, October 10, 2001). In other transcripts, ABC was full of praise for Al-Jazeera, reminiscent of the network's pre-September 11, 2001 representation on US television and taking note of Al-Jazeera's relative independence in a "troubled" region where the media are usually state-controlled:

> Stephanopoulos: *This Arab satellite news network, which some call the CNN of the Arab world, is also the network of choice for Osama Bin Laden, who regularly releases videos to the station and grants them interviews when he has a message to relate to the world. Watched by an estimated 35 million people worldwide, Al-Jazeera gets credit for revolutionizing the Arab world's tradition of state-censored media … Many of its journalists have been trained by the BBC and its formats mimic BBC News and current affairs programs … In fact, you know, last week, Colin Powell went to the Emir of Qatar and said, "Can you tone down the anti-American coverage?" But in the past, it's been the Arab governments who've complained about Al-Jazeera and say they're giving too much time to American and pro-Israeli viewpoints.* (ABC, *Good Morning America*, October 9, 2001)

In fact, ABC's anchor encouraged US officials to fight the emergent information war *with* Al-Jazeera and not oppose it. Stephanopoulos stated his belief that US officials should talk to Arabs directly through Al-Jazeera and persuade them that the war is against terrorism and not against Islam:

> Stephanopoulos: *Just yesterday afternoon, the White House got a request from Al-Jazeera to have President Bush go on. They still have it under consideration. They're looking at having other officials to go on as well. But the White House is doing a broad effort now to speak to the Arab world. We also found out that they're now air-dropping thousands of transistor radios, wind-up transistor radios into Afghanistan so they can give a direct message to the Afghani people as well.*
>
> Gibson: *If you were advising the President, would you tell him to go on Al-Jazeera?*
>
> Stephanopoulos: *I'd do it, absolutely. Go straight to the source.* (ABC, *Good Morning America*, October 9, 2001)

Similarly, CNN's anchors strongly argued for Al-Jazeera's credibility. Howard Kurtz, host of CNN *Reliable Sources* (October 10, 2001), argued on the show against the allegations for a link between Al-Jazeera and Osama Bin Laden, repeating Al-Jazeera's argument that the US networks would also have broadcast Bin Laden's message if presented with the opportunity because it was "inherently newsworthy":

> Woodruff: *So not a reason to be suspicious that they're the ones who got the Bin Laden tapes?*
>
> Kurtz: *They claim that this was given to them by an intermediary, and I know some people say, well, gee, if they're putting this on the air, they're giving a terrorist a platform. I would suggest that any Western news organization that got that videotape, however it might have been obtained, would have put it on the air, because although it was horrifying and chilling it was newsworthy. Clearly newsworthy.* (CNN Reliable Sources, October 10, 2001)

During the studio discussion, Judy Woodruff described the dilemma facing the US media regarding the re-presentation of Bin Laden's messages "...we're getting into a very, very sensitive area, where American press, obviously patriotic, cares about the country that we live in, but at the same time wants to try to report the news in a fair and – in a fair way" (CNN *Live Events*, October 10, 2001). Kurtz revealed that the US networks were under enormous pressure from conflicting forces: "On the one hand, they do not want to aid the enemy, but on the other, they also do not want to "black out the other side." Kurtz noted that the current dilemma was similar to that experienced by CNN during the 1991 Gulf War: "People said: 'Why are we hearing those messages?' Because it's important to know what the other side is saying in this kind of new war" (CNN *Live Events*, October 10, 2001).

Ultimately, the analysis found that following the Bush Administration's 'flak' regarding the airing of Bin Laden's messages, CNN chose to play a double game in an attempt to satisfy both its journalistic needs and the demands of patriotism, complying with National Security Advisor Condoleezza Rice's request not to air unedited Bin Laden messages (and later, with Rumsfeld's request not to air graphic images of war casualties) while refusing to frame its content partner as a mouthpiece for Bin Laden. This policy is similar to CNN's overall reporting policy after September 11, as it needed to balance between commitments to global (CNN International) and local (CNN US) audiences, as illustrated in McChesney's (2002) analysis of the differences between CNN international "transnational" angle of events versus CNN US patriotic angle .

On November 1, 2001, Al-Jazeera broadcast a new message it received by fax from Bin Laden. The statement called the Afghanistan war "a battle of religion between Christians and Muslims" and criticized Pakistan for being "under the banner of the cross." This letter was followed by a video message on November 3 in which Bin Laden claimed the US had no proof to justify its attacks on

Afghanistan and also attacked the United Nations, calling it "an instrument of crime against Muslims."

This time, the White House responded to Bin Laden's message within two hours of its broadcasting, fighting back in the propaganda war by addressing Arab viewers directly through Al-Jazeera. The Bush Administration defined both Bin Laden messages as "more of the same propaganda" and "explained" to Americans that Bin Laden is now feeling the pressure of US-led attacks on Afghanistan. The Administration also attacked the contents of the message, which, they claimed, alienated moderate Arab states such as Egypt, Saudi Arabia and other Arab League members (as Bin Laden was attacking the United Nations). Furthermore, former US Ambassador to Syria Christopher Ross appeared on Al-Jazeera and, in fluent Arabic, labeled Bin Laden's message as "lies" and "propaganda."

The networks sided with the Administration. For NBC, Ross's appearance (NBC *Nightly News*, November 5, 2001) was part of a new White House public relations offensive aimed at discrediting Bin Laden and the Taliban within the Arab world. The NBC anchors persistently referred to an emergent information war between Bin Laden and the Bush Administration on other broadcasts and even in the context of war images, thus giving weight to the idea of a propaganda war. On another news show, NBC anchors noted that the propaganda war was exacerbated after Al-Jazeera aired some "troubling images of civilian casualties" (NBC *Nightly News*, November 4, 2001), linking it with the airing of Bin Laden videos. NBC's pro-Administration stand is illustrated by its support of US propaganda efforts: "Tonight White House officials are declaring a major victory in the public relations war" (NBC *Nightly News*; November 5, 2001). On the Fox News network, anchor John Gibson asked *Weekly Standard* Editor Bill Kristol for his insight on an emergent problem: [non-] Penetration of the American view of the war on terrorism in the Muslim world. Gibson pointed to both Bin Laden and Al-Jazeera as major factors responsible for radicalizing Muslims against America, asserting "...and it seems like there's a billion Muslims around the world who are quickly becoming very radicalized by Al-Jazeera and Osama Bin Laden and the rest. What are we supposed to do about this?" (Fox News, *The Big Story*, November 2, 2001). CBS also cheered the Administration's offensive and its importance in fighting the information war. In its report, it aired an excerpt from President Bush's address to the leaders of Eastern and Central European nations gathered at a conference in Warsaw, in which he called upon the European community to align with America to fight the War against Terrorism and isolate the terrorists. Bush mentioned that the coalition includes many Arab and Muslim countries and that the head of the 22-nation Arab League denounced Bin Laden's actions (CBS, Early Show, November 6, 2001). CBS interviewed the Egyptian Ambassador to the United States, Nabil Fahmi, who confirmed that Egypt and other Arab countries stand behind the United States in its war on terrorism and called on the entire international community to join the global War on Terror (CBS, *Face the Nation*, November 4, 2001).

On December 11 (according to Al-Jazeera), Bin Laden recorded another video message. Bin Laden's appearance was intended to show that he had survived the US airstrikes and attacks on Afghanistan that were carried out with the aim of capturing him [dead or alive] and thereby dismantling the infrastructure of the Taliban and Al-Qaeda. Al-Jazeera claimed the video was recorded around December 11 to mark the three-month anniversary since the September 11 terrorist attacks and two months of American military action in Afghanistan. In the video, Bin Laden claimed that the Muslim counterattack has "just begun" and will not end even if he is killed in the process. Bin Laden again referred to the Palestinian issue, suggesting that Al-Qaeda will continue to target Americans as long as it supports attacks on Palestinian children.

Although Bin Laden referred to specific events in November 2001, the networks still questioned Bin Laden and Al-Jazeera's account that the video was recorded on December 11 (which was intended to show that Bin Laden had survived the airstrikes). CBS's Charles Osgood reported that the video was broadcast by Al-Jazeera, "Bin Laden's usual outlet" and that "this tape may be more than a month old, made before the bombardment of Tora Bora, so Osama could have been killed since then" (CBS, *The Osgood File*, December 27, 2001). NBC's Brian Williams asserted that despite the video, Bin Laden's fate is still open to speculation over whether he is dead or still alive (NBC *Nightly News*, December 26, 2001). Fox News' John Gibson also questioned Al-Jazeera's account that the video was made recently: "... is there a way to place when it was made? Al-Jazeera said it was a week ago, but who knows how they figured that?" (Fox News, *The O'Reilly Factor*, December 26, 2001).

As noted, the US Administration dismissed the contents of Bin Laden's message as "more of the same propaganda." Accordingly, the networks followed the Administration's line in dismissing the message's content, choosing instead to focus on Bin Laden's physical appearance. To illustrate this, consider CNN's Miles O'Brien's reporting of the video: "All right, let's talk first of all about the content of the message, because I don't think we have to spend too much time on it. In the excerpt that has been released it seems like the same old propaganda and nonsense that we've been hearing from this man all along" (CNN, *Mornings with Paula Zahn*, December 27, 2001).

The other networks also used Bin Laden's appearance as evidence that his health had deteriorated since the September 11, 2001 attacks and the ensuing US attacks in Afghanistan. At the same time, the networks ignored that the tape proved the Administration had actually failed its mission to capture Bin Laden – the declared goal of the war in Afghanistan. Charles Osgood discussed Bin Laden's physical condition before airing the tape, stating: "On this tape, he looks like hell, beard white, voice strained, the face drawn" (CBS, *The Osgood File*, December 27, 2001). ABC speculated that "his gaunt looks remind intelligence analysts of reports that Bin Laden has long suffered from kidney problems" and quoted a US official who said: "We are glad at least that that damn smile we saw in the earlier tape has been wiped off his face" (ABC *World News Tonight*, December 27, 2001). Fox News counter-terrorism expert Larry Johnson joked: "I am sure Al-Jazeera's not going to be signing him up to do health club ads. The guy looks, you know, like a walking skeleton in this thing" (Fox News, *The O'Reilly Factor*, December 26, 2001).

While the treatment of the Bin-Laden messages clearly illustrates the disagreement between Al-Jazeera content-partners (CNN and ABC) and the other stations regarding Al-Jazeera's link to Al-Qaeda, on January 31, 2002, CNN changed its tune and joined the other channels in demonizing Al-Jazeera, a move that affects the CNN-Al-Jazeera relationship until today.

CNN's Exposé of Bin Laden's Al-Jazeera interview

On January 31, 2002, CNN aired the only interview conducted with Osama Bin Laden after September 11, which it claimed to acquire from "non-government" sources. In that interview with Al-Jazeera's Tayseer Allouni on October 21, 2001, Bin Laden provided the most explicit testimony (to that date) that he was behind the September 11 attacks in his answer to one of the questions: "If avenging the killing of our people is terrorism, let history be a witness that we are terrorists. Mr. Speaker, they are terrorists and history will judge them as such." (CNN, *Wolf Blitzer Reports*, February 1, 2002). For US officials, Bin Laden's words "underscored the importance of winning the war on terrorism" (CNN, *Wolf Blitzer Reports*, February 1, 2002).

Although the tape was recorded by Al-Jazeera, the network did not release it but rather decided to self-censor it. CNN obtained the tape through "other sources" and decided to air it despite Al-Jazeera's resistance, thus breaking its content-sharing agreement with Al-Jazeera. As a result, CNN and Al-Jazeera severed their relationship. According to CNN, Al-Jazeera initially denied that such an interview even existed; later, Al-Jazeera said it did not air it because it did not meet the network's standard and was not newsworthy. In response, CNN's Chief News Executive Easton Jordan said: "Once that videotape was in our possession, we felt that we had to report on it and show it because it's extremely newsworthy and we really were dumbfounded as to why Al-Jazeera would decide not to air or even acknowledge the existence of the interview" (CNN, *Wolf Blitzer Reports*, January 31, 2002). Jordan emphasizes that he considered the interview "extremely newsworthy," adding that although CNN worked hard on its relationship with Al-Jazeera, this was a "tough spot": "Clearly a lot of interesting material has fallen into Al-Jazeera's hands" (cf. El-Nawawy and Iskandar, 2002, p. 170). Next, Blitzer mentioned CNN's Chief News Executive, Easton Jordan's assertion that Al-Jazeera "... has some very tough questions to answer: Among them, why was the interview not ever televised, why did Al-Jazeera initially deny the existence of the tape, and what other tapes does Al-Jazeera have, or did it have, that had never been acknowledged or televised" (CNN, *Wolf Blitzer Reports*, January 31, 2002). Similarly, CNN's terrorism expert Peter Bergen's statement (both on *Wolf Blitzer Reports*, January 31, 2002 and on Mornings with Paula Zahn, February 1, 2002) that in the video, Bin Laden "almost explicitly" takes credit for the September 11 attacks also criticizes Al-Jazeera's decision not to air the video:

> *I mean that's obviously the main kind of news there, and to me as a journalist it's absolutely mystifying why Al-Jazeera would choose to basically sit on what is the scoop of the – certainly the decade, if not the last 20 years, which is the only television interview that existed. It's puzzling, I think it was newsworthy. He takes a bit of a pass on the anthrax question. These are things, I think, the public would have been interested in knowing at the time and still are of interest now.* (CNN, *Wolf Blitzer Reports*, January 31, 2002)

Notably, Bergen speculated that the Al-Jazeera interviewer, Tayseer Allouni, who had a good relationship with Bin Laden, was among Bin Laden's "inner circle" (CNN, *Wolf Blitzer Reports*, January 31, 2002). Al-Jazeera's executives refused to appear on CNN to discuss the Bin Laden interview and announced that Al-Jazeera would sever its relationship with CNN. CNN's anchor read Al-Jazeera's response to the airing of this interview:

> *Al-Jazeera refuses to appear on CNN to discuss its unaired interview with Osama Bin Laden. Al-Jazeera denounces the fact that CNN resorts to such illegal ways to obtain this tape. Al-Jazeera would have expected CNN to use its judgment and respect its special relationship*

with Al-Jazeera by not airing material that Al-Jazeera itself chose not to broadcast. Al-Jazeera does not feel it's obligated to explain its position and its reasoning of why it chose not to air the interview. Al-Jazeera will, nonetheless, respond to CNN's airing of the interview using its own means and its own ways. Furthermore, Al-Jazeera will sever its relationship with CNN and will take the necessary action to punish the organizations and individuals who stole this video and distributed it illegally. (CNN, *Wolf Blitzer Reports*, January 31, 2002)

While it is legitimate to question Al-Jazeera's motives for not airing the tape, a few questions also remain regarding CNN's decision to do so: (a) the tape, that was Al-Jazeera's property, was aired against its will and in violation of the business agreement that the networks signed; (b) after nearly two years of close cooperation with Al-Jazeera, CNN Chief News Executive Easton Jordan expressed his suspicions regarding the network's overall credibility; and (c) CNN displayed extraordinary decisiveness in determining that Al-Jazeera's decision not to air the tape was a wrong one. Despite criticism of Al-Jazeera's self-censorship of the video, Al-Jazeera's assertion that the video was not "newsworthy" was actually backed by *Chicago Tribune* reporter Collin McMahon in a CNN broadcast. Addressing Howard Kurtz's question regarding whether Bin Laden's video was newsworthy, McMahon said:

You know, I looked at it, I didn't feel it was that newsworthy. I mean, I think they should have aired it when they had it. I don't think there is any question about that. It was another piece of information of the story of our generation, and I think that they were wrong not to air it at that time. But the fact that we're talking more about whether or not they should have aired it, and the relationship between Al-Jazeera, shows that the substance of the tape itself was not that important, was not that illuminating itself. (CNN Reliable Sources, February 2, 2002)

Finally, note the double standard in the denunciation of Al-Jazeera's decision to self-censor the video. In several previous instances, US networks knew about or possessed controversial footage that could damage US Government policy and summarily shelved it. In 1991, for example, during the First Gulf War, NBC acquired but declined to air footage of Iraqi conscripts carpet-bombed with "explosives, napalm, radioactive DU (depleted uranium) ... a slaughter described by one American officer as a 'turkey shoot' "(Sontag, 2003, p. 66). None of the US networks criticized NBC for censoring these newsworthy images at that time.

Following this incident, CNN became more suspicious of Al-Jazeera and questioned the authenticity of several of its news items. Consider the treatment of Al-Jazeera's report of an Al-Qaeda video on April 15, 2002. Al-Jazeera aired a preview of a documentary from a production company linked to Al-Qaeda entitled *The Will of the Martyrs of New York and Washington Conquest*, showing Al-Qaeda training camps, and a statement from one of the September 11 hijackers who was aboard the United Airlines flight 93 that crashed in Pennsylvania, providing very clear evidence that Al-Qaeda was responsible for the September 11 attacks. Al-Jazeera announced that the video would be aired in full on April 22, claiming the tape was recorded in Kandahar six months before the September 11 attacks. Pentagon officials, however said that the tape appeared to be only a few months old (NBC, *Today*, April 16, 2002). The networks questioned Al-Jazeera's claim regarding the time the tape was made. CNN's reporter Daryn Kagan declared it "not possible" because a portion of the tape shows an apparently electronically inserted background of the burning World Trade Center Towers, asserting it was likely that "later in production someone went ahead and electronically inserted that picture behind the hijacker" (CNN *Breaking News*, April 15, 2002).

Next, on *American Morning with Paula Zahn*, the CNN host asked Al-Jazeera's Hafez al-Mirazi how long Al-Jazeera held the tape, referring to allegations that the tape is undated and expressing suspicion regarding Al-Jazeera's handling of it. The question is reminiscent of Easton Jordan's February 1, 2002 assertion regarding the "interesting material" that fell into Al-Jazeera's hands without being aired (see above). NBC's anchors also questioned whether the tape was updated, citing Pentagon officials who claimed that it appeared to be months old. On the same show, terrorism expert Steven Emerson speculated that the video was made within weeks of the September 11 attacks and that the background is superimposed: "... in fact, they're sitting in front of some type of Hollywood set" (NBC, *Today*, April 16, 2002). On April 18, CNN discovered that Al-Jazeera would not air the tape in full on April 22 (as initially announced). On *American Morning with Paula Zahn*, the "big question of the hour" was: "Is the US fighting back in the propaganda war in an attempt to counter what they say is Al-Jazeera's clout in the Arab world?" On the show, Zahn asked Al-Mirazi why Al-Jazeera decided not to air the entire video, as opposed to some of Bin Laden's other messages that were aired in full. The underlying accusation behind this question implies that Al-Jazeera is biased in censoring self-indicting messages from Bin Laden while emphasizing those that feature his anti-Western propaganda. Zahn also questioned Al-Mirazi about the length of time that Al-Jazeera held the tape. Al-Mirazi estimated that Al-Jazeera waited about a week before airing it:

> *We were trying first to make sure that that hijacker, Okma Hasnowi, is really one of them. We compared that the images of that person with the images on the Web site of the FBI and*

> *we found almost identical resemblance between both of them. However, so far we haven't heard from the FBI or the Intelligence Committee in the US to confirm that this is really one of them.* (CNN, *American Morning with Paula Zahn*, April 18, 2001)

In return, Zahn questioned the credibility of Al-Mirazi's version of the events: "That's interesting, because I know Senator Shelby, who sits on the Intelligence Committee, said that ... his committee members have seen this tape. How did you find out about this tape? Was it something that was sold to you?" (CNN, *American Morning with Paula Zahn*, April 19, 2002). It is interesting to note this spontaneous hostile response, as it demonstrates how Al-Jazeera's partisan character caused even liberal networks that initially supported it and cooperated with it, such as CNN, to adopt a suspicious and jingoistic reporting style.

Throughout the following weeks, the frame parity vanished between Al-Jazeera's partners CNN and ABC and the other US networks (CBS, NBC and Fox News) as CNN shifted to the ranks of stations that perceive Al-Jazeera as a mouthpiece for the enemy. For example, consider the self-censorship of a June 22, 2002 video message from al-Qaeda's spokesman, Sulaiman Abu-Gaith, aired on Al-Jazeera, assuring Arabs that Osama Bin Laden and "98% of the Al-Qaeda leadership" were alive and well. Abu-Gaith said the American operation was not able to destroy the organization. The Bush Administration downplayed this video, saying that although there is some speculation that Bin Laden is alive, there is no definitive proof. Accordingly, US networks mostly ignored the contents of the message; when re-presented, it was only mentioned briefly, with CBS, ABC, and NBC all giving it a single five-second mention (ABC *World News Tonight*, June 23, 2002; CBS, *Sunday Morning*, June 23, 2002; NBC, *Today*, June 24, 2002). Fox News did not consider the report important, as its officials "pointed out that Abu-Ghaith is a known liar and Al-Qaeda propagandist" (Fox News, *The Big Story with John Gibson*, June 24, 2002).

During the build-up to the war in Iraq, that was taking place throughout this period, messages from Arab insurgents actually supported the Administration's stance, as they served as an exposé of the imminent terror threat that still faced America; furthermore, such messages strengthened the US Administration's argument that there is a link between Al-Qaeda terrorists and Saddam Hussein. During this period, the Administration did not oppose the airing of Bin Laden's message to the same extent that it did earlier.

On September 10, 2002, a day before the anniversary of September 11 and a month before Congress passed the resolution declaring war on Iraq, Al-Jazeera aired a new Al-Qaeda tape. The first part contained an audio message from

Bin Laden, in which he praised the September 11 hijackers. The second contained interviews with some of the [deceased] plane hijackers, who revealed unknown details of the attacks, such as the initial plan to target US nuclear power stations. For the US Administration, these messages reinforced the observation that Americans were still not safe a year after the attacks and that the threat of Muslim terrorism was imminent. They were also useful in convincing Arabs that America's war is not on Islam but on terrorism.

The networks framed the video as an exposé of the imminent terror threats that Al-Qaeda still posed to the free world. CBS (CBS *Morning News*, September 10, 2002) and CNN (CNN *Live on Location*, September 9, 2002) stressed that the video interviews with the plane hijackers were highly valuable because they served as conclusive proof that Al-Qaeda was responsible for the September 11 attacks to a disbelieving Arab audience. Next, on October 7, 2002, Al-Jazeera broadcast the tape in which a voice, purported to be that of Bin Laden, warned Americans that "militants will continue to fight you until you stop your oppression." (NBC, *Today*, October 7, 2002). Subsequent discussions of this message focused primarily on its authenticity.

In conclusion, the analysis reveals that the US networks systematically re-presented Bin Laden's messages in line with the Administration's stance, thus emphasizing messages that linked Bin Laden to the September 11 terrorist attacks but self-censoring messages that challenged the official US position. Furthermore, the re-presentation of the Al-Qaeda messages was often accompanied by denunciation of the messenger, Al-Jazeera, thus positioning both the message and the messenger within the "sphere of deviance."

CHAPTER SEVEN

THE WAR IN IRAQ

The US invasion of Iraq was one of the greatest media events in history. More than 3,000 journalists from around the world flocked to Kuwait City and Baghdad to cover the war. The US Army applied a new control mechanism by embedding reporters with the troops, allowing journalists to join units and allocating them places inside tanks and army bases. From a technical perspective, the Embed Program, in which the Pentagon attached some 600 print, radio, and TV reporters to coalition forces for the Iraq invasion, gave reporters unprecedented access to the battlefield, allowing them to file uncensored views of the action in real time. In return, embeds vowed not to reveal anything that would endanger operational security – such as troop strength, location, and strategy (Hoskins, 2004). The Pentagon's embed strategy, however, was somewhat ingenious because giving broadcasters access to highly newsworthy action footage from the front line encouraged focus on the actions of US and British troops from the perspective of "us" versus "them" (the enemy), thereby sidestepping the journalistic values of impartiality and objectivity. Hoskins (2004) maintained that the story was all about winning and losing rather than consideration of the context in which the war was fought and television reports even inflated exchanges of small-arms fire into major shootouts.

Many of the 2,000 reporters that functioned as "unilaterals," trying to file reports from the relative safety of hotel lobbies (and thus often called "hotel warriors"), still depended on the army for access to and contextualization of events. Several complained about the second-class role to which they were relegated, as well as broken promises by the military (Schaffer 2003), as they were prevented from covering the war in many areas, especially in the southern cities of the invasion's wake: Basra, Umm Qasr, Nasiriyah and Safwan. *New Yorker* war correspondent Jeffrey Goldberg estimated that only 50 to 70 of the 600 embeds saw any interesting combat during the conflict and that others found themselves embedded in units that saw little action or were never deployed (Ibid.). Unilaterals were often in grave danger from both enemy and allied fire.

At the same time, the US Administration decided to change strategy and aimed at improving its relationship with Al-Jazeera to better its image in the "hearts and minds" of the Arab world. In early March 2003, several Central Command public information officers even attended a barbecue at the home of Al-Jazeera Public Relations Director Jihad Balout to talk about cooperation throughout the war. Managing the war from a base outside Al-Jazeera's home city of Doha, the US military offered the network's reporters extra spots as embedded journalists. Along with this privilege, Al-Jazeera maintained access to areas behind enemy lines that were off limits to embeds and unilaterals alike.

Nevertheless, it took only four days for harmony between the US-led Coalition and Al-Jazeera to evaporate. On March 22, 2003, the fourth day of the war in Iraq, Al-Jazeera aired a video showing the charred bodies of four US soldiers lying face up and interviews with five US prisoners of war. These soldiers, ambushed near the southern Iraqi city of Al-Nasiriyah, were not frontline fighters, but were serving in Maintenance Unit 507. The video showed individual interviews with the five prisoners, several of whom appeared extremely frightened. Shoshanna Johnson, the only woman among the prisoners, had a large bandage around her ankle and one of the men was lying on a blanket and had to be assisted to sit up. When asked why he had come to Iraq, one soldier said "I came to fix broke stuff;" another (who said he was from Texas) answered "I follow orders." The airing of images of frightened and beaten US soldiers at such an early stage of the war ridiculed the US Army, demonstrated its vulnerability and could have damaged morale in the US. The global spread of these images further undermined the notion of US military superiority. In light of their traditional "rally round the flag" reporting style when the military goes to war, US networks would have been expected to have censored the report altogether. The CBS program *Face the Nation*, however, broadcast once the footage without obscuring the faces of the dead. CNN and NBC also aired still images of the event. The reports were discussed on no fewer than 26 shows on CNN, NBC, ABC and CBS during the following four days. Furthermore, several American news outlets – both network and cable – aired the footage (either totally or partially blurring the faces of the POWs and dead soldiers).

This is sursprising, as the broadcasting of these images broke several taboos and thus violated traditional reporting patterns. First, it contravened the "good taste" principle declaring that "US blood" and particularly "the naked face" are rarely shown (Sontag, 2003, pp. 68–70). This guideline, established during the Second World War, was firmly adopted as a broadcasting value by all US networks after the Vietnam War. Sontag noted that "this is a dignity not thought necessary to accord to others. The more remote or exotic the place, the more likely we are to have full frontal views of the dead and the dying," such as the graphic close-ups of African victims in Biafra during the late 1960s (Sontag, 2003, pp. 68–69). For the Administration, then, Al-Jazeera's decision to broadcast close-ups of the faces of dead US soldiers killed in action, some of them lying face up in pools of blood, was particularly controversial. The argument was that the graphic close-ups of the faces and wounds of deceased US soldiers violated the principle of good taste, even though the *New York Times* presented graphic images of the faces of dead Iraqi soldiers on its front page just a day before the killing and kidnapping of the US soldiers.

Second, the airing of images of POWs and their rebroadcasting by television networks worldwide broke the tradition asserting that during wartime, immediate family members should not have to learn of their loved ones' death or capture in a military operation through the media. In this case, some parents indeed first found out about the incident on television. For example, Nikki Johnson, mother of POW Shoshanna Johnson, learned about her daughter's capture through the Spanish-language television station, Telemundo (Agencies, 2003–see http://edition.cnn.com/2003/US/03/25/sprj.irq.pow.johnson). In response, the Administration sent requests to all news agencies worldwide not to air these images at least until family members were notified. Al-Jazeera agreed to comply (although it was already too late).

Third, in the rare cases that such images were presented, it was at times of major controversy between US officials over the decision to go to war (in contrast to the wide agreement amongst officials to go to the war in Iraq). In Vietnam, for example, images of execution were self-censored during the first year of the war and the famous scene of General Loan executing a Vietcong soldier was only shown in light of the major debate and disagreement between Republicans and Democrats about the question of the moral justification of the war in light of the Tet offensive (Hallin, 1986). Similarly, the airing of images of the body of a US soldier dragged through the streets of Mogadishu in 1993, the only occasion on which US networks willingly displayed the "naked face" of a dead soldier, took place only under heavy opposition after the Clinton Government called for withdrawal from Somalia.

Considering the above taboos, how can we explain the airing of the Al-Nasiriyah images on CBS and CNN? It is reasonable to argue that this development demonstrates the ability of counterhegemonic news reports to *force* images on the US media: On March 22, Al-Jazeera reports dictated the global news agenda of the day, despite the US Administration's request to censor the images. This happened not only because of the high newsworthiness of the images but also because of Al-Jazeera's global reach. Although Al-Jazeera borrowed the images from Iraqi television, its distribution system allowed it to spread the images faster than any other comparable station. PBS's *Wide Angle* show, that examined the spread of the images, explained: "Because of Al-Jazeera's more advanced technology, the network was able to broadcast some of this footage before even Iraqi state television could" (http://www.pbs.org/wnet/wideangle/uncategorized/handbook-the-geneva-conventions/240/).

The images, in turn, were aired not only on non-Western channels worldwide but also on television stations in countries that were the US's closest allies. Notably, the transnational news network Sky News, aired the images with the soldiers' identifiable features countless times throughout the day, with blocked faces. Another well-known example is the broadcasting of Al-Jazeera's images by Australian media, that refused US requests (through the Australian Defence Department) to pixelate the images and thus "meet…obligations under the (Geneva) Conventions." Australian media executives argued that the Geneva Convention applies only to the behavior of combatants, not observers (Holloway, 2003) and therefore the images must be shown in the name of impartiality. According to a CNN report (see http://www.cnn.com/2003/WORLD/asiapcf/auspac/03/24/sprj.int.australia.media), the Australian Broadcasting Corporation also pointed to the "many previous examples of prisoners of war footage being shown" as justification for their position. The reports were re-presented on all UK newspaper front pages the following day (Hoskins, 2004, p. 23). Hoskins observed:

> *…in effect, the fact that Al-Jazeera made these images available to the global audience provided an excuse for Western broadcasters (particularly in the UK) to use them. Firstly, they were able to cite that these were 'already in the public domain', and secondly, Al-Jazeera broadcasting this footage became as significant a part of the news story as the actual capture of the POWs. (Hoskins, 2004, p. 67)*

Finally, the news anchors themselves attest that the networks felt compelled to air the images. In accordance with the global spread of the images and the US Administration's failure to stop their display even on the screens of its closest allies, CBS reporter Susan McGinnis noted that Al-Jazeera has "put images for all the world to see" (CBS *Morning News*, March 24, 2003). Such statements render it reasonable to claim that the global spread of this footage *forced* these reports on US networks.

Does this compulsion mean that the Al-Jazeera Effect is similar to the CNN Effect as it succeeds in showing local atrocities to global audiences, including those of the US itself? For a moment, the concept of a "global public sphere" was proposed. This significant turning point in the history of war reporting deserves a closer examination of the framing of the event. As noted in Appendix E, most scholars agree that the interpretation of images depends on their contextualization. In this case, the networks immediately contextualized the images by subscribing to the Administration's allegations that their airing violates the Geneva Conventions. Furthermore, to explain the images to viewers, the networks began an unprecedented attack on their source. The demonization of Al-Jazeera is important, as there is a close correlation between re-presentation of reports of foreign origin and representation of their sources. A non-credible source is naturally more likely to air falsified images. The next section examines the framing of the images and the source as "deviance."

Discrediting the Message: The Double Standard in Image Censoring

In re-presenting the video of the dead soldiers, some US news anchors did not apply the journalistic code of *detachment* and expressed their grief over the images. On the CNN *Live Event/Special*, Aaron Brown said the images are "chilling for us and I suspect many of you" (CNN *Live Event/Special*, March 24, 2003). On NBC, Kelly O'Donnell also shared her feelings about the footage with the viewers: "Many of us, not only those in uniform but those of us covering the story, were deeply moved and disturbed by it... it's a very sensitive topic here and the images of Al-Jazeera caused a great deal of concern" (NBC, *Today*, March 24, 2003). NBC's anchors denounced Al-Jazeera's "controversial" decision to air the "disturbing" videos as well (NBC, *Dateline*, March 23, 2003). ABC's news presenters stated that the images of dead soldiers were "too brutal to air on TV" (ABC, *World News Tonight*, March 23, 2003). When censoring the images, Fox News, NBC and ABC explicitly explained to their audience that Al-Jazeera did not comply with the Western norm of "good taste."

The networks' description of the images subscribed to the Administration's unsubstantiated allegations that the soldiers were executed, a symbol of the enemy's cruelty and a violation of the Geneva Conventions, without questioning their validity. The only reporter to challenge this allegation was NBC's Jim Miklaszewski, who noticed that the wounds could demonstrate that the soldiers died in battle:

> *I must add this caveat, however, Katie, that in taking a close look at the tape it appears that some of them had other wounds. They may have been killed elsewhere, their bodies taken to this building. And even those who appear to have been executed could have been shot elsewhere and brought into the building.* (NBC, *Today*, March 23. 2003)

Initially, CNN and CBS only partially censored the images. CBS showed a glimpse of the footage of dead American soldiers and blackened out their faces, while the voice-over read 'Donald Rumsfeld cautioning all of us when we see these fixed location shots, it is just giving us a small sliver of an idea of what is going on' (CBS, Face the Nation, March 23, 2003). The CNN *Live Event/Special* and NBC *Evening News* shows (23 March 2003) declared they had made a decision not to show the "disturbing" images. Instead, they screened a single image of a dead soldier with no identifiable features. Following several requests by the US Administration and off-screen contact with the Pentagon, CBS and CNN apparently agreed to censor the images (Hoskins, 2004, p. 67).

There was on-screen pressure to censor the images as well. In an interview on CNN *Live Event/Special* on March 23, 2003, Donald Rumsfeld declared that networks that choose to air the images were doing "something which was unfortunate" because the Geneva Convention "makes it illegal for prisoners of war to be shown and pictured and humiliated" (CNN *Live Event/Special*, March 23, 2003). The US networks, in turn, not only agreed to Rumsfeld's request to self-censor and denounce the messages but also adopted the Administration's allegation that the footage violates the Geneva Convention.

However, while US reporters openly condemned Al-Jazeera's March 22 footage of dead US soldiers, ABC was broadcasting similar images of Iraqi soldiers on or about the same day. Furthermore, when Al-Jazeera aired a video of Keith Matthew Maupin, the first soldier captured by Iraqis during the occupation/liberation, on April 16, 2004, confirming he was alive, the Geneva Conventions were not mentioned in any of the 28 transcripts concerning this item, because the context (unlike that of the dead US soldier images) was *good news* for Americans, namely that Maupin was not killed in action at Abu Ghraib (west of Baghdad) on April 9 when his convoy came under attack by rocket-propelled grenades and small arms fire. CBS interpreted the images for Americans:

> *It's hard to call a picture of an American soldier held hostage "good news," but at least it means the 20-year-old Maupin, one of nine Americans missing since their convoy was ambushed and went up in flames last Friday, is alive and apparently in good condition. Yesterday, there was*

> *a prayer vigil for him in his hometown and today you can hear him speak his name.* (CBS News Transcripts, April 16, 2004)

In the case of Maupin, there were hopes that the Reverend Jesse Jackson would negotiate with his captors through Al-Jazeera, according the network an exceptional key role in supplying positive news for US viewers. In stark contrast to the case involving the first video of dead soldiers and interviews with prisoners of war in 2003, however, this time the Defense Department did not denounce Al-Jazeera for airing the video and did not mention the Geneva Conventions.

In retrospect, it may be argued that The Geneva Conventions have been invoked selectively in accordance with national interest. In Somalia, 1993, the US media chose to air similarly graphic images of dead US soldiers and an interview with a POW Michael Durant without a mention of the Geneva Conventions. To elaborate, late in 1992, the wrenching pictures of starving Somalis in the wake of famine (sparked by virtual dissolution of the central government) encouraged humanitarian assistance (known as Operation Restore Hope), delivered by the military and organized by George H. W. Bush's Administration. This aid was the result of the last presidential decision made by Bush, who wished to leave office with a reputation for being humanitarian (after having been defeated by Clinton, who during his campaign had accused Bush of lacking compassion). However, that humanitarian task soon metamorphosed into a war between US forces and Muslim resistance led by Somali warlord Mohamed Farah Aidid. A manhunt for Aidid commenced following the violent deaths of twenty-four Pakistani peacekeepers on June 5, 1993 at the hands of his troops. After US soldiers also died in a similar ambush, Clinton announced on September 28, 1993 that he would place new emphasis on getting US forces out of Somalia. However, a few weeks before the US Army's planned retreat, Somalis again ambushed US soldiers who had raided a house occupied by Aidid's men on October 4, 1993, resulting in 18 dead US soldiers, 65 wounded and the loss of two Black Hawk helicopters. One helicopter pilot, Michael Durant, was taken hostage. Subsequently, a crowd of enraged Somalis dragged one of the dead US soldiers through Mogadishu's streets, a scene captured by *Toronto Star* photographer Paul Watson (who later won a Pulitzer Prize for the images). The images were no less horrifying than the ones shown on Al-Jazeera on March 22, 2003. In Somalia, the networks showed the dead soldier's face, while US networks interviewed Watson and encouraged him to describe the scene in detail, as illustrated in the following interview on the CBS *Evening News*:

> Watson: *You could see quite clearly that his face had been mutilated and that he had a large gash wound along one of his thighs. This crowd followed it down the street and around a*

corner, pausing every once in a while for people to kick at the corpse, to spit on it and to stomp on it. (CBS Evening News, October 4, 1993)

Coincidentally, the images of the dead soldier were followed by an interview with the American hostage – a format similar to that of the March 23, 2003 Gulf War video. The nightmarish aspect of media coverage was heightened when CNN aired a videotape of this interview, provided by Aidid's faction (recorded by a Somali freelance cameraman). Like the US POWs taken hostage in Iraq, Durant looked frightened and severely beaten. Michael Durant's image, appeared on the *Time* Magazine cover on October 18 1993; the headline reads: "What in the world are we doing?" (see http://www.time.com/time/covers/0,16641,1101931018,00.html). US television stations aired the video nonetheless (although it was clearly made for propaganda purposes) throughout the day and until Durant's release ten days later, on October 14. A search for "Durant" on the *Lexis-Nexis* database reveals that CNN referred to the tape in 69 reports, CBS 84 and ABC 8 (NBC – n/a; Fox News was not yet established in 1993). Furthermore, the US networks did not mention that the interview with Durant violated the Geneva Conventions. A search for the term "Geneva Conventions" in CNN, ABC, NBC and CBS transcripts of coverage during the airing of the video and Durant's release ten days later (October 4–14, 1993) yielded only one result: A discussion of Durant's fate on the October 5 edition of CNN *Live Report*, illustrating the US's double standard regarding the airing of war reports in general and those violating the Geneva Conventions in particular.

As the next section illustrates, denunciation of this footage was accompanied by a ruthless attack on the credibility of its source.

Discrediting the Messenger: Building the "Al-Jazeera is Biased" Frame

Hallin's study of war reporting in Vietnam found that during wartime, mainstream US media use techniques of exclusion, condemnation and exposure to attack or undermine "those political actors and views which journalists and the political mainstream of the society reject as unworthy of being heard" (Hallin, 1984, p. 142). These "unworthy" voices are presented as operating within a "sphere of deviance" in which the media play the role of "*exposing, condemning, or excluding* from the public agenda those who violate or challenge the political consensus. It marks out and defends the limits of acceptable political conflict"

(Ibid.). Al-Jazeera's placement in the sphere of deviance is comparable to the categorization of Communist perspectives as propaganda during the Cold War. Hallin noted that Federal Communications Commission (FCC) guidelines for application of the Fairness Doctrine state: "It is not the Commission's intentions to make time available to Communists or to the Communist viewpoints" (Hallin, 1984, p. 142). In the case of the Vietnam War, Hallin determined that the exclusion, condemnation and exposure methodology was rigorously applied to reports about the antiwar movement, as the US Administration viewed such dissent as damaging to its efforts. In Iraq 2003, Al-Jazeera turned into a "victim" of such treatment after the global spread of its "culturally congruent report" threatened to show US viewers morally discouraging images that did not conform with the traditional patriotic reporting angle. The Arab news angle thus became the deviant one.

For NBC, Al-Jazeera's airing of the images supported one of the Administration's central arguments for the war, namely that the enemy does not respect international law. In this context, "the enemy" refers not only to Saddam Hussein but also to Al-Jazeera. The decision to air the footage, that allegedly violates the Geneva Conventions, has been compared to the allegations against Saddam Hussein for violation of international law by holding weapons of mass destruction. The NBC anchor stated that Al-Jazeera's airing of the images has "certainly…borne out the Bush Administration's allegations that the Iraqi regime and the Iraqi military are entities that do not adhere to all of the conventions or the rules of warfare" (NBC, *Today*, March 23, 2003).

At the same time, the networks fell silent during a subsequent wave of attacks on Al-Jazeera. This new trend began with the ousting of Al-Jazeera from the trading floor of the New York Stock Exchange (NYSE) on May 25, 2003 for "irresponsible" coverage. NYSE officials revoked the media credentials of two Al-Jazeera reporters during the Iraq War. Al-Jazeera executives contended that this measure was taken in retaliation for its coverage of the conflict and the broadcast of the controversial footage of the dead US soldiers and prisoners of war. NYSE spokesperson Ray Pellecchia denied the allegation, noting that during this period, several other media organizations were removed from the accreditation list for new "security reasons" that limited the space allocated for journalists. Pellecchia stated that the NYSE "was now only providing access to those media outlets that focus on responsible business coverage" (NBC *Evening News*, March 25, 2003). When asked to identify other media organizations that were denied access, however, Pellecchia refused to provide any examples (see http://money.cnn.com/2003/03/25/news/nyse_aljazeera). The US news networks failed to make any comment regarding violation of freedom of the press in the expulsion of Al-Jazeera reporters from the stock exchange floor. NBC and Fox News emphasized the Administration's version that the expulsion has nothing to do with the nature of that network's coverage:

> Soledad O'Brien, anchor: *Two Al-Jazeera reporters have been booted from covering the New York Stock Exchange. Officials say it was for security reasons and not because of Al-Jazeera's coverage of the war or American POWs.*
>
> Matt Lauer: Right. *Real, real quickly. The New York Stock Exchange banned two Al-Jazeera reporters from the floor on Monday, saying that they were restricting access to "responsible networks." What reaction has that generated?*
>
> Ron Insana: *Well, it's a little early here to see what the reaction is, but apparently there were some people concerned about their presence here. Maybe some traders on the floor voiced their displeasure at it, but the – the – the statement itself speaks quite – speaks volumes, that those covering responsibly, the business community will be allowed to stay. So, kind of a mixed message from the exchange this morning.* (NBC, *Today*, March 25, 2003)

Fox News also emphasized the NYSE spokesman version of the story, relating it to Al-Jazeera's "irresponsible news coverage":

> *Brit Hume: ... And two reporters covering the New York Stock Exchange for Arab – the Arab TV network Al-Jazeera are no longer allowed into the New York Stock Exchange. Al-Jazeera says the move is due to its coverage of the war in Iraq. Al-Jazeera has showed over and over gruesome images from Iraqi TV of American prisoners who had apparently been executed as well as POW interviews. But Exchange spokesman, Ray Pellecchia says the move was for "security reasons." He told the AP that access had been limited to networks that focused, quotes, 'on responsible business coverage.* (Fox *Special Report with Brit Hume*, March 25, 2003)

The US networks' silence on violent acts against Al-Jazeera continued when its website was attacked by Western hackers. John William Racine, a 24-year-old Californian web designer, was later fined and sentenced by a US court for the offense. The networks did not denounce the action taken by Boston-based Akamai Technologies, whose refusal to offer its services to Al-Jazeera, without explanation, left its website vulnerable to attackers. Interestingly, Akamai also operates the US Army's recruitment website. Its spokesperson Jeff Young refused to explain the reason for this denial of service.

The media's policy of ignoring US Administration attacks on Al-Jazeera continued throughout the occupation/liberation of Iraq. A few months after the attack, Al-Jazeera's Baghdad bureau chief wrote to the Bush Administration that the station was subjected to "strafing by gunfire, death threats, confiscation of news material, and multiple detentions and arrests, all carried out by

US soldiers" (Robert Fisk, writing in the London *Independent*, August 1, 2003). Michael Hudson, Professor of International Relations at Georgetown University (2005) commented: "Judging by the facts, Washington's strategy of intimidation has been well-calculated and deliberate."

Most importantly, the networks failed to denounce the second bombing of Al-Jazeera offices and the killing of Al-Jazeera reporter and cameraman Tareq Ayoub on April 8, 2003 when US tanks fired on the Palestine Hotel, known to be inhabited by journalists. Before that incident, the US Army fired on Al-Jazeera and the Abu Dhabi TV offices in Iraq on the banks of the Tigris River. Al-Jazeera executives insist that they provided the US military with the exact location of the network's studios in the Palestine Hotel to avoid just such an incident. In response, the US Army claimed that insurgents fired on troops from the hotel's lobby. Eyewitnesses at the hotel – including several well-known and respected Western journalists – denied that any weapons fire came from inside the building (CNN *Live on Location*, April 8, 2003). Knightley (2003, p. 11) considers the attack on Al-Jazeera's offices to be a deliberate attempt to show that the Pentagon will not tolerate any more reporting from the enemy side. The *Independent* reporter Robert Fisk notes that US journalists did not even investigate the killing of Tareq Ayoub, warning them that "they should – because they will be next" (*Independent*, April 26, 2003, p. 17; cf. Hoskins, 2004, p. 72).

CNN was the only one of the five networks that provided extensive coverage of the killing of Tareq Ayoub; NBC and ABC both gave the event a single five-second mention, while Fox News and CBS ignored the incident. CNN included eyewitness reviews claiming that the attack was deliberate:

> Unidentified male (through translator): *Our colleagues, who were at the offices confirm and believe that this bombing was deliberate. They were hit by two missiles, not one. And the second bombing of Abu Dhabi offices confirmed their views.*
>
> *Brahimi: That second bombing took Abu Dhabi TV off the air for four hours. A US State Department spokesman said on Al-Jazeera TV that the bombing was not deliberate.* (CNN *Live on Location*, April 8, 2003)
>
> Brahimi: *Tareq Ayoub was a very good correspondent. He's also worked for CNN at one point in Jordan when Al-Jazeera had been banned temporarily from this country and everybody here has obviously very, very good memories about him.*
>
> *It's a very sad day for us in the journalistic community, as you know, Bill. Tareq Ayoub, a 35-year-old journalist, leaves behind a little baby and a wife.*
>
> *After the Al-Jazeera building was hit, apparently the Abu Dhabi TV building, that's just next door to the Al-Jazeera building, was also hit. It got, its reporting or its live coverage from the Abu Dhabi House in Baghdad was taken off air for something like four hours.* (CNN *Daybreak*, April 8, 2003)

While the networks merely denounced the violence against Al-Jazeera, that was aimed at disrupting its broadcasts, they persistently decried what they perceived as Al-Jazeeera's consistent "bias," positioning it as a "deviant" news source. In particular, they attempted to link the 1967 credibility crisis between Arab media and their audiences to the Iraqi defeat, thus drawing a line illustrating that Arab media could not be believed throughout their first five decades of broadcasting and are still not credible as they enter their sixth. As noted in chapter 4, a major outrage and distrust in the system emerged during the 1967 Six-Day War with Israel, when Arab radio broadcast false reports of Arab victory, even though Israel had crushed the Egyptian Army. Consequently, until the advent of Al-Jazeera, Arabs did not trust the media in their own countries.

The US networks rebuilt this "Arab media is biased" frame in light of reports on the Iraqi Army defeat from April 9, 2003. These well-known images of US Marines welcomed in Baghdad (mostly by Sunni Iraqis) with cheers and even flowers, along with images of Iraqis welcoming US soldiers and toppling a huge statue of Saddam, were used to show not only the defeat of Saddam Hussein's regime but also the Arab media's lack of credibility. Through these news items, the networks managed to link the images of Arab military defeat to a defeat of the Arab media as well. Consider the commentary accompanying those images on CNN, Al-Jazeera's former content partner in the US:

> Octavia Nasr, Senior Arab Affairs Editor: *These pictures, especially on Al-Jazeera, sounded like an apology: You have all these anchors and reporters trying to explain to their viewers, telling them that although we're bringing you first images of this demise of the Iraqi regime, but in no way are we in support of it. We're trying to play fair here. We're trying to bring you an objective view from inside Baghdad... It is very interesting to see them try to apologize to their viewers... And the Al-Jazeera reporters, Abu Dhabi, Al Arabiya, LBC, all of them are trying to explain to their viewers that these celebrations are real, they are genuine, and they're trying now to play the objective journalism game.* (CNN *Live on Location*, April 8, 2003)

Fox News commentary on the images was even more direct. The Fox News anchor, Brit Hume, quoted a government employee in Cairo who said: "Now no one believes Al-Jazeera anymore." Hume asked the network's news analyst whether Al-Jazeera, that had done little to prepare its audience for this defeat, lost its credibility and clout after the airing of these images (*Fox Special Report With Brit Hume*, April 10, 2003).

In the same spirit, other reports continued to frame the fall of Baghdad specifically as the loss of Arab media credibility (ABC, *Good Morning America*, April 1, 2003; NBC *Nightly News*, April 1, 2003; CNN *Live On Location*,

March 31, 2003; Fox News, *The O'Reilly Factor*, April 1 and April 3, 2003). Some even claimed that Al-Jazeera does not represent Arab public opinion. On CNN's *American Morning with Paula Zahn*, Dr. Mamoun Fandy of the International Institute for Strategic Studies commented on Al-Jazeera's airing of anti-US demonstrations in Baghdad:

> *I think in certain areas, it had an effect that the United States is an occupying power and all the rest. But really, on balance, Daryl, you have to look at it in general that all the demonstrations we saw on Al-Jazeera TV screens and other things were not exactly the feelings of the Arab world. I mean, not many people were shedding a tear on Saddam Hussein's falling statues.*
>
> *You look around, and there were no single American soft target or single American who was hurt in the Arab world during the most intense fighting for 20 days in one of the major Arab capitals. So this is a big surprise, I think.* (CNN, *American Morning with Paula Zahn*, April 12, 2003)

In the next 12 months, the networks imported from Al-Jazeera mostly news items concerning insurgency in Iraq, including graphic images of the beheadings of citizens by terror groups, as well as messages from terrorists. These images served as proof for US viewers that the network is indeed a mouthpiece for Islamic terrorism. During this period, two further incidents contributed to the notion that Al-Jazeera was not a credible source: The first took place on August 6, 2004, when US Defense Secretary Rumsfeld again alleged that Al-Jazeera reporters in Baghdad had been on Saddam's payroll. This allegation is based on documents obtained by the London *Times* which apparently show that three Iraqi agents worked inside Al-Jazeera from August 1999 to November 2002 to secure favorable coverage for the Saddam Hussein regime. The documents showed that Al-Jazeera's General Manager, Mohammed Jassem Ali-Ali, who helped set up and run the network since its inception, was in touch with these agents. Jassem was sacked in June 2003.

At the same time, the networks ignored Al-Jazeera's images of US soldiers humiliating Iraqi citizens. In fact, Al-Jazeera repeatedly aired images throughout this period insinuating that the US Army humiliates and even tortures Iraqi prisoners, including an image of Iraqi prisoners wearing sacks on their head as "punishment." The networks willingly self-censored the images, but they generated outrage online (see Chapter 8). Similar images were only presented on March 28, 2004, with CBS as the source, again showing that Al-Jazeera cannot be the source that admonishes US military behavior, even when it documents inappropriate conduct.

However, Al-Jazeera (together with Al Arabiya) managed to surprise and challenge the US Administration again on April 2004, as they were the only witnesses to the alleged massacre of civilians in Fallujah.

The Battle of Fallujah: "Why Show Civilian Casualties?"

On March 31, 2004, Iraqi insurgents ambushed a convoy in Fallujah, west of Baghdad, that included four US contractors from the Blackwater private security firm. The four were dragged from their cars, beaten and set ablaze. Their burned corpses were then dragged through the streets before being hung over a bridge crossing the Euphrates. Photos of the event were released to news agencies worldwide, causing a great deal of outrage in the United States and prompting the announcement of an upcoming "pacification" of the city. Following the event, the US military made an unsuccessful attempt to capture the city of Fallujah in April 2004, code named Operation Vigilant Resolve.

Al-Jazeera and Al Arabiya were the only sources in Fallujah. The stations showed the high death toll of civilians, that Al-Jazeera later estimated at 6,000. The Pentagon's argument this time was that Al-Jazeera is "surprisingly close" to events and that it has evidence of the network's cooperation with insurgents. This line of reasoning developed since the rise of insurgency towards US forces throughout the liberation/occupation of Iraq, with neoconservatives calling Al-Jazeera the principal source of the anti-Americanism prevailing in the Arab world. In summer 2003, Assistant Secretary of Defense Paul Wolfowitz had already attacked Al-Jazeera for "inciting violence" and "endangering the lives of American troops" in Iraq. In September 2003, the US-appointed Iraqi Governing Council banned Al-Jazeera from Iraq as a result of these allegations. In late November 2003, Rumsfeld again claimed that his top military advisors had evidence that Al-Jazeera and Al Arabiya cooperated with Iraqi insurgents to witness and videotape attacks on American troops. Articles in US media called for a "military solution" to the Al-Jazeera problem. Robert Alt wrote in the conservative journal *Weekly Standard* (2004) :

> *While telling half of the story is bad enough, there is substantial evidence that outlets like Al-Jazeera are in fact acting in concert with terrorists to generate overtly false and misleading news reports. Colonel William Rabena, who commands the 2nd Battalion, 3rd Field Artillery Regiment Gunners in the Adhamiya region of Baghdad, related a scam coordinated between anti-Coalition elements and Al-Jazeera in his area of operation. A gunman would go to the*

mosque, where Al-Jazeera, as luck would have it, would be setting up. The man would open fire in order to draw fire from the Coalition. After he was inevitably taken down by the Coalition, a bystander would rush over to check his condition, and in the melee secret away the firearm. Al-Jazeera then would swoop in for the story: Coalition guns down unarmed man in front of mosque! And as in Fallujah, they would have the pictures to prove it.

Indeed, the networks willingly self-censored Al-Jazeera's images again concerned not with the atrocities themselves but Al-Jazeera's role in the battle. General John Abizaid of the US Central Command blamed the Arab media, in particular Al-Jazeera and Al Arabiya, for:

> *...portraying their [US Army] actions as purposely targeting civilians, and we absolutely do not do that, and I think everybody knows that. It is always interesting to me how Al-Jazeera manages to be at the scene of the crime whenever a hostage shows up or some other problem happens to be there. So they have not been truthful in their reporting. They haven't been accurate. And it is absolutely clear that American forces are doing their very best to protect civilians and at the same time get at the military targets there.* (CNN *Live Event/Special*, April 12, 2004)

On the same show, senior military spokesman Mark Kimmitt had a suggestion for Iraqis who saw civilian deaths on Al-Jazeera: "Change the channel to a legitimate, authoritative, honest news station. The stations that are showing Americans intentionally killing women and children are not legitimate news sources. That is propaganda, and that is lies" (CNN *Live Event Special*, April 12, 2004).

In the same spirit, CNN interviewer Daryn Kagan (who replaced Wolf Blitzer on *Wolf Blitzer Reports* that day) interviewed Al-Jazeera's Editor-in-Chief Ahmed Al-Sheik, asking him why the network focuses on civilian deaths when this was not actually the journalistic story:

> Kagan: *I want to get to another point that we heard General Abizaid – because there was another news conference today with two other generals, General Abizaid and also General Sanchez from Baghdad today that was seen here in the US. And he made some interesting comments where he said – he said, to him: "It's interesting how Al-Jazeera always manages to be at the scene of the crime or when a hostage shows up. They have not been truthful in their reporting and they have not been accurate." How is it that Al-Jazeera does get the videotape of these hostages?*
>
> Al Sheik: *In our bureau in Baghdad, we have 85 people working there. We have correspondents and pictures in almost in every Iraqi city, south and north, west and east. We are well equipped there and we have very good contacts there.*
>
> Kagan: *Isn't the story, though, bigger than just the simple numbers, with all due respect to the Iraqi civilians who have lost their lives – the story bigger than just the numbers of people who*

> *were killed or the fact that they might have been killed by the US military, that the insurgents, the people trying to cause problems within Fallujah, are mixing in among the civilians, making it actually possibly that even more civilians would be killed, that the story is what the Iraqi insurgents are doing, in addition to what is the response from the US military?* (CNN, *Wolf Blitzer Reports*, April 12, 2004)

In dealing with the "damage" that the images caused to the US Army profile, Donald Rumsfeld could not deny the authenticity of Al-Jazeera's images or the number Al-Jazeera was putting on the death toll. Instead, when pushed to explain US military behavior, Rumsfeld blamed Al-Jazeera for biased reporting and urged the reporter to turn the fire back at Al-Jazeera:

> Rumsfeld: *I can definitively say that what Al-Jazeera is doing is vicious, inaccurate and inexcusable.*
>
> Question: *Do you have a civilian casualty count?*
>
> Rumsfeld: *Of course not. We're not in the city. But you know what our forces do. They don't go around killing hundreds of civilians. That's just outrageous nonsense. It's disgraceful what that station is doing.* (CNN *Live Today* . . ., April 15, 2004)

Finally, as the following transcript from CNN's *Lou Dobbs Tonight* indicates, US anchors were not focusing on the content of Al-Jazeera's reporting of the casualties in Fallujah but rather on what to do about the "Al-Jazeera problem". In this CNN interview, member of the US House of Representatives Lynn Woolsey, particularly refers to the term "soft power," describing the US's ambition to control nations without military conquest by tempting them to believe in capitalist values, and Al-Jazeera's ability to disrupt these attempts. In return, Dobbs vehemently adopts Rumsfeld's unsubstantiated allegations against Al-Jazeera and the interview turns into a brain-storm about the best way to win the information war. The following transcript is the strongest evidence that even the "global" CNN, Al-Jazeera's content partner during the early days of the war in Afghanistan, had joined the anti Al-Jazeera camp:

> Woolsey: *An awful lot of that could be done, a lot more than is, could be done overtly. There's a lot of things we could do to win the war – the so-called soft-power war of influence. I think it's amazing that in Iraq still the principal broadcasters are either Arabic language from Iran, which are very hostile to is, or Al-Jazeera. We invented mass media, we invented radio for Europe and we're not doing nearly as well as we should in those areas.*
>
> Dobbs: *Speaking of mass media, Al-Jazeera, the Secretary of Defense Donald Rumsfeld today lashed out at Al-Jazeera. Effectively calling it a tool of the Islamists and Sunni Ba'athist loyalists in Iraq. What should be done?*

Woolsey: *I think there's a lot to that. Occasionally they'll put somebody on with a different point of view. I've been on there once or twice and other people are occasionally, but generally speaking, it really is a propaganda organ for the Islamists, that is, I think, the totalitarian point of view.*

Dobbs: *Well, help me out. Al-Jazeera is owned by the government of Qatar, which are allies, at least presumptively of the United States. Why in the world should that be going on as if the United States were indifferent in that relationship?*

Woolsey: Because some rulers like to have it both ways.

Dobbs: *But it's our choice, is it not? This President said he wanted democratization in the Middle East. Why not be straightforward and insist upon it?*

Woolsey: *I would think particularly given how bad it's gotten, pointing out rather forcefully for the government of Qatar what a service it is doing for terrorism. By the way, Al-Jazeera broadcasts would be something the United States government should have done some time ago, but certainly should do now.* (CNN, *Lou Dobbs Tonight*, April 15, 2004)

In conclusion, in Fallujah the US media again self-censored Al-Jazeera's images. The key issue was the challenge that Al-Jazeera posed to the US military rather than a professional discussion of the explicit images of civilian casualties. Shockingly, CNN's Daryn Kagan asked Al-Jazeera's executive why the network focuses on civilian casualties "when the real story is insurgency."

The Abu Ghraib Photos and the "Information War"

On April 28, 2004, CBS's 60 Minutes aired scenes of leering American soldiers taunting naked Iraqi prisoners forced to assume humiliating poses at Abu Ghraib Prison, the same facility at which Saddam Hussein's regime tortured opponents. The photos were revealed a few weeks after the US Army announced that 17 soldiers in Iraq, including a brigadier general, had been removed from duty following charges of mistreating Iraqi prisoners. A few days later, on May 1, 2004, the New Yorker reported it had a copy of Major General Antonio Taguba's report, which is said to conclude that Iraqi prisoners were subjected to "sadistic, blatant and wanton criminal abuses." At the same time, the Daily Mirror published pictures of a soldier urinating on a hooded Iraqi prisoner sitting on the floor. Following the airing of the images, the US Senate unanimously (92–0) passed a resolution that "condemns in the strongest possible terms the despicable acts at Abu Ghraib Prison and joins with the President in expressing apology for the humiliation suffered by the prisoners in Iraq and their families" (http://www.foxnews.com/story/0,2933,119546,00.html). On April 30, 2004, the US military charged six soldiers with torturing Iraqi prisoners. The images caused outrage around the world, particularly because of fears that torturing prisoners had become common among Coalition troops. The Bush Administration argued that this behavior was not representative of US military conduct but was an exceptional case of "mistreatment" and abuse performed by junior soldiers. Liberal voices, however, expressed their disapproval of Bush's tactics. Senator Edward (Ted) Kennedy, for example, vehemently attacked US policy.

Traditionally, the broadcasting of such images was seen as capable of revitalizing the Vietnam Syndrome by showing the "ugly face of war" (see chapter 3). However, the US media described the events as "abuse" rather than "torture," in line with the Administration approach (Bennett, Lawrence and Livingstone, 2007). While some commentators assume that this pro-Administration coverage was the result of weak opposition and Democratic presidential candidate John Kerry's failure to criticize the Administration, the information war with Al-Jazeera might also have affected this patriotic stance, as the images were aired only a month after Al-Jazeera's report on the atrocities in Fallujah, creating anti-American sentiment and posing an external threat to US interests. Two of Fox News transcripts reveal what the other channels did not perhaps dare to say on air and indicate that the information war might have been a factor in the decision to frame the treatment of Iraqi prisoners as an exception and not the rule in order not to strengthen Al-Jazeera's status:

> O'Reilly: *Allies like Pakistan's Musharraf will now have an even harder time convincing Muslims to cooperate with America against terrorists. America- haters like Al-Jazeera now seem almost justified in their vile portrayal of the USA. Anti-American partisans both abroad and here at home can now lace their propaganda with this incident.* (Fox News, *The O'Reilly Factor*, May 3, 2004)

> David Gergen, former presidential adviser:...*And, you know, you only have to believe that Al-Jazeera and the others making such political gain out of this at our expense, that it's going to make it more difficult to bring security there and to turn over or to build a secure democracy. What worries me a lot though, Greta, is that we're going start – there is going to be a build-up of sentiment just to cut tail and run, and we have to prevail here ultimately.* (Fox News, *Fox on the Record with Greta Van Susteren*, May 3, 2004)

US networks also backed President Bush's decision to ignore Al-Jazeera and to be interviewed on the topic only on the newly-launched US-sponsored channel Al-Hurra and on Al Arabiya, as "punishment" for Al-Jazeera's "anti-US slant." The networks cheered the Al-Hurra interpretation of the event as one that will be investigated, in contrast to their condemnation of Al-Jazeera's assertion that the incident was part of a policy of torture. Furthermore, opposition members such as Ted Kennedy who criticzed US troops were put under the same sphere of deviance as Al-Jazeera for condemning US military conduct:

> Kate O'Beirne: *Now, for the first time, Iraq strikes me as Vietnam, when I hear what liberal Democrats are saying about this. They apparently are not just going to oppose the war with Iraq, they're going to do, as they did with Vietnam, slip into blaming America. Teddy Kennedy's a disgrace. We've reopened torture chambers under US management? I mean, that sounds like an Al-Jazeera editorial. And despite their – everybody serving so honorably, they're going to imply that widespread number of people in uniform are somehow possibly guilty of the same sort of thing. They're going to wind up smearing the troops. By overplaying it like that, they're going to lose the public.* (CNN, *The Capital Gang*, May 15, 2004)
>
> David Lee Miller: *One of them is the fact that the former Minister for Humanitarian Affairs here in this country has come out to say publicly that he believes the abuses are continuing. And, secondly, satellite news channels, like Al Arabiya and Al-Jazeera, continue to fan the flames of anti-US rhetoric saying that there's going to be a lot more of this type of abuse and that they downplay the apologies and the fact that there are ongoing investigations and court-martials that will soon take place.* (*Fox News Live*, May 10, 2004)

To conclude, as an important eyewitness to several war atrocities, Al-Jazeera has played a role in American war reporting throughout the war in Iraq. As early as the third day of the war, Al-Jazeera compelled US networks to show images of dead soldiers and interviews with prisoners of war, thus exposing American military vulnerability. The response was a fierce attack on the credibility of Al-Jazeera rather than, as hyperglobalists expected, a presentation that supports (or at least includes) an extraterrestrial view of the war as a bloody one with casualties on both sides. The US media further ignored the subsequent physical attack on Al-Jazeera's facilities, that reached its peak with the killing of Al-Jazeera reporter Tareq Ayoub.

In April 2004, when Al-Jazeera was the only source behind enemy lines in Fallujah, the chief issue discussed was not the Al-Jazeera images and their meaning but why Al-Jazeera chose to focus on civilian casualties and not on the insurgents.

Finally, analysis of the undercurrents and dilemmas facing US media as they framed the story of humiliation of Iraqis incarcerated at Abu Ghraib reveals that Al-Jazeera's presence does have some impact: Presentation of the story as "single abuse" rather than "systematic torture" was, as the Fox News anchor put it, an attempt to avoid strengthening Al-Jazeera's framing of the war.

CHAPTER EIGHT

THE DARLING OF THE ALTERNATIVE MEDIA WEB SITES: ENGLISH.ALJAZEERA.NET

Al-Jazeera launched an official English-language version of its Arabic website, english.aljazeera.net on September 1, 2003, a few months into the liberation/occupation of Iraq. According to its mission statement, the website was designed "to fill a niche for English speakers who want to get the other side of the story, the Arab perspective" by breaking the traditional "language barrier" (Dube, 2003) between Western audiences and the Arab television network. The launch of this English language news service represents Al-Jazeera's first attempt to directly target a Western audience directly with news from behind enemy lines without the mediation of their media.

As noted in chapter 7, immediately after its launch in 2003, the English site was attacked by several hackers, who launched denial-of-service attacks, and by an engineer named John William Racine, who posed as an Al-Jazeera employee to get a password to the network's site and redirect visitors to a site featuring an American flag. In November 2003, Racine, was sentenced to 1,000 hours of community service and a $1,500 US fine for the online disruption. The perpetrators of the denial-of-service attacks remain unknown.

This chapter, however, explores a less known dimension in the interplay between Al-Jazeera English and Western surfers throughout the occupation/liberation of Iraq. Although the analysis presented here, of an online cross-cultural dialogue, is anecdotal in comparison to the wide attacks on Al-Jazeera's website which were highly documented above, it is required to complete the map of the Al-Jazeera-Western surfers interplay. The chapter explores the re-presentation and representation of three randomly selected reports from Al-Jazeera's coverage of the US occupation of Iraq and Afghanistan from October 1 to November 30, 2003, and seeks to determine whether the web served as a better platform than mainstream media for news exchange between Al-Jazeera and Western content providers. The first, *The Picture Which Shames US Army* (October 17, 2003) by Yvonne Ridley, depicts US soldiers searching young Afghan children in the village of Zermit. The photograph, taken secretly, was given to Al-Jazeera by the Islamic Observation Centre. The article quotes US Army Major Peter Mitchell's response that the children could have carried explosives. The second report, *Shocking Images Shame US Forces* (November 10, 2003), by Yvonne Ridley and Lawrence Smallman, showed US soldiers tying up Iraqi women and children in their homes, while the third, *US Continues to Humiliate Iraqis* (November 23, 2003), by Lawrence Smallman, depicted US soldiers searching young Iraqi girls for explosives. The piece quoted an Iraqi father who promised that if US soldiers intended to humiliate his daughter in such a way, he would rather die "and take a few soldiers with him." During the month that the images were presented on Al-Jazeera (October 17 to November 23, 2003), US mainstream media completely ignored these reports. Throughout this period, the five major networks presented material from Al-Jazeera on 31 occasions, mostly to present messages from Bin Laden (strengthening the notion among viewers that the network is indeed "the mouthpiece of Al-Qaeda").

The Al-Jazeera.net reports appeared on 118 English websites, 102 originating in Western countries or operated by Westerners, 88 of them based in the US, six in the UK, six in Canada and two in Ireland. The results were retrieved through searches on *Google* and *Alta Vista* to maximize the number of results and avoid exclusions resulting from individual search algorithms.

Re-Presentation of english.aljazeera.net Reports

Table 1 classifies the 102 websites that re-presented reports from Al-Jazeera by type. A majority (55) could be characterized as *alternative media*. Given the substantial number of alternative media organizations that reported on various elements of the War in Iraq and Afghanistan, this result is not surprising. The

Table 1: Websites that Re-presented Al-Jazeera Reports

Type (N=102)	Re-presentations
Alternative	55
Unaffiliated	19
Blogs	11
Hate groups	4
Mainstream	2
Unclassified	11

Table 2: Political Affiliations of Websites Re-presenting Al-Jazeera Reports

Type/orientation (N=102)	Liberal	Conservative	Other (Unclassified/ Unaffiliated)
Alternative	47	5	3
Blogs	6	3	2
Politically Unaffiliated	4	7	8
Hate groups	1	3	---
Unclassified	---	---	11
Mainstream	---	1	1
Total	58	19	25

number would have been much larger if the study had included the blogs that frequently re-presented the Al-Jazeera reports, as blogs are sometimes considered a component of alternative media. The study distinguishes between blogs and alternative news websites, however, seeking to assess the differences in representation between these distinct formats. A single user usually operates a blog, while alternative news websites are often semiprofessional operations (see Indymedia citations, below). Moreover, many blogs follow mainstream media and thus cannot be classified as "alternative" in content or perspective.

The ratio between alternative and mainstream media (55:2) mentioning the Al-Jazeera reports is the most surprising result of the study, especially considering the online "buzz" that Al-Jazeera's exclusive images created (as shown below), the follow-ups to several of the reports that appeared in Western forums and the availability of the reports and images (in English) to Western news outlets.

As Table 2 shows, an overwhelming number of the surveyed websites openly declared a political orientation (66 of the 102 websites examined). The table shows that the ratio of re-presentation between liberal and conservative-oriented websites was more than 3:1 (58:19). This result is hardly surprising, considering that Al-Jazeera implicated US soldiers in questionable activities and was presented from the Arab perspective. Moreover, alternative liberal-oriented media specifically aim at publishing reports (and using sources) that contradict mainstream US media, naturally rendering Al-Jazeera an invaluable source for news.

Finally, the relatively small number of "hate" websites is a surprising result. Such websites may have focused on Al-Jazeera's perceived anti-American bias rather than re-presentation of its reports. It may be argued that by posting those reports, hate websites acknowledged the de facto importance of Al-Jazeera.

What Did Western Internet Users Derive from Al-Jazeera Reports?

Overall, representations were favorable towards Al-Jazeera on alternative websites, mixed on blogs and unaffiliated websites and generally hostile on hate websites and websites affiliated with the mainstream media. Given the overwhelming number of re-presentations on alternative websites, the analysis revealed a slight tendency to embrace Al-Jazeera as a credible news source.

How do alternative media websites – the principal sites that used Al-Jazeera reports – differ from mainstream media websites? First, while mainstream media seek to maximize profits or sell advertisers access to a specific audience, alternative media are often non-profit or free and thus can target a broad and non-elite audience. Second, it has been argued that powerful social institutions (particularly corporations) control mainstream media that seek to reinforce elite hegemony and hierarchical social relationships (Chomsky, 1997). By contrast, the alternative approach is structured to "subvert society's defining hierarchical social relationships, and sees itself as part of a project to establish new ways of organizing media and social activity" (Albert, 2003).

Western-based alternative media organizations originated out of recognition that mainstream media are restricted or controlled by a few agents or corporations that share a similar sociopolitical ideology. Many alternative news sites clearly have their own agendas, some declaring them openly in their mission statements. For example, the Centre for Research on Globalization (CRG) presents itself as "an independent research and media group of progressive writers, scholars and activists committed to curbing the tide of 'globalization' and 'disarming' the New World Order" (http://www.globalresearch.ca/about). Thus, while Al-Jazeera was consistently framed in mainstream media as a mouthpiece for Osama Bin Laden, a significant number of liberal-oriented alternative websites embraced the Arabic network as a credible news source. Typical examples include the following posting on Indymedia Vancouver and Portland, respectively:

> ... *thank god we have Al-Jazeera and other news media that present an alternative view to the US propaganda machine. Have you not already learned how many lies the US Administration and main stream media have fabricated to justify this illegal and atrocious war? Your attempt to justify treating women and children as such only reveals your true racist agenda.* (Indymedia Vancouver, November 10, 2003)

> ... *last night I listened to the founder and owner of the Aljazeera network speak. He spoke about the s*** they get from the US for showing certain things, but he said he also*

*gets the same s*** from every country in the Middle East for reporting 'not so nice things' about them too. Now that's Fair & Balanced.* (Zach, Indymedia Portland, November 10, 2003)

Bloggers expressed mixed feelings regarding using Al-Jazeera as a news source. While some argued that the images are important per se regardless of their source, for others the fact that Al-Jazeera came up with the story means that it is phony: "I'm sure this actually does cause international outrage – but consider the source, Americans. This is coming from Al-Jazeera, aka the Bin Laden Network. My guess is the story that goes with these pictures is not the one told in the article" (Riz's blog, November 10, 2003).

Like many alternative news websites, bloggers often noted that Al-Jazeera reports were not picked up by mainstream US media, and were therefore happy to post them as part of their perceived job to uncover issues that the manstream media fails to put on the agenda: "... no wonder the world is hating us. the arab world is seeing these pictures. and the american media will never show them" (Blog for America, November 12, 2003). In another interesting post, the author ponders Al-Jazeera's reputation versus his admittance that he finds it a credible news source:

I hesitated to put this link here, because after all it is Al-Jazeera and it could somehow be a fake (although I have found, to my surprise, that one of the best places to get fairly unbiased news lately is their site). Anyway, since TGS and Dongi mentioned the dire possibility, here it goes: Shocking images shame US forces. I really don't know what to make of it. You may judge for yourselves. (Whiskey Bar blog, November 15, 2003, http://billmon.org/archives/000883.html)

Websites with no political affiliation were the source of the most heated debates regarding the nature and credibility of Al-Jazeera, particularly because such forums invite users with less defined or rigid views. Exposure to such counter-hegemonic images and subsequent debate might lead to questioning of government policies and affect future voting preferences. Govteen.com, a non-profit US-based corporation that aims "to provide interactive and engaging educational opportunities for teenagers by teenagers," logged more than 50 postings after its re-presentation of the Al-Jazeera report on the restraining of Iraqi women and children. This is interesting because the participants are American teenagers whose opinions regarding the war could be significantly shaped by the content of these forums. "Weejoby," the first user to post a message about the article, wrote: "Why did i have to go to aljazeera to find out about this? Can anyone find it on CNN for me?" (Govteen.com, November 12, 2003). Other users supported this perspective. "Cicero17" wrote: "You think they would show this on CNN? Of course they wouldn't; our media is VERY biased" (Govteen.com, December 4, 2003).

Some forums, however, took a distinctly oppositional stance towards Al-Jazeera and reflected the hatred that many bodies in the US have against the station. On Rantburg.com, a discussion board "dedicated to a civil, well-reasoned discourse," the editors of the website distorted the original Al-Jazeera article by adding "entertaining" side notes. For example, in response to the photograph of the US soldier frisking the Afghani child, one side note read: "Get his name! I want him court martialed!" Another side note, next to the text recounting the US army's response to the photograph, reads: "At least the major had the good grace not to burst out laughing in their faces" (Rantburg, November 24, 2003). This spirit of mockery was clearly present in many of the succeeding talkback postings.

The fourth and smallest group consisted of websites affiliated with mainstream media. A reference to the Al-Jazeera report on the frisking of the Afghani children on Opinionjournal.com – the Wall Street Journal's editorial page website – characterizes Al-Jazeera as an unworthy voice. James Taranto called the report a "fascinatingly weird, and rather funny, example of Islamist propaganda." Taranto then purported to "expose" the article's source as unreliable, claiming that the spokesman for the Islamic Observation Centre (responsible for releasing the photograph to Al-Jazeera) was "known as the mouthpiece of Al-Qaeda in Britain" and that he had sought asylum in Britain after fleeing Egypt, where he had been convicted and sentenced to death for a bomb attack that killed a 12-year-old girl. Taranto also revealed that the author, Yvonne Ridley, was a Muslim convert who made "the extraordinary claim that Western intelligence agencies tried to get her killed to bolster public support for the air strikes on Afghanistan" (Taranto, Opinion Journal, October 23, 2003, http://www.opinionjournal.com/best/?id=110004208). (This is the place to mention that Ridley was sacked shortly after the publication of the articles, and sued Al-Jazeera on the grounds of unfair dismissal (a trial in which she won in 2008). Ridley is currently working for the Iranian Press TV).

Hate websites, constituting the fifth group, rely on the Internet to present and propagate their hate-based perspective to a worldwide audience of like-minded individuals. A US Senate Judiciary Committee review of hate websites in the late 1990s defined hate messages as messages that "can be interpreted as threatening to some groups [and] may demonstrate a degree of criminal intent" (Currie, 2002), differentiating them from the content of extremist alternative news websites. In this study, some of the hate groups that discussed the Al-Jazeera reports included anti-gay websites. The following posting from Thundermonkey (noisyprimate.com, a website that identifies itself as a forum for extreme right-wing groups) typifies the perspective towards Al-Jazeera on these sites:

> *Listen up you hypocritical m***********s. If you savages didn't use any and all methods of employing civilians to wage your jihad maybe our soldiers wouldn't have good reason to frisk 4 year old children. In the mean time while you goat r****s continue to pull stunts like this one don't complain when our troops get a little jumpy doing the dirty work of rebuilding your country, sans fascism. Aljazeera.Net - The all whiney maggots, all the time, channel.* (Thunder monkey, October 17, 2003, http://www.noisyprimate.com/archives/ 000188.html)

This analysis has demonstrated that the more liberal and "alternative" the website (alternative news media and blogs), the more willing it is to use Al-Jazeera reports and the more likely to accept Al-Jazeera as a credible news source. In contrast, websites related to the mainstream media and hate groups rarely use Al-Jazeera reports and regard Al-Jazeera as a mouthpiece for Osama Bin Laden.

Implications

Analysis of the presentation of Al-Jazeera's reports on the abuse of Iraqi and Afghani civilians reveals the emergence of a counterpublic that debates news articles from Al-Jazeera's website on alternative news websites, blogs and (to a lesser extent) politically unaffiliated Websites. Ethnographic studies of online debates show that media-savvy surfers go to these websites to seek more information about news events proactively after watching the news on mainstream media. The analysis here discovered that although many users took the Al-Jazeera reports "with a hefty pinch of salt," the general tendency was to accept Al-Jazeera as a credible news source. Many of the Western websites that republished the reports were popular news hubs for Internet users, thus dramatically increasing Al-Jazeera's exposure. For example, dailykos.com is ranked of the most visited political blogs on Alexa's global ratings and won the Forbes "best blog" award; this means that the Al-Jazeera reports reached a substantial Western audience (although nowhere nearly as large as that of the mainstream media).

As global and mainstream US news networks block culturally incongruent images, a new bond forms between Al-Jazeera and liberal alternative websites, blogs and online forums, that are constantly searching for credible alternative news sources because of their dissatisfaction with the mainstream media. These platforms thus perceive Al-Jazeera as an ally in fighting the "bias" of the mainstream media, rendering Al-Jazeera part of an emerging counterpublic that I term a "coalition of alternatives," as it unites several forces that challenge mainstream discourse. While global debate concerning the war on terror takes place in society at large and through mainstream and global news networks, the coalition of alternatives invents and circulates a global debate that should be the focus of future globalization studies.

These findings support the conclusions of a comprehensive study (Michalsky & Preston, 2002) of audience reception in the aftermath of the terrorist attacks on September 11, 2001, noting the emergence and growth of "skeptic" and non-affiliated audiences. The study found that the proliferation of transnational news channels and alternative news sources generated a heightened awareness of a diversity of perspectives on political events among those able to access such sources. The study noted that general distrust of available television and print media news sources "was the single biggest reason given for the vastly increased use of Internet sources following September 11" (Michalsky & Preston, 2000, p. 37). In other words, "skeptic zappers" are those who characteristically flip between television channels to compare and contrast different news bulletins (e.g. CNN vs. BBC vs. Al-Jazeera). As they "display relatively high levels of cynicism towards all news media regardless of language or source and tend to be highly skilled and competent alternative news-seeking surfers" (Ibid.), they supplement their consumption of TV news bulletins with highly selective but extensive use of Internet and other news and current affairs source material. In turn, these media consumers view Al-Jazeera to complete the picture provided by their own mainstream media. This suggests that for some people, at least, the Internet is more important than any other information technology in creating the wider narrative or world picture; accordingly, television becomes simply a receptacle for images understood through the Internet rather than through the media that channel them. Al-Jazeera thus assumes an important role in disrupting conventional media by framing and context indualizing media stories for these skeptic zappers. While Michalsky & Preston's study found that skeptic zappers are usually multilingual, the present study uses Al-Jazeera to illustrate that it is not necessarily so, as there are numerous skeptic zappers who only speak English. Instead, some Internet users who operate or frequently rely on alternative websites simply come to view CNN and Fox News as "unreliable". Among such users, Al-Jazeera is perceived as an ally that shares the goal of fighting the corruption of their own mainstream media. While mainstream media often filtered out Al-Jazeera's original news angle, an identifiable cross-cultural dialogue is occurring among their alternative online counterparts.

CHAPTER NINE

AL-JAZEERA ENGLISH IN THE US

On November 15, 2006, exactly 10 years after the launch of Al-Jazeera Arabic, Al-Jazeera launched a 24/7 English news channel. Al-Jazeera English represents Al-Jazeera's objective to be upgraded from the category of a regional ethnic media provider to that of a major international news network. The channel's main target-audience groups are (a) viewers from developing countries who want to replace or complement their BBC World News and CNN viewing with a channel that gives a non-Western perspective of global news events, (b) second and third generation Arab and Muslim immigrants in English-speaking countries who feel more comfortable with English than Arabic but want to watch global news from an Arab angle, and (c) Westerners familiar with the Al-Jazeera brand interested in receiving news directly from the channel (rather than through re-presentation of material from Al-Jazeera Arabic on local channels). In its mission statement, the channel explicitly declares its high aspirations: "...Al-Jazeera English is destined to be the English-language channel of reference for Middle Eastern events, balancing the current typical information flow by reporting from the developing world back to the West and from the southern to the northern hemisphere" (http://english.aljazeera.net/aboutus/2006/11/2008525185555444449.html).

Al-Jazeera English has easily acquired viewers in the first two target groups: Those from developing countries and Arab and Muslim immigrants living in the West. After three years of broadcasting, the channel declares access to 150 million viewers in 50 countries, which signifies that it is already more popular than rivals CNN and BBC World News in the areas of Africa, Asia, South America and the Middle East (Mason, 2009). It also has a large following amongst Arab viewers in the West who have actively set up their satellite dishes (using location coordinates) to receive the channel.

Al-Jazeera has also gained significant success amongst its third target group in Europe; Major cable and satellite distributors in France, Germany, Italy, the

Netherlands, Norway, Sweden, Switzerland, Danmark, and the United Kingdom have secured distribution deals with the new channel. Interestingly, in the UK, Al-Jazeera English is carried on BSkyB, owned by media mogul Rupert Murdoch, who also owns Fox News, which illustrates the demand for Al-Jazeera in the country. Al-Jazeera English has even gained success in securing distribution in Israel, where Israelis can watch the channel on satellite carrier *Yes*, which has access to 600,00 households. Moreover, the position of Al-Jazeera English on *Yes*'s channel listing is adjacent to the other major international news networks (CNN is positioned on channel 102, Sky News - 103, France24 – 104, Fox News -105, BBC World News – 107 and Al-Jazeera English on channel 108). Such order means that when flicking through the international news channels throughout a crisis, Israelis are likely to reach Al-Jazeera English (accidently or not).

The real challenge for Al-Jazeera English, however, is in its ability to secure distribution deals with its most important customer in the West, which holds the keys to the single most lucrative and politically-important television market in the world: the US cable and satellite carriers. Predictably, in light of Al-Jazeera's problematic reputation in the US, the channel is still stuggling to find major distributors there. To this end, it is trying to ensure a clear distinction between the Arabic and English channels. Al-Jazeera English's commercial Director Lidsay Oliver reportedly refused space on the Arabic tier of an American cable company in order not to be identified with Al-Jazeera Arabic (Tischler, 2007). Josh Rushing, one of Al-Jazeera English's presenters, reveals that at some point before the channel's launch he suggested to the first managing Director Nigel Parsons to market the channel under a different name in order to contribute to its distribution in the US (Ibid.).

The aim to distance itself from Al-Jazeera Arabic is evident not only in the marketing strategy of the new channel but also in the content of its broadcasts: Al-Jazeera Arabic focuses on the Arab world in 60.2 percent of its stories compared to only 12 percent on Al-Jazeera English. Instead, 57 percent of all stories on Al-Jazeera English focus on the "developing world" (Sudweeks, Hrachovec & Ess 2008).

A further move to gain credibility in the West is also evident in the new channel's recruitment strategy of capitalizing on the reputation of well-known TV figures. One famous American face on Al-Jazeera English has been Dave Marash who had a long career beside Ted Koppel on ABC's *Nightline*. Being an American Jew, Marash contributed to Al-Jazeera English's image as a channel that goes beyond borders and religions. Another famous recruit was Sir David Frost. One of the most famous TV news personalities in the UK, he is also well-known to many (especially older) viewers in the US. Already in the early 1960's, NBC bought the rights to produce an American version of Frost's political satire show "*That Was the Week That Was*". When Frost moved from political satire to tough interviewing in the late 1960's, the TV group Westinghouse selected him to anchor a US version of the daily interview show *The Frost Report* (which won him Emmy awards for the show in 1970 and 1971). In the 1980's Frost returned to US screens after NBC bought the rights to his show *Spitting Image*, a British satirical puppet show. In 2006, Frost made waves in the US again following the success of the *Frost/Nixon* the London theater-play, which is based of Frost's set of interviews with Richard Nixon in 1977 (in which Nixon first denied and later admitted to the Watergate affair). In 2008 Ron Howard and Universal Pictures turned the play into a Hollywood film. In light of Frost's reputation, which earned him knighthood in the UK, his decision to finish his successful career at Al-Jazeera English won the headlines of dozens of leading news channels in the US, Britain, Australia, and Canada, improving the channel's public relations and promoting curiosity towards its launch. Another famous recruit of the channel is Riz Khan. Khan was on the founding team and one of the first news anchors at BBC World News in the early 1990's. In 1993, he moved to CNN, where he served as a senior news anchor and hosted an interactive interview show *CNN: Q&A with Riz Khan* from 1996. Other well-known faces on the channel former CBS's David Hawkins, former CNN and BBC news anchorwoman Veronica Pedrosa, former BBC World News senior anchor Stephen Cole, and former BBC reporter Rageh Omaar. The most surprising Western face to join the channel is a former US marine, *Captain* Josh Rushing, who gained fame after the success of the 2004 documentary film *Control Room*, (which portrayed Rushing's interaction with the Al-Jazeera team at The United States Central Command (US CENTCOM) in Doha, Qatar during the early days of the war in Iraq). In the documentary, which gained success in US cinema, Rushing admitted on camera that he began to question his ethics when he realised that while watching Al-Jazeera's images of Iraqi civilian casualties he did not feel the same pain he felt while watching the hurdles of US soldiers on CNN. In a later interview to the New York City newspaper *The Village Voice* Rushing re-stated his disappointment that the US media does not show the human suffering of Iraqis. As a result, Fox News Sean Hannity posted his face above the caption traitor. As a result of this controversy, Captain Rushing left the US army after 13 years of service to join Al-Jazeera English.

Beyond its recruitment strategy and it attempts to distance itself from its Arabic sibling, the English channel's efforts to appeal to the US market also includes the decision to choose Washington as one of its four broadcasting centers (together with Kuala Lumpur, Doha and London). The Washington bureau has over 150 staff and is responsible for 4 hours of broadcasting each day during US prime-time. This choice of location is not obvious and is possibly based on the failure of BBC World News to gain US viewership, in light of its strategy of keeping its broadcasting center in London. (As a result of its image as a foreign source, it took the BBC World News 11 years to find a major distributor in the US. It still suffers from low ratings in the US. Consequently, BBC America - an entetainment channel that caters to US palate with shows such as reality cooking shows with celebrities - was launched in 1998).

Furthermore, Al-Jazeera English offers hard to refuse business offers to US cable and satellite carriers to carry the channel (which might be the reason that carriers who decline to carry the channel do not mention money but bandwidth as the reason). Of those that have agreed, Burlington Telecom is carrying the channel for free (see below) until 2011 and Buckeye Captains report that they closed a "sweet" deal with Al-Jazeera English without disclosing the full details.

To further help promote its status in the West, Al-Jazeera English hired a high-profile Manhattan-based PR agency Brown Lloyd James (BLJ). The firm, whose clients include The Walt Disney Corporation, *Forbes* magazine, Harper Collins Publishers and the Telegraph Group, monitors anti-Al-Jazeera English messages 24/7 on television, in newspapers and on the web and responds instantly to negative commentary about the channel. BLJ also launched a global advertising campaign, which includes the website "I want Al-Jazeera English" (http://www.iwantaje.net/), dedicated to defying "myths" about the Al-Jazeera brand. The website stresses that Al-Jazeera has a Code of Ethics and that it does not show beheadings, that the chanel is watched in Israel and conducts more interviews with Israeli officials than CNN and BBC, that it always edits videos from Bin Laden and Al-Qaeda members and that it does not support terrorism in any manner. The website calls on Americans to proactively support Al-Jazeera's English distribution by writing to their local cable and satellite providers asking them to carry the channel:

> *...unlike the rest of the world, most North American audiences remain in the dark. In a world that is growing increasingly smaller and more interconnected each day, it is more important than ever to have full access to international news. Al-Jazeera English is dedicated to providing a voice to the voiceless, and now you have the opportunity to have your voice heard. If you live in the United States or Canada, this website is your opportunity to show your support for Al-Jazeera English.* (http://www.iwantaje.net/speak/)

Before and during the launch of Al-Jazeera English, the US media's response to the channel varied. The *New York Times* op-eds and articles voiced the most positive support. A day after Al-Jazeera's launch Alessandra Stenley the *New York Times* television critic, wrote: "Yesterday, most Americans could watch it only on the Internet at english.aljazeera.net. It's a shame. Americans can see almost anything on television these days, from Polish newscasts to reruns of 'Benson.' The new channel, Al-Jazeera English, will never displace CNN, MSNBC or Fox News, but it provides the curious — or the passionately concerned — with a window into how the world sees us, or doesn't" (cf. Stanley, 2006). Of all the op-eds regarding the new channel, the most surprising support came from Judea Pearl, the father of Wall Street Journal reporter Daniel Pearl, who was kidnapped and beheaded in Pakistan in early 2002 by al-Qaeda members. Pearl wrote in a January 17, 2007 column that the US should give the channel a chance despite Al-Jazeera Arabic's persistent bias against the US and the fact that they employ a Muslim cleric that preaches terrorism (referring to cleric Yusuf Al-Qaradawi, host of "Sharia and life") in the name of the freedom of speech:

> *I wouldn't call for banning Al-Jazeera English in the United States even if that were possible. It is important to extend a hand to the network because it can become a force for good; but it is as important for our news organizations to scrutinize its content and let its viewers know when anti-Western wishes are subverting objective truth. As Al-Jazeera on the whole feels the heat of world media attention, we can hope that it will learn to harness its popularity in the service of humanity, progress and moderation.* (http://www.nytimes.com/2007/01/17/opinion/17pearl.html?pagewanted=print)

USA Today and *The Boston Globe* also published op-eds by liberal commentators and peace advocates supporting Al-Jazeera English. In addition, panelists on public TV and radio channels PBS and NPR expressed almost unanimous support of the channel. The PBS panelists (which included Washington Post columnist Colbert King, political commentator Mark Sheilds and National Public Radio legal affairs correspondent Nina Totenberg) agreed that putting Al-Jazeera English on cable was a test of the belief in the "full, free flow of ideas."

However, reaction to Al-Jazeera English was different on the commercial new stations which raised questions about the new channel's ideology and terminology. CNN questioned the values of the channel after Riz Khan told correspondent Frank Sesno on November 16, 2006, a day after the launch of Al-Jazeera English that "he is not to judge" whether Hezbollah and Hamas are terrorist organizations. Considering that both Hamas and Hezbollah are officially registered as terrorist organizations in the US (Hamas is also considered a terrorist organization by Canada, the European Union, Isreal, Japan, Australia and the United Kingdom and

Hezbollah is on the terrorist list of 6 Western countries), predictably, Khan's reply strengthened anti-sentiment towards Al-Jazeera English in the US blogosphere.

Another harsh, fierce welcome for the new channel came from Fox News, which portrayed the launch of Al-Jazeera English as a joke:

> Hume: *Finally tonight, the new English language Al-Jazeera Network is not being carried on a single major American cable or satellite TV provider, but you can take my word for it, it will soon be a huge hit here. With promos like this, they can't miss.*
>
> (begin video clip)
>
> Announcer: *Coming soon to the United States, it's the Al-Jazeera Network for America. The leader for news, sports, and quality entertainment in the Middle East is now available in the land of the great Satan. Check out exciting dramas and hilarious sitcoms. Shows like I Love Uzi, Kurd Your Enthusiasm, 30 Rocks, Dancing with the Shiites, Extreme Makeover: Cave Edition, Saddam Squarepants, My Name is Oil, and, of course, Everybody Hates Israel. The Al-Jazeera network for America. Call your Zionist controlled cable company today.* (*Fox Special Report with Brit Home*, November 20, 2006).

Initially, however, the signs regarding the adoption of Al-Jazeera English in the US had been positive. Before its launch, the channel was reportedly on the verge of signing a distribution contract with *Comcast*, the largest cable provider, to carry the channel on the Detroit cable system. Such a distribution deal seems natural in light of the concentration of Arab-Americans in Detroit (it is estimated that 200,000–300,000 of the 1.8 million Arabs living in the US live in the area). In *Al-Jazeera: The Inside Story*, Hugh Miles reported that all the satellite dishes in Dearborn "are glued to Al-Jazeera" (2005, p. 396). However, a few days before Al-Jazeera English's launch, Comcast backed out from the negotiations and announced that it would not carry Al-Jazeera. Comcast's decision was a major blow for Al-Jazeera for two reasons: First, it meant that no major body would distribute its broadcasts on its launch day. Second, Comcast is the number one cable carrier in other Arab centers in America, which set a precedent against carrying Al-Jazeera in other strategic regions. After the Comcast announcement, Nigel Parsons, the founding Managing Director of Al-Jazeera English asserted that Comcast had turned to Al-Jazeera first and not the other way around. Parsons stated his belief that the decision was based on "political pressure" rather than "lack of bandwidth". Furthermore, in an interview with the entertainment magazine Variety on Comcast's decision, an Al-Jazeera employee said on condition of annonimity: "We thought we were just awaiting signatures." (Jaafar, 2006).

Throughout the next few months, Al-Jazeera English's negotiations with the other major cable carriers – Cox Communications and Time Warner – also failed. Regarding the satellite carriers, Al-Jazeera's luck was only slightly better: After negotiations with the major sattelite carriers DirecTV and Echostar's Dish network (which carries Al-Jazeera Arabic in the US) failed, Al-Jazeera secured a deal with a smaller carrier whose mother company is French: The France Telecom subsidiary provider Globecast. Viewers interested in watching Al-Jazeera English need to pay Globecast a one-time fee of 179$ in addition to a 200–300$ connection fee. Taking into consideration that Globecast is considered a provider of "ethnic" TV, which carries a variety of Iranian and Afghan channels to immigrants, and due to the high price of adding Al-Jazeera English to the viewing package, it is reasonable to assume that most of Globecast's Al-Jazeera English subscribers are Arab-Americans.

As a result, when Al-Jazeera English launched in November 2006, only two small cable carriers had agreed to carry it – Burlington *TV* (BT) in Vemont and Buckeye in Toledo, Ohio. Buckeye's decision to carry the channel was based on the large Arab population that lives in Toledo. With Burlington Telecom, a city-chartered and privately financed cable company, the decision was based more on the alternative nature of the cable carrier and the progressive nature of the city of Burlington than on the nature of Al-Jazeera. Burlington is known as a city that defies norms and fights monopolies. Vermont's Progressive Mayor Bob Kiss supported the idea of starting a local initiative to counter the monopoly of Adelphia (which was bought by Time Warner and Comcast in 2006) in line the Vermont Progressive party ideals (the party does not take donations from corporations in order to be clean of corporate interests). BT, a municipal fiber-optic information roadway which provides phone and cable services for a very low cost to the community, does not have to report to shareholders (who might have opposed Al-Jazeera English) and depends entirely on revenues from its small subscriber base of 2500 (as it is not subsidized in any form by the city). Due to these unique circumstances, BT only offers news channels that deliver their content for free. According to its deal with Al-Jazeera English, BT will carry the channel without paying for it until 2011 (although it costs about $18 more than a standard package to get Al-Jazeera).

What is interesting in both cases is the amount of pressure from the public as well as from lobbyist groups, particularly the conservative group Accuracy in Media, placed on these two small cable carriers to stop offering Al-Jazeera English, undoubtedly illustrating the consequences to other carriers who might have considered carrying the station. Accuracy in Media, a media watchdog founded in 1969 is a powerful and experienced organization that systematically criticizes "leftist propaganda" in US media and has persistently managed to affect the US media market in the last four decades. Their open campaign against Al-Jazeera English began with a poll that it comissioned from the research and consulting firm The Polling Company on September 7–10, 2006, a few months before the launch of the channel, which aimed to find whether Americans oppose its arrival in the US (http://www.pollingcompany.com/cms/files/AIM%20Omnibus%20Analysis%20to%20Client.pdf). The poll found that 53 percent of those asked oppose the channel and think that the US government should not give it access to the US media market. Of these 53 percent, 38 percent said that they strongly oppose the new channel and 15 percent "somewhat opposed" it. 29 percent said they supported it. Since the survey was conducted before Al-Jazeera English's launch, viewers who opposed the channel did not actually have the option of watching it and therefore their opinion was based on feelings and some familiarity with Al-Jazeera Arabic. Accuracy in Media also did not mention on its website figures that could have countered its cause: For example, 15% of the television viewers polled said that they were undecided whether they support or oppose the new channel (perhaps because they had not watched the channel), which would have made a major difference to the figures (the statistics come out to 97% response rate but the poll does not indicate whether 3% abstained from answering the survey). Second, and more important, Accuracy in Media did not mention that young adults aged 18–24 were more divided about the channel with 42% supporting it versus 41% opposing it (!).

Accuracy in Media declared that following the survey's results (which were widely aired in the US), it decided to launch a campaign against the broadcasting of Al-Jazeera English in the US. On a website "stop Al-Jazeera.com", it airs a video titled "terror television" whose main message is that Al-Jazeera is behind the insurgency in Iraq. It also shows Saddam Hussein's son Uday Hussein meeting with Al-Jazeera's former General Manager Mohammed Jaseem Al-Ali in March 2000 as well as interviews with wanna-be suicide bombers who came to Iraq from different countries, and "admitted" that Al-Jazeera's TV images prompted their decision. Further, the video mentions the arrests of Al-Jazeera cameramen Sami Al Hajj and reporter Tayseer Allouni on charges of terrorism activity. The campaign calls on Americans to take action against Al-Jazeera English by writing, calling or emailing the two Senators and one member of the House representing, Accuracy in Media asking them to verify that carriers will not carry the channel. It suggests the following text be used:

> *I am writing to urge you to introduce a congressional resolution saying that Al-Jazeera International should not be granted access to the U.S. media market. Al-Jazeera television has served as an outlet for propaganda from terrorist organizations such as al Qaeda, Hamas and*

Hezbollah; refers on the air to suicide bombers as "martyrs;" and has inspired violence against Americans, as demonstrated by videotaped confessions of captured terrorists.

Dissent against Al-Jazeera English can also be found in progressive states such as in Vermont, where a small group called Defenders Council of Vermont formed in 2007 "to educate the citizens of Vermont about the nature, reality and threat of Islamic Jihadismse". The group argues that Al-Jazeera English should be dropped from BT since it promotes anti-Jewish sentiment and "insults American patriots". It is also part of a larger anti-Muslim campaign, with it's website containing articles that warn Westerners against the secret formation of a "Worldwide Islamic State" as well as other anti-Muslim sentiment.

The anti-Al-Jazeera English lobby has gained partial success in its mission to disrupt the adoption of the channel and force the carriers in Burlington and Toledo to question their decision to carry it. In early May 2008, Burlington Telecom General Manager Chris Burns attempted to drop the channel "in response to 'dozens' of complaints from angry customers". However, Mayor Bob Kiss issued a Stay of Execution and called for town hall meetings to discuss the fate of the channel. The first meeting was conducted on May 27, 2008 but was attended by only 75 residents, despite the Defenders Council of Vermont calling for "as much support as possible." Two weeks later, a further meeting was hosted by Burlington Telecom's Advisory Committee and was attended by nearly 200 citizens, most of them supporting the decision to leave Al-Jazeera English in Burlington. However, no final decision was made during the meeting. Although the pressure to drop Al Jazeera English continued, online more than 300 residents signed a petition to keep Al Jazeera English on BT where it continues to be carried. The petition read:

To: Burlington Telecom

The City of Burlington, Vermont should be a city that tolerates all views and opinions on the Middle East and U.S. policy in the Middle East. The "dozens" of letters you (Burlington Telecom) have received in an attempt to force you to stop carrying Al-Jazeera English is against the basic principle of free speech. This is a calculated attempt to politically censor dissenting views from the Middle East that are all too often excluded from the main stream media. This anti-Arab and Islamophobic drive to force you to discontinue Al-Jazeera English is at odds with Burlington's long history of defending and celebrating diversity. Al-Jazeera English keeps Vermonters informed and aware of U.S. foreign policy and politics in the Middle East, providing a valuable service to the state. Vermonters need more access to a variety of information, opinions and views, not less! We will not let anti-Arab, Islamophobic and divisive elements limit our access to news and differing views.... This attack on Al-Jazeera is an attack on free speech! We the undersigned urge Burlington Telecom to keep Al-Jazeera English as part of its programming. Sincerely, http://www.petitiononline.com/BTSpeech/petition.html

Al-Jazeera also experienced difficulties in Toledo, Ohio. The cable service provider Buckeye decided to carry the channel in part because of the large Middle Eastern population in the area and after receiving some (but not overwhelming) demand. Like in Burlington, they received complaints following the channel's launch, including a letter sent by about 50 subscribers threatening to cancel their subscription to Buckeye and calling the company's chairman "a traitor at wartime". However, the company's executives reported that despite these threats, very few canceled their subscription in practice. The controversy over Buckeye's decision to carry the channel also became the talk of the day on online local forums, where hundreds of Toledo citizens took part in the heated debate. Accuracy in Media also protested the Buckeye decision, arguing that as Toledo is a center for Arab-Americans, Al-Jazeera will radicalize them in the same manner that it has radicalized British Muslims. They refered campaigners to an MA thesis written at the University of Leeds by Mohamed Ben Moussa "The role of mass media in shaping identity construction among British Muslim Diasporas after 9/11" which (they argue) notes that transnational media promoted mistrust in local media amongst British Muslims immigrants and reinforces their sense of belongings to their own communities (p. 15, http://ics.leeds.ac.uk/pg%20study/ma%20showcase/Ben_Moussa.doc). While Ben-Moussa indeed argued that watching Al-Jazeeera increases British Muslim's sense of connection to their community, Accuracy in Media wrongly deducted that Al-Jazeera English encouraged the actions of the July 7, 2007 terrorists in London. Ultimately the pressure to drop Al Jazeera English in Toledo failed. According to Tom Dawson, Buckeye's director of government and community affairs, this was due to the many phone calls received in support of the channel resulting in Al-Jazeera English receiving "a similar number of compliments as complaints" (Moss, 2007).

Beyond the hurdles that Al-Jazeera faced to keep the channel on the two small broadcasters that initially adopted it, it took another blow with the publication of an article in December 2007 in the business magazine *Fast Company* which revealed that US advertisers were not likely to buy any airtime on the new channel. Reporter Linda Tischler called the major commercial buying companies - OMD, Starcom, MediaVest, MindShare, Carat – in order to ask them about their intentions to buy ads on Al-Jazeera English. They all reportedly "refused to respond or politely declined to comment". The magazine quoted one account executive who said on condition of anonymity: "Politically, this is a nightmare. Never in a billion years would I bring this to our client." The magazine further quoted Marketing guru Ernest Lupinacci, formerly CEO of the ad agency Anomaly, who explained why US companies will never advertise on Al-Jazeera English: "If you're a marketer, your worst nightmare is to wake up and read a headline on the Drudge Report: 'U.S. Widgets to Buy Airtime on Al-Jazeera.' Next thing you know, you're a tape loop on Howard Stern" (Tischler, 2007).

A further blow came in March 2008, when senior anchor Dave Marash announced that he was leaving the channel due to its "anti-American" bias. As noted above, Dave Marash was the American face of Al-Jazeera and his decision to quit has caused the Al-Jazeera English brand great damage. In an interview to *Columbia Journalism Review*, Marash explained in detail what instigated his decision. He claimed a decision to move him, the only anchor with an American accent and perspective, from the anchor chair (where he could make editorial decisions) to the role of correspondent symbolized the channel's overall aim to minimize Washington's role as an important news bureau. This, he stated, was to promote Arab interests at the expense of the original cosmopolitan perspective gained from broadcasting from four broadcasting centers with equal footing. To support his argument, Marash revealed that although he and his team thought that a documentary series planned by Doha titled "poverty in America" was stereotypical and handled the matter in an accusatory rather than an analytic way, the planning desk in Doha sneaked in a team to film the documentary under their nose anyway. According to Marash, the change of spirit from a cosmopolitan to a pan-Arab channel stems from recent political developments: The strengthening of the relationship between Al-Jazeera and Saudi Arabia, and the weakening of Qatari ties with the US (Cunningham, 2008).

However, despite all these difficulties, in April 2009, the channel did manage to secure a distribution deal in the US with MHZ networks, a non-commercial broadcaster that focuses on newscasts from around the world. According to the deal, MHZ will distribute Al-Jazeera English to its 5 million subscribers in the Washington area and gradually extend this number to 18 million households in 20 US cities. According to Tony Burman, Al-Jazeera English Managing Director, this signifies a change of attitude toward Al-Jazeera with the transition of Administrations. Burman believes that Obama's entry to the White House "has changed the game dramatically, as America reengages with the wider world, the appetite for more international news is there" (cf. Helman, 2009).

In light of its failure to secure a deal with major commercial cable and satellite carriers, Al-Jazeera English has turned to the internet as an alternative distribution channel. Online, it is much easier to secure distribution deals due to the great number of providers and competition between IPTV carriers. Russell

Merryman, editor-in-chief of Web and New Media, reported that already in July 2007 10,000 people were watching the channel online (of which 20% are subscribers). Al-Jazeera English is avalable on numerous sites in addition to the live streaming available on its own website. It is available on the Livestation, Vingo, and JUMPTV (and formerly also on Virtual Digital Cable and Jalipo) platforms. These services either offer the channel either for free or for a very small fee of around 9$ a month (depending on the quality of the broadcasts). Interestingly, the most popular platform by far for Western viewers to watch Al-Jazeera English news items is not through live stream but on its branded *Youtube* channel which has over 62,000 subscribers and over 4.4 million views. Currently, over 60% of its traffic originates in the US (this equates to over 36,000 subscribers and 2.5 million views). During crises such as the 2008–9 Operation Cast Lead (the war in Gaza) the numbers rose tenfold. In addition, Al Jazeera English is running a successful Twitter service, where it updates news items regularly to more than 112,000 registered subscribers. But however this relative success online is it is important to see these numbers in perspective. Al-Jazeera English's tens of thousands of US viewers is still a drop in the ocean, especially when compared to its viewership in tiny Israel, where it is available to 560,000 households.

To conclude, it is hard to determine which factor has been the most determinant in Al-Jazeera English's failure to secure a distribution deal with a major commercial broadcaster in the US. The bottom line is that this is in stark contrast to its reception in Europe and Israel on major cable and satellite carriers, Al-Jazeera English only appears on ethnic (and one progressive) cable carriers in the US. In some respect, Al-Jazeera English is facing even more obstacles than Al-Jazeera Arabic, despite its declared global perspective, perhaps because it aims to broadcast to US viewers directly what the Administration perceives as "propaganda".

CHAPTER TEN

CONCLUSIONS

Drawing an alternative map of the emerging global news order and its impact on local reporting, this book concludes that the rise of non-Western global news stations has increased nationalism, centralization and ethnocentrism in US war reporting. Through the example of Al-Jazeera, the analysis exposes that the advent of counter-hegemonic contra-flow has impeled local stations towards a defensive and at times even offensive stance regarding "foreign" reports perceived as threatening their national sovereignty. It reveals that the Pentagon and the Administraion have persuaded US media to demonize the network and self-censor newsworthy information in light of a perceived information war with the Arab world.

As such, reports of gory images of civilian casualties (victims of the "glorified" airstrikes), of US soldiers' cruelty to Iraqi and Afghani citizens and Bin Laden's messages emphasizing the US's failure to capture him and the reasons behind the attacks were automatically self-censored. Comparative analysis of the re-presentation of similar reports during previous crises reveals the double standard as similar images had been traditionally considered newsworthy (consider the low magnitude of Al-Jazeera reports on the October 23, 2001 massacre of 122 Afghani civilians versus the wide coverage of CNN's reports on the bombings of the bunker in Al-Amariya during the 1991 Gulf War – see Chapter 5).

In the rare cases of "forced footage," when US networks were compelled to react after Al-Jazeera exposed "US shame" to global audiences, they "forced" the reports back into conventional boundaries by framing both the reports and their "foreign" source as "deviant." In such cases the US media contrived a new "Arab media are biased" scheme to ensure that such reports would be interpreted as an attack on American values rather than according to their actual content, that often exposed the ugly face of war or the vulnerability of the US Army. Al-Jazeera reports were thus considered "contaminated" and automatically categorized as "propaganda". Therefore, when Al-Jazeera showed graphic images of dead US soldiers and interviews with US POWs on the fourth day of the war in Iraq the Administration distracted attention from them and blamed Al-Jazeera for violating the Geneva Conventions.

Furthermore, the networks fell silent on the Pentagon's ensuing intimidation tactics, including the ousting of Al-Jazeera from the New York Stock Exchange floor, the refusal of US companies to host Al-Jazeera's website and finally, the killing of Al-Jazeera reporter Tareq Ayoub and the wounding of Al-Jazeera cameramen in what some argued was an intentional, planned attack. Therefore, in contrast to the popular globalist view, Al-Jazeera has not exposed US viewers to the atrocities of war and the Arab perspective throughout the war on terror.

This policy of labeling Al-Jazeera as a deviant network and the US media accepting their role to "expose, exclude or condemn" Al-Jazeera's material in accordance with Bush Administration policy resembles the treatment of Communist voices throughout the Cold War (Herman and Chomsky, 1988). During the Korean War, President Truman set up a Psychological Strategy Board aimed at fighting and reversing Soviet propaganda. During the Vietnam War, voices of dissent from the antiwar movement were viewed as damaging to US efforts and dismissed as "Communist propaganda," in accordance with FCC guidelines for application of the Fairness Doctrine: "It is not the Commission's intentions to make time available to Communists or to the Communist viewpoints" (cf. Hallin, 1984. p 142). Hallin determined that voices within the sphere of deviance faced exclusion, condemnation and exposure of their (alleged) bias (Ibid.). In this way, shortly after the September 11 attacks the Bush Administration started the Office of Global Communications (OGC) together with the Pentagon. The OGC used tactics such as intimidation, flak (negative responses to media output) and unsubstantiated "anti-terrorism" arguments to block counter-hegemonic images and challenging events from reaching US viewers.

Noam Chomsky, co-author of *Manufacturing Consent*, who has long argued that US media are subservient of the Administration, addressed an interviewee question as to whether there were any attempts to stop the free flow of information after September 11:

> *There are, however, some startling examples of US Government efforts to restrict free flow of information abroad. The Emir of Qatar confirmed that 'Washington has asked Qatar to rein in the influential and editorially independent Arabic Al-Jazeera television station,' BBC reported. The Emir, who also chairs the Organization of Islamic Conference that includes 56 countries, informed the press in Washington that Secretary of State Powell had pressured him to rein in Al-Jazeera: to 'persuade Al-Jazeera to tone down its coverage,' Al-Jazeera reports.*

> *Asked about the reports of censorship, the Emir said: 'This is true. We heard from the US Administration and also from the previous US Administration' (BBC, October 4, 2001, citing Reuters)... There has also been remarkably little use of the Bin Laden interviews and other material from Afghanistan available from Al-Jazeera.* (Chomsky, 2001, pp. 113–14)

This pressure by the US Administration to silence the anti-hegemonic reporting of Al-Jazeera is illustrated in Herman and Chomsky's propaganda model (1988). Herman and Chomsky assert that five filters determine which information will be censored. Most relevant here are the fourth and fifth filters: "Flak" and anti-ideology. Flak refers to the negative responses to media broadcast, and anti-ideology refers to demonization of the enemy's ideology. In the case of the interplay with Al-Jazeera, flak has worked on numerous occasions, mostly notably in the case of the images of dead soldiers and prisoners of war from Februrary 22, 2003. After CBS and CNN aired glimpses from the images, they were persuaded to drop them after hearing from the Pentagon (Hoskins, 2004, p. 67). In the case of the anti-ideology filter, here both the message and the messenger were demonized, as Al-Jazeera was framed as a deviant source on several occasions, particularly after its images threatened the sanitized presentation of the war by US networks.

In light of this hostile atmosphere, it is not surprising that Al-Jazeera's new 24/7 English channel is blocked by major US cable and satellite carriers, although it is heavily populated by media personnel that US viewers are familiar with (i.e. Sir David Frost, former BBC and CNN's anchor Riz Khan, former ABC's correspondent Ricard Gizbert, former CBS and CNN reporter David Hawkins). Comparison with the online realm shows that some of Al-Jazeera's images such as those portraying the humiliation of Iraqi and Afghani civilians, as well as Iraqi prisoners, did attain exposure online. The analysis illustrates that the real potential of an online global news exchange is among small groups of counterpublics - [US] viewers frustrated by their media's patriotic coverage seeking to complete their news consumption on alternative platforms including Al-Jazeera's English website. As such, it is hardly surprising that the web serves as a promising platform for a global public sphere.

To conclude, the book warns that not only do news reports threatening local coherence not necessarily refine traditional reporting within nations (and consequently the local public sphere), they may actually lead to a growing offensive and enmity between news networks that follow significantly different worldviews. Under this new environment, local reporters act as soldiers in a war and their actions are characterized by cultural protectionism and a systematic self-censorship of news events that might disrupt cultural congruency. Al-Jazeera has become the scapegoat of the US Administration and a way to distract attention away from the real causes of its failures in Iraq and Afghanistan. This draws boundaries around the extent of cross-cultural cooperation and signifies the polarization of the global news order, underscoring the myth of media globalization.

APPENDIX A

METHODOLOGY

Studying the effect of an international station on politics and public discourse can be a difficult task, since it is extremely hard to measure and determine the exact impact of a phenomenon and to separate it from its context. While a laboratory environment allows control over different variables, a real-life situation does not. For example, when we consider the Al-Jazeera effect we need to to take into account other important factors that influence the mood of journalists, such as the overall perspective of US news reporting in the wake of the events of September 11, 2001. Here, it has been argued that after the attacks and during the ensuing war on terror, journalists were looking to support and comfort US citizens rather than provide objective reporting, adopting an "us" against "them" rhetoric (Schudson, 2002, p. 36). This has been considered part of an overall process of a "re-nationalization" (Carey, 2002, p.87). After the 2003 Iraq War, political communication scholar Lance Bennett (2003) argued: "If the first Iraq war was named Desert Storm, the second might be called Perfect Storm. The run-up to the 2003 war witnessed an extraordinary convergence of factors that produced near perfect journalistic participation in government propaganda operations". This inability to take into account all the factors surrounding the Al-Jazeera encounter with US media such as the patriotic stance of the stations illustrated above is indeed the main weakness of the research presented in this book.

To overcome the problem of studying an effect in an uncontrolled environment (particularly the inability to take into account all the processes affecting the decision-making of US media) the research relies on a comprehensive analysis of 2723 articles throughout three years during the war on terror, which aims to ensure longtitunal analysis as well as to ensure that the findings are based on persistency and are not anecdotal.

Secondly, the study uses *multiple* sources of evidence at the data collection stage. This strategy, termed the "triangulation of sources" (Denzin, 1989, pp. 234–48), gives the study a clear advantage over those using a single method since it increases the *construct validity* (correct operational measures for the concept being studied, see Yin, 2002 p. 35) of the findings. This research report synthesizes data from three research methods: Comparative analysis, frame analysis, and news visuals analysis. The choice of the *comparative analysis* method stems from its popularity amongst scholars who have examined the ability of international networks to influence international politics. Robinson (2002), Strobel (1997), Jakobsen (1996) and Mermin (1996, 1997, 1999) all used the comparative analysis method to evaluate CNN's ability to drive political decisions in the 1990s due to *its ability to sensitize* the researcher to variation and similarity. This often enables a deeper perspective of the impact of the new agent (Hallin and Mancini, 2004, p.2) as well as the "capacity to render the invisible visible" (Blumler and Gurevitch, 1975, p. 76). In other words, thanks to a comparison between a "before" and "after" effect, the comparative analysis has the ability to illuminate various aspects that other methods fail to. To study the Al-Jazeera effect, I have specifically borrowed Jonathan Mermin's (1996, 1997, 1999) tactic. Mermin conducted a comparative analysis to study the the traditional media behavior *before* the arrival of CNN to global consciousness in 1991 (including the crisis in Grenada, Panama, and the bombing of Libya) versus the decision-making-mechanism and presentation of events *since* CNN's arrival to globl fame (including the Gulf War, Operation Restore Hope in Somalia and the humanitarian crisis in Haiti). Building on Mermin's method, this study will compare the US media-Administration nexus during wartime before and after Al-Jazeera's rise to global fame in the wake of September 11. The analysis will pay special attention to "double standards" between the re-broadcasting of reports originating from US sources throughout former crises and the re-broadcsting of reports on similar events that came from Al-Jazeera throughout the war on terror.

The analysis also relies on *qualitative frame analysis* as a second research method. During crises, the media selects specific facets of news events in order to promote a specific problem definition. Accordingly, media frames are defined as those "persistent patterns of cognition, interpretation, and presentation, of selection, emphasis and exclusion, by which symbol-handlers routinely organize discourse, whether verbal or visual" (Gitlin, 1980, p. 7). Scholars found that the higher the repetition of the framing words and images, "the more likely the framing is to evoke similar thoughts and feelings in large portions of the audience" (Entman, 2004, p. 6). The research method of frame analysis, in turn, has been established as a "unified thread" in political communication research (Entman, 2004, p. 170), despite the criticism that it is imprecise since it means different things to different researchers. The analysis in this book will examine the re-presentation of the Al-Jazeera news material through a critical framework that pays special attention to the framing of the following themes: (a) the military frame, which examines the re-presentation of Al-Jazeera's reports on military issues; (b) the humanitarian frame, which examines the "importing" of the Al-Jazeera reports on civilian casualties. This frame focuses on the extent to which the US networks re-present Al-Jazeera's news material of un-sanitised and sometimes gory images of war casualties, since it has been argued that this "techno war" frame alienates audiences from the atrocities of war (Thussu, 2003; Sontag, 2003) and portrays war as a "non-event" (Baudrillard, 1995); and (c) the "enemy's voice" frame, which seeks to evaluate whether the networks gave stage to Bin Laden's messages that challenged the Administration's policy.

The last method used in the analysis of the re-presentation of Al-Jazeera's images on US media is *news visuals analysis*. Researchers have identified that each news item on television is "doubly encoded" - while images appeal to audiences' feelings and attitudes about the news events, the accompanying text mainly transforms the *ideational* message of a news item (Meinhoff, 1994). Visuals and their accompanying text are thus an integral part of media output (together with written and verbal text), and in turn, play a crucial role in the transmission of information and the media's engagement with its audiences (Cottle, 1998, pp. 191–2). Studies showed that the interpretation of television images does not "stand-alone" but is rather highly dependent upon its accompanying news commentary (Glasgow University Media Group, 1980; David and Walton, 1983). Accordingly, Al-Jazeera's footage and its accompanying US news commentary are analyzed separately, since they are not integral news items but a "hybridization" of a news item produced by a pan-Arab network and re-presented to viewers by US producers. The analysis examines the presentation and contextualization of the textind and images and the interrelations between US media's text (e.g. voice-over) and Al-Jazeera's original visual material.

The experienced reader might wonder why the study does not include interviews with decision-makers in the US media industry. Here, repeated attempts to interview producers and senior editors in the US failed time after time as soon as I mentioned the name Al-Jazeera. As several media scholars have noted and I had to closely learn myself, the media is often willing to question every aspect of society but when it comes to questioning its own decisions, especially on a controversial topic such as Al-Jazeera, it shies away from exposure and self-examination. In one instance, when I gave a more blurred description for the interview as one that would focus on "media reporting after September 11", I did manage to get an interview with a senior news producer at CBS, but as soon as

I started turning the conversation towards the interplay with Al-Jazeera I was told that the interviewee time was over.

To conduct the research, I gathered data from television news transcripts and videos (ABC, CBS, NBC, CNN, Fox News and Al-Jazeera). To compile the television news transcripts, I used the *Lexis Nexis* news database. To enhance accessibility to reports and images, I also purchased video files from The Television News Archive Collection at Vanderbilt University. I searched the *Lexis-Nexis* news and the Vanderbilt database for transcripts from the five major TV networks: CNN, NBC, ABC, Fox News and CBS using the search term "Al-Jazeera" between September 11, 2001 and September 4, 2004, the day the Iraqi regime expelled Al-Jazeera from Baghdad. I have filtered and deleted "multiple results" (numerous search results for the same news-show). Since US media did not always credit Al-Jazeera for its footage, I have extended my search further in order to find representations of Al-Jazeera reports that were not credited. However, for technical reasons (lack of a search engine that can track captions on footage), I was not able to recover all the non-credited footage and/or transcripts.

Selection of Media and Titles

There is a vast amount of written and broadcast material produced by US media regarding Al-Jazeera and the war on terrorism. This research will limit itself to a sample analysis of US television, since this is the parallel medium to the Al-Jazeera television network and since two television networks – CNN and ABC – signed content-exchange agreements with Al-Jazeera during the war in Afghanistan. Specifically, within the US television industry, I have chosen the Columbia Broadcasting Systems, the National Broadcasting Company, and the American Broadcasting Company as representatives of commercial free-to-air TV news networks. In addition, I have chosen two representatives from the commercial television news industry: Cable News Network and the Fox News Channel. I have chosen Fox News since it has been the most popular cable news network since 2003 (Ibarra, 2009) and CNN since it retains a coordinator (Octavia Nasr) in Qatar and is the only US network that had business links with Al-Jazeera prior and after the events of September 11. The televised analysis is augmented by analysis of the Al-Jazeera effect online through a small-scale study of the re-presentation of Al-Jazeera.net news material on US-based websites.

APPENDIX B

DISCOURSES OF THE GLOBAL PUBLIC SPHERE

The term "public sphere" was first coined by Jurgen Habermas in his work *The Structural Transformation of the Public Sphere* (1962; translated to English in 1989) that examined the relationship between communication and social change. Habermas argued that a new [public] sphere emerged between the church and the state with the emergence of Enlightenment and Capitalism in the seventeenth and eighteenth centuries in Western European Feudalist societies. For Habermas, during this "golden age" period, governments encouraged political participation through rational public debate rather than public representation (e.g. election), thus bringing together "private people ... as a public" (Habermas 1989, p. 27). Within this environment, citizens read highly- political media, such as newspapers, novels, letters, and political advertising (frequently party-owned, and thus committed to the party's ideology), and then they gathered in public places to discuss political matters. These public places were the theatres, concerts, public parks, salons, coffee shops, debating societies and libraries open to the public, and permitted rational debate among citizens in a highly political environment. For Habermas, the "public sphere" eliminated the domination of authoritative power, therefore enabling the establishment of a government that represented the public's will.

Habermas, however, argued that the golden age of the public sphere ended in the nineteenth century with the commercialisation (which he calls "re-feudalisation") of the public sphere. For Habermas, under the highly commercialised and centralised media environment, public relations experts, "spin doctors", and advertising agencies replaced the monarchs, churches and feudal lords. Thus, debate moved back into parliamentary circles, and the public was asked only to approve government decisions. For Habermas, commercial mass media again blurred the boundaries between "rational communication" and public representation of private interests. In turn, he asserts, the representation of issues is currently structured according to commercial or political interests rather than reason and rationality. For Habermas, in the twentieth century, the power of information management and manipulation through public relations has made contemporary debate a "faked version" of a genuine public sphere, where public affairs are nothing but a display of power in the style of the feudal courts (Habermas 1989, p. 195).

Herman and McChesney (1997) support Habermas' re-feudalisation argument and argue that social exclusion of less-privileged groups indeed occurs in the highly-concentrated corporate media environment, and that a genuine public sphere is threatened by both government censorship' and media self-censorship. They observe increased self-censorship through the private interests of media owners, and warn that this might lead to manipulation according to ownership interests and "interconnectedness" (through mergers and acquisitions, cross-ownerships, joint-ventures and content cooperation) between commercial and political bodies.

However, Habermas' concept of the public sphere has been subjected to wide criticism. Some, such as Thompson (1995) argue that he failed to identify the audience's ability to resist governmental propaganda. Thompson argued that while Habermas claimed audiences are passive and absorb media messages without question, he ignored contradictory claims from the works of Adorno and Horkheimer, authors who inspired his ideas in other areas (Ibid.).

Another line of criticism sees that, due to his German background, Habermas failed to acknowledge public rituals (such as concerts) as events that encourage the emergence of a public sphere. For Peters (1995), Habermas' German roots and despising of the Nazis are major components causing him to see concerts and other rituals as undemocratic acts that leave no room for 'rational debate'. (Habermas considered public representation (e.g. concerts, ceremony and rituals) as 'irrational debate', due to his Germanic roots).

Another important criticism of Habermas' work relates to the historical accuracy of his theory. Applying Habermas' ideas to U.S. history, Schudson (1992) argued that citizen participation rose in the U.S. specifically following 1865, with the liberation of Afro-Americans after the Civil War, and with the "enfranchisement" of women and the civil rights laws in 1965, and not as argued by Habermas in the eighteenth century. Schudson argued that in the eighteenth century, colonial media was not political and did not encourage citizens to political action. He also noted that during this period, books in the U.S. were addressed only to small and educated groups. In addition, Schudson argued that during the nineteenth century, with the advent of previously less prioritised groups in the public arena, literacy became more accessible to the masses and the politically oriented press actually increased political participation.

Similarly, Curran (1991, p. 40) argued that Habermas' account of the public sphere in Britain was misinformed, and that instead ... the newspapers celebrated by Habermas were engines of propaganda for the bourgeoisie rather than the embodiment of disinterested rationality (Curran 1991, p. 40).

Another important line of criticism refutes Habermas' argument regarding the re-feudalisation of commercial media in the twentieth century. It argues that commercialisation of the media actually resulted in a massive extension of the public sphere, since it forced the media to be more inclusive and appeal to a much wider audience (La Mahieu 1988; cf. Sparks 1998), both in terms of vocabulary and presentation (Scannell 1989 cf. Sparks 1998; see also Hallin 1994).

In the context of the U.S. media, Hallin (1994) offers a somewhat ambivalent view of the relationship between commercial media and the public sphere. For Hallin, the U.S. media underwent a process of 'professionalization', specifically through the reporting of the Vietnam War, which positioned the journalists as a surrogate public sphere (1994, p. 4), independent from government as well as from commercial interests. However, Hallin argued that the culture of 'professionalised' media ... is largely hostile to politics, preferring technical and administrative expertise or cynical detachment to engagement in the public sphere (1994, p. 6).

Thus, he argues, the "professionalised" media tend to frame and analyse events in terms of strategy and tactics, success and failure, rather than through political or public debate (for example, when CBS' Walter Cronkite reported on the struggle for political support in the villages of Vietnam, which was the ultimate goal of the war, he structured his report around technical and effectiveness issues such as the computerised evaluation system and the number of casualties from a US tank rather than the significance and the context of the events, see Hallin, 1994, pp. 21–2).

Finally, critics of Habermas point to the authenticity of his argument regarding the seventeenth century public sphere, and the ability of certain groups to participate in the public debate. For Thompson (1995), the most obvious weakness of the concept of the public sphere is that Habermas failed to acknowledge that free access to the "bourgeois public sphere" was limited to the educated and financially stabilised male citizens, rather than (as Habermas claimed) by all citizens equally. Therefore the public sphere was not universal in nature but rather based on exclusions. Fraser (1992) further notes that by marking the domestic sphere as private, men were able to exclude issues central to women:

> The view that women were excluded from the public sphere turns out to be ideological; it rests on a class- and gender-biased notion of publicity, one which accepts at face value the bourgeois public's claim to be the public. In fact . . .the bourgeois public was never the public. (Fraser 1992, p. 116)

Fraser goes as far as stating that there is a "Gramscian moral from the story", since (she argues) the official "bourgeois public sphere" served as a "… prime institutional site for the construction of the consent that defines the new hegemonic mode of domination" (Fraser 1992, p. 117).

Notwithstanding these criticisms, the concept of the public sphere remains influential to this day, as it serves as one of the best means of measuring the impact of two decades of privatisation of public media and increased commercialisation of private media on participatory citizenship. Indeed, the concept of the 'public sphere' continues to play a key role even under the current environment of increased globalisation, as suggested by Habermas himself.

With the emergence of increased globalisation in the 1980's and 1990's, Habermas referred to an "emerging global public sphere" as a key development that may conceivably be a harbinger of a "new universalist world order" (Habermas 1992, p. 444). The call for a "global public sphere" was re-iterated by other scholars who saw that in the current environment, where international news interacts with the national and produces growing tensions between the national and the transnational, there was a place for the extension of both political accountability and the public sphere from a national to a global level (Garnham 1990, p. 18; Held 1995, p. 126).

In conjunction, various scholars began to identify that the globalisation of media "create(s) an extension of organizations and societies across space and time", which "weaken the cultural hegemony of nation-states" (Held 1995, p.126) and thus erodes the borders of the nation-state. Similarly, for Tomlinson, globalisation's "bright side" is that it "dissolves the securities of locality, it offers new understandings of experience in wider-ultimately global-terms" (Tomlinson, 1999, p. 30). Garnham (1992, pp. 361–2) went as far as arguing that the development of a global market means a crisis for the national:

> …the development of an increasingly integrated global market and centers of private economic power with global reach are steadily undermining the nation-state…We are thus being forced to rethink this relationship and the nature of citizenship in the modern world. (Garnham 1992, pp. 361–2)

APPENDIX C

POLITICAL COMMUNICATION THEORIES OF WAR REPORTING

The research field of political communication seeks for the relationship between media, government and democracy and its influence on media reporting. In the context of this study, it is particularly important to examine this relationship in the context of foreign policy and wartime news reporting. Therefore, this appendix begins with a review of the major theories of wartime news coverage.

Political communication scholars, who examined the relationship between the media and Administration during conflict, are in agreement regarding the Administration's overwhelming power in influencing media reporting (see Entman 2004, p. 4). The major debate remains regarding the *extent* of this control, particularly in the post Cold-War era and with the increase of globalisation. According to Entman (2004, p. 4), there are currently two major approaches to understanding the Administration-media relationship in foreign policy in the US: Hegemony and Indexing. Both approaches see that the media is too submissive to the Administration, and both encourage more deliberation of democracy in foreign policy (See Entman 2004, p. 6). Hegemony theorists assert that the information that the government allows to flow to the public is kept within such narrow boundaries that it does not permit democratic debate. They assert that although government officials are sometimes in conflict, there is a constant major agreement and even a state of harmony on "first principles". This consensus on first principles, they argue, prevents essential information from flowing to the public and produces propaganda and subsequently public consent. Herman and Chomsky wrote:

> The beauty of the system... is that... dissent and inconvenient information are kept within bounds and at the margin, so that while their presence shows that the system is not monolithic, they are not large enough to interfere unduly with the domination of the official agenda'. (Herman and Chomsky 2002, p. xii)

In contrast, the "indexing" approach puts the elite's disagreement at the centre of its analysis of the media-Administration nexus. The theory sees that the media reporting reflects elite debate. Thus, indexing theorists see that the media follows (rather than, as we would expect, is independent of) elite debate, and does not initiate critical analysis of the White House policy unless it comes first from members from the government. Contrary to hegemony theory proponents, indexing theorists sees that it is within the boundaries of elite debate that the media fulfils its role, and thus moves to something more similar to "objective reporting" that can affect foreign policy rather than simply spreading propaganda.

Notably, both theories do not see that the advent of alternatives to mainstream Western media – the Internet, alternative media groups, and non-Western global players such as Al-Jazeera – poses a threat to the status quo. Hegemony theorists Herman and Chomsky (2002, p. xvi) mention the barriers of access to the Internet for lower class, computer-illiterate and less-developed countries versus the advantages of big corporations in running and advertising on their websites and reaching large audiences, as well as the increased commercialisation of mainstream news websites and the ability to track citizens' behaviour online. As for Al-Jazeera, as noted earlier, Chomsky (2001, pp. 113–15) saw that the US media used its news material in a "surprisingly scarce" manner, thus supporting the government propaganda through emphasis of Bin Laden's messages.

Similarly, leading "indexing" theorists do not count Al-Jazeera as a major development that influenced mainstream US media reporting in the wake of September 11. In an article that reviews the ten predominant influences on the US media reporting during the War on Terrorism, Bennett (2003) does not even mention Al-Jazeera in his list of 10 things that influence US media coverage in the wake of September 11.

The Indexing Theory

Daniel Hallin's study of media reporting of the Vietnam War (1984) broke a tradition of studies that saw the media as straightforwardly "oppositional" to the Administration, particularly on the context of the reporting during the Vietnam War. Here, in the late 1960s, various political science studies showed, through public opinions polls, a rise in public cynicism and decline of trust toward the American government (e.g. Miller 1974; Lipset and Schneider 1983).

Subsequent studies argued that one of the main reasons for this public distrust was the transformation of American media from being a "passive and conservative institution" in the 1950s toward a being a "critical and oppositional institution" against state authorities in the 1970s (Huntington 1975, pp. 98–9). Huntington argued that the advent of the half-hour nightly news broadcast in 1963 has led to greater dependency of the American public on news and thus, increased the impact that television news had on its audiences and contributed to the emergent media criticism of "established institutions". For Huntington, in turn, the media has become "the most notable national power" in the 1970s (Ibid.).

The evidence for the "oppositional media" argument was established with Miller, Erbring and Goldenberg's (1974) empirical study of the impact of newspapers on public confidence. This study combines survey data from the 1974 American National Election Study on the denouncement of the Watergate affair with content analysis of the front page of 94 newspapers, to examine the relationship between political criticism found in newspapers and their readers' trust in the government. The researchers concluded that the media's style of reporting had a significant impact on their readers, and that readers of the more critical newspapers were more distrustful toward the government. Moreover, the researchers found that the level of exposure had an impact as well with higher exposure to criticism leading to higher levels of cynicism (Miller et al. 1974, pp. 80–1).

Hallin (1994, pp. 41–2), however, argued that the above mentioned studies' critical flaw is in its confinement to a limited period of time, which does not allow the assessment of *changes* of news content over various periods and different trends. Hallin saw that this element is critical in order to assess claims about the role of the media on political distrust. Secondly, Hallin (1986) argued that the study ignored the constraints under which the media operates and the media's 'interconnectedness' with political institutions. To address these methodical flaws, Hallin conducted a content analysis study of the television coverage of the war in Vietnam over more than 7 years (20 August 1965–27 January 1973) through a random sample of 779 television broadcasts (Hallin 1994, p. 42).

Hallin's finding dismissed the "oppositional media" theory. The findings support the argument that the media was actually favourable toward American policy in the first years of the Vietnam War and up until around the time of the Tet offensive in 1968. Hallin found that it was only after the Tet offensive that the US media criticised the South Vietnamese regime. Hallin argued that the shift toward critical stance after the Tet offensive stems not from the media's natural critical stance but rather from the media's following of "establishment positions", since after the Tet offensive the oppositional voices against the Vietnam War become "mainstream". In turn, Hallin argued, the media followed the shift of the elite debate over the Vietnam War, thus moving from the "sphere of consensus" stance to the 'sphere of legitimate controversy' stance in the wake of Tet Offensive (Hallin 1994, pp. 53–4).

To elaborate, Hallin (1994, pp. 53–4) suggests the journalist's world is divided into three regions: the first is the sphere of consensus, where voices and values that are not considered controversial rest (the region of motherhood and apple pie). Within this sphere, the media takes a "patriotic" rather than critical stance. Next, outside the sphere of consensus lies the sphere of legitimate controversy (which reflects, for example, elections coverage, legislative debates, or in our case, official controversy during wartime), where objective journalism takes a neutral rather than a pure advocacy stance. For Hallin, it is within this sphere that media takes an objective stance during wartime. Hallin argued that the move to this sphere depends on elite debate; for him, in post-Tel-offensive Vietnam, the press continued its normal business of citing official leaders – it just so happened that they were at odds with one another (Hallin 1994, p. 52). In turn, Hallin argued that the US media "mirrors the version of reality government officials would like to present to the public" (Hallin 1994, p. 52).

Importantly, beyond the sphere of legitimate controversy lies the "sphere of deviance", where we can find the views discarded by mainstream society. In the context of the Vietnam War, these include the voices of dissent coming from the anti-war movement which the US Government viewed as damaging to its efforts and which were dismissed as "Communist propaganda"; this dismissal stands in line with the Federal Communications Commission (FCC) guidelines for application of the Fairness Doctrine state: "It is not the Commission's intentions to make time available to Communists or to the Communist viewpoints" (cf. Hallin, 1984. p. 142). Hallin determined that the voices within the sphere of deviance face exclusion, condemnation, and exposure of their (alleged) bias (Hallin 1984, p. 142).

Following Hallin's findings, and based on his own empirical research of a a four-year media coverage of the congressional policy in Nicaragua. Bennett argued and explained that the Nicaragua affair was an ideal case for testing the "indexing hypothesis": After this occurred, the Reagan Administration battled with the congress over support to the 20,000 "contras" (or, in Reagan's terms, "freedom fighters", see http://www.reagan.utexas.edu/resource/speeches/1986/31586a.htm), who fought against the pro-Soviet regime that took power in Nicaragua in 1979. Since the beginning of this policy in 1983, a majority coalition in the House of Representatives questioned the legality and efficacy of the military solution in Nicaragua, and thus, the House rejected military aid requests. In 1986, the Reagan Administration finally won its battle with Congress and secured a $100 million military aid package for the contras. This assault on Congress was termed "outrageous" by the Chair of Senate Intelligence Committee, which was one among many opposition voices. For Bennett, with the collapse of the opposition, a 'watchdog media' should have given stage to interest groups that were still committed to the congress and to public opinion polls that showed opposition to the Reagan, while "indexing media" would ignore opposition voices with the Congress' collapse. Bennett's findings significantly backed his hypothesis and he concluded that "journalistic patterns both before and after the shift in congressional policy on Nicaragua are best explained by continuing application of the indexing norm, at the expense of the democratic ideal" (1990, p.113).

Lance Bennett (1990) has developed the "indexing" hypothesis, which argues that the news is indexed to the range and dynamics of governmental debate with only minor relation to expressed public opinion. For Bennett, journalists and media owners might consciously choose to "index" issues under the impression that, since the government represents its electorates, the government's definition of reality represents the variety of voices within democracy. This, Bennett argued, might lead to the emergence of a passive press in America. To support this argument, Bennett brings his personal encounters with the ABC news' Vice president, who defended the broadcasting of a news segment that he admitted was inaccurate because, he claimed, it was based on the government's analysis. For the ABC news executive, Bennett argues, quoting official sources was enough in order to categorise the piece of information as "responsible journalism" (Bennett 1990).

Similarly, Bennett (1990) documents that another US news executive admitted the technical hurdles journalists experience when they try to cover war without the Pentagon's cooperation: Bennett recalls that when NBC's Tom Brokaw was asked in a press conference why the media stopped questioning the integrity of civilian leaders in El Salvador after the 1984 election victory of the Christian democrats, "frustrated" Brokaw said the media could not report on the issue after the government "fell silent" on it. Thus, Bennett offered, Brokaw could not even imagine how to cover a conflict without the support of government officials. Here, it would be interesting to see whether the new unprecedented access to Al-Jazeera, which significantly weakens the reporter's dependency on the Administration for access to news reports from behind the enemy lines, has influenced traditional indexing.

Subsequent studies of media behaviour during wartime, most of them using the methods of content analysis of critical versus supportive patterns of media coverage over wartime period, reaffirmed the Indexing hypothesis. Entman and Page's (1994) and Bennett and Manheim's (1993) studies of the coverage of the Gulf War have concluded that media coverage at each stage was restricted to "official" debate. Other studies that support the Indexing hypothesis are Solomon's (1992) analysis of news frames in El Salvador, and Nacos' (1990) study of the media coverage of the Cuban missile crisis, the Dominican invasion of 1965 and the Grenada invasion of 1983.

In a recent account, Entman has tried to update the indexing theory in line with the changes taking place in the post Cold-War era with a revised "cascading activation" model. The model is more interactive than its predecessors and gives special significance to public opinion. It illustrates the cascading flow of influence linking each level of the system: the Administration, other elites, news organization, the text they produce, and the public (Entman 2004, p. 9).

Similarly to Hallin's idea of the three spheres, the model sees that the media promotes habitual and culturally congruent frames, while ambiguous events (meaning events that bear Administration debate) are presented in a contested manner, and culturally incongruent reports are "blocked" altogether. Interestingly, Entman notes that in order to deal with ambiguous events, the media produces new schemas, which simplify the events for its viewers and fit within the traditional norms of reporting. As an example, Entman mentioned the "domestic terrorism" frame, which the media "knitted" to explain Americans the ambiguous event of the 1993 Oklahoma Bombing (Entman 2004, p. 17). The cascading activation theory is still new and needs to be empirically tested by other scholars; however it provides various new insights, which will prove very useful at the stage of data analysis at various places in this study.

From here, we now move to review the second major perspective in relation to US media's reporting of foreign crises: the Hegemony paradigm.

The Hegemony Paradigm

One of the most controversial yet influential studies within the political-communication field is Herman and Chomsky's (1988) idea of the "propaganda model". The model focuses on the general notion of inequality of wealth and power, and the media's tendency to mobilise support for state organs. The model looks at what Herman and Chomsky see as the ways government and dominant private interests are able to filter out the news fit to print, marginalise dissent and get their message across to the public. The "news filters", which determine the news that will be filtered in accordance with government and private interest, are: size and ownership of the prominent media firms, advertising, media dependency on official sources, negative responses to media reports by officials (flak), and anti-communism messages. According to Herman and Chomsky, raw material becomes "newsworthy" only after passing these filters.

This theory, however, suffered wide criticism. The following section notes the main criticisms of the propaganda model and Herman and Chomsky's reply to their critiques. Here, a popular critique is that the model resembles a "conspiracy theory" Schudson (1989, p.270) and others dismiss Herman and Chomsky's propaganda model and claim that such political economy studies are "often characterized and caricatured as 'conspiracy theory' or as a simpleminded notion that there is a ruling directorate of the capitalist class that dictates to editors and reporters what to run in the news". To this, Herman (2003) replied that critiques are "too lazy" to engage with their idea and suggest that these critiques approach the model as a "guided market system", where "institutional factors can cause a 'free' media to act like lemmings in jointly disseminating false and even silly propaganda" (Herman 2003, see http://human-nature.com/reason/01/herman.html).

Secondly, the argument states that the propaganda model ignores cases where reporters bring their own stories, the rare occurrence of editor-publisher meetings, and that most reporters are not even familiar with the board of directors of their organisations. To this, Herman replies that most journalists are not even aware of the way they promote the general ideology of the media organizations they serve (Herman 2003). Chomsky (1997) adds to this account that the big corporations "filter" independently-thinking reporting and "teach" others that those who comply to the system's values are getting promoted while "there are all sorts of filtering devices to get rid of people who are a pain in the neck and think independently"; for Chomsky, these people are "weeded out" along the way (Chomsky 1997). As far as ownership influence goes, Herman and Chomsky's allegations were established in studies of the increased control of media corporations over content: Hickey' study (1998), for example, exposed that the politics of media mogul Rupert Murdoch is highly reflected in his Fox News reporting.

Thirdly, for authors like Hallin (2000), the reality of market-driven journalism and commercialisation are more complex than how Herman and Chomsky's argued, due to the deep-rooted journalistic value of professionalism. Hallin sees that the call for professionalism in the 1970s has increased a shift that was already in progress toward a "social responsibility" model of the press, and the development of an ethics of "public service". (the call for media professionalism came from the commission of Freedom of the Press in 1947, and suggested "that the press look upon itself as performing a public service ... there are some things that a truly professional man will not do for money" (Commission on Freedom of the Press, 1947 p. 92 cf. Hallin, 2000). Hallin asserts that today's journalism is more analytic and reports events with better perspective than ever. Hallin further sees that news-entertainment hybrids such as news talkshows (e.g. CBS *60 Minutes*) represent real "democratisation", since the public can directly engage in political debates. Herman addressed Hallin's arguments by arguing that professionalism was embraced by corporations in order to give credibility to their news, and due to internalised commercial values such as using inexpensive sources. He mentioned that Hallin himself acknowledged that professionalism increases government control through the subsequent domination of sources (see Hallin 1994, pp. 64, 70).

APPENDIX D

THE RELATIONS BETWEEN QATAR, ISRAEL AND THE US

Qatar's relations with the US are usually kept out of the public eye. They began when a US embassy was established in Doha in 1973, but only warmed up in the 1991 Gulf War, as Qatar helped fend off an Iraqi attack on coalition troops in Saudi Arabia. In 1992, Qatar signed a defense treaty with the US. Since then, the US has become involved in Qatar's internal affairs. Some argue that it was behind the military coup in Qatar, in which Sheikh Hamad bin-Kalifa el-Thani revolted against his father and that the American Administration's swift recognition of the coup serves as clear evidence of its support of the new Emir.

The Emir's Sheikh Hamad's reforms undoubtedly served US interests regarding democratization of the Middle East. In July 1998, the Sheikh El-Thani set up a framework for elections, emphasizing universal suffrage with no race, gender, creed or social status restrictions. For the first time, women were able to run for national office. The move was lauded in the West as a major step towards liberalization of the Middle East (although all six women candidates were defeated). In July 1999, the Emir formed a 32-member commission charged with drafting a constitution, clearly defining Qatar's future policies: "We want a constitution... that fulfils our needs and aspirations... [one that] fosters progress and advancement rather than [causing] ossification and stagnation, a constitution that entrenches affiliation to this homeland" (cf. "Qatar takes first step toward setting up elected parliament", *Middle East Mirror*, July 14, 1999). The permanent constitution was drawn up and approved by referendum in 2004. These efforts join the bold steps the Emir took to promote freedom of speech: In 1996, for the first time in Qatar's history, no appointment was made to the post of Minister of Information; in March 1998, the Ministry of Information was abolished.

Besides these reforms, Qatar promotes steps towards privatization. In July 2005, one month after Sheikh Hamad's military coup, the Doha Stock Market was established, opening the Qatari market to private investors and promoting privatization. In April 1998, the Chamber of Commerce was elected by 3,700 Qatari businessmen and not, as in previous instances, by royal decree, thereby guaranteeing prosperity rather than nepotism. The privatization of Qatar is evident in various other fields as well: In 2004, Qatar reformed its educational system by turning 140 of the 220 local public schools into self-managed independent schools that adhere to international curriculum standards. Qatari-US business ties are also stronger than ever: In November 2005, Qatar and the US launched a $14 billion joint project to build the world's largest liquefied natural gas plant. Most of the gas is exported to the US.

The US and Qatar also cooperate in the military sphere. Following Sheikh Hamad's military coup, Qatar became the principal staging area for American ground forces in the Middle East. On September 29, 2001, during preparations for the War in Afghanistan, 4,000 US troops landed at the Al Udeid base. Access to this base enables US forces to counter potential threats from Iran and Iraq. Currently, Al Udeid is the most important base for the US outside its national boundaries (excluding the Philippines) (Da Lage, 2005, p. 59). The Emir actually admitted that he built the base in 1996 with the hope that the US would use it in the future: While Qatar's air force has only a dozen aircraft, the base can host more than a hundred. In 1999, the Emir reportedly told US officials that he would like to see as many as 10,000 US servicemen permanently stationed at Al Udeid. Furthermore, since preparations for the August 2002 War in Iraq, US forces have been occupying the Qatari As Sayliyah base, the world's largest prepositioning base for the US, used by the army component of the US Central Command (US CENTCOM) and the international media teams covering the war.

Secrecy goes across the board in the case of Qatar-Israel ties as well. Regular meetings between Qatari and Israeli officials are also conducted away from the camera's eye, although a few were made public. Israel and Qatar began business ties soon after the military coup, once the 1994 Oslo Accords were signed. Topics for discussion included Qatar's supplying Israel with natural gas and conducting a mutual feasibility study worth $1 billion as part of Qatar's goal to become the leading gas provider in the region. To "explain" these ties to the Arab world, Qatar declared that they were intended to "know the enemy." In September 1996, an Israel Trade Office was established in Doha following an October 1995 meeting between Qatari Minister of Foreign Affairs Sheikh Hamad bin Jassim and his Israeli counterpart Shimon Peres in New York. It is very difficult to estimate the scope and extent of the Qatar-Israel business relations, as most are kept discreet, but recently publicized negotiations between Israeli company IDB and Qatar Gas to import liquefied natural gas to Israel through the Aqaba port, estimated at billions of dollars, illustrates their vast large scope. Further, this deal illustrates the involvement of both governments in the business ties: As Qatar Gas is controlled by the Qatari government (90%) and the French corporation Total (10%), the Israeli and the Qatari governments are highly involved in this potential deal.

Qatar maintained secret ties with Israel that remained unbroken even throughout the Al Aqsa (Second Palestinian) *Intifada*. Soon after its outbreak, Qatar hosted the Organization of the Islamic Conference (OIUC) Summit Meeting (November 12–13, 2000) and was subjected to heavy pressure to sever relations with Israel. Although officially, Qatar surrendered to Arab pressure, particularly from Saudi Arabia, Libya, Iran and Iraq, that threatened to boycott the conference if Qatar maintained ties with Israel, in practice the Israel Foreign Ministry said that it received no formal announcement terminating business ties with Qatar. Moreover, the two Israeli diplomats at the Trade Office apparently did not leave Doha but were working from their hotel suite throughout the Intifada (Da Lage, 2005). During that same period, Sheikh Hamad bin Jassim met Israeli foreign ministers in Paris: Shimon Peres in July 2002 and Silvan Shalom in May of the following year. After the Intifada and the subsequent Israeli disengagement from Gaza, Qatar renewed ties with Israel publicly. The Emir declared that Qatar aspires towards normalization of its relations with Israel even before the establishment of a Palestinian state (Somfalvi, 2005). In accordance, on April 14, 2005, the Qatari ambassador to the UN, Nasser El-Nasser, asked Israel's Ambassador Danny Gillerman to support Qatar's candidacy as UN Security Council representative in Asia.

During the 2006 Israel-Lebanon War, Qatari Foreign Minister Hamad bin-Jaber El-Thani again refused to shut down the Israel Trade Office in Qatar, stating his support of Israeli presence in the Middle East. On April 17, 2008, Qatar hosted Israeli Foreign Minister Zipi Livni, a visit that was widely publicized on Al-Jazeera. Livni said she felt that Qatar was willing to go "all the way" towards normalization of its relations with Israel. On August 12, 2006, Qatari Prime Minister Emir Hamad bin-Jassim el-Thani visited Israel for four hours and met with Livni, Prime Minister Ehud Olmert and Defense Minister Amir Peretz. In August 2009, Qatar declared that it will re-open the Israeli chamber of commerce (which was closed during the Decmber 2008 Operation Cast Lead) if Israel will agree not to build in the West Bank settlement.

Normalization of Qatar's relations with Israel may also be illustrated by tourism and sports. According to the Israel Trade Office, since 1999, more than 400

Israelis received tourist visas and arrived in Qatar, most of them business persons traveling in organized groups. Dozens of guests from Qatar land in Israel each year, primarily Christians on Holy Land pilgrimages, as well as Palestinian and Jordanian workers. ISSTA, an Israeli travel agency primarily for students, openly sells tickets to Qatar. In sports, Qatar, a serious candidate for hosting the 2018 Olympics in Doha publicly declared that Israel is "invited – and more than that" to participate despite the opposition of other Arab countries. In February 2008, Shahar Peer, Israel's leading tennis player, was invited to participate at the Doha tournament. The Qatari press warmly welcomed her at the airport and her visit was widely documented in local media.

Al-Jazeera also contributed to Qatari-Israeli relations at times: It is the first Arab network offering a platform to Israeli officials – including Shimon Peres, Ehud Barak and former Deputy Director of Israel's National Security Institute Gideon Ezra – to express their views, thereby assumedly facilitating normalization of Arab-Israeli relations and demonstrating that Israelis are "human beings" rather than "pigs and monkeys" (their description in audiocassettes distributed in the Palestinian territories and in several Islamic textbooks). During the Al Aqsa Intifada, Al-Jazeera aired interviews with Israeli officials despite Palestinian allegations that their leaders are not accorded similar treatment on Israeli television. Furthermore, throughout the Israeli disengagement from the Gaza Strip, Al-Jazeera repeatedly aired images depicting the pain of Jewish-Israeli settlers forced to leave their homes, despite outrage from its Muslim viewers who were not interested in seeing the Jewish perspective of events. The content of Al-Jazeera in English is a bit softer and more balanced towards Israel than the Arabic version: For example, a study found that while the Arabic depiction of the killing of two Palestinian militants reads: "Two martyrs in new raid" (L: May 14, 2007), the English version sticks to the facts: "Israel hits Hamas targets in Gaza" (L, M1: May 14, 2007).

In turn, Al-Jazeera benefits somewhat from the close relations with Israel. In a region in which every country that is not an enemy is important, Israel treats Al-Jazeera's oppositional reporting with patience because it maintains diplomatic relations with its host country. Al-Jazeera's offices remained open throughout the Intifada despite its repeated airing of statements by Palestinian suicide bombers, while other stations, such as Abu Dhabi TV, were closed because of inflammatory reporting (Da Lage, 2005).

APPENDIX E

THE IMPACT OF WARTIME IMAGES ON PUBLIC OPINION

Photographic images have been a way of presenting events to the public since the inception of cameras in 1839. Images have affected public opinion from the U.S. Civil War, where "sidewalk exhibits of both the dead in Antietam and prisoners in Confederate prisons" prompted fierce pubic debate (Zelizer 2002, p. 52) to the First World War, where photos of heavy combat, which were only published after the war due to war censorship, revealed the scope of tragedy and the extent to which the news had been manipulated (Goldberg 1991, p. 196).

However, in Zelizer's view (2000, p. 52), photography only came of age during the Second World War, where more photographers covered the war than any previous struggle (Ibid.). During the first two years of war, U.S. media was not allowed to publish images of dead American soldiers for fear of demoralisation at home. Nevertheless, on February 1943, *Life*'s photographer George Strock photographed the death of three American soldiers on Buna beach (see image in chapter5). The censors let the story through but not the photographs. *Life* magazine editors complained, and in response, James Byrnes, chief of the Office of War Mobilisation, suggested to President Roosevelt that photos of American casualties could stimulate the morale of American civilians, who were indifferent to the war and critical to administration's will to wage cuts for war bonds. President Roosevelt agreed to the policy of publishing the photos, and indeed, this publication – which illustrated that U.S. soldiers suffered their share of the atrocities of war - significantly mobilised civilian purchase of war bonds and wide consent for wage deductions to support the war (Goldberg 1991, p. 199). Coincidently, *Life* reported that a psychologist who examined the impact of four thousand headlines on 109 "average persons" had concluded that headlines reporting that the enemy is losing produce civilian lethargy, while headlines that reports that U.S. is losing stimulate the greatest public will to win, (cf. *Time*, 'Headlines and Heartbeats', September 4, 1943, p. 54).

In Vietnam, shots of the savagery of the war – such as the widely publicised photos of the Saigon police chief executing a Vietcong suspect during the Tet offensive, the photo of the 1969 My Lai massacre, and the 1972 photo of a young girl (Phan Ti Kim Phuc) fleeing a napalm attack on Highway 1 - were considered to be contributors to the escalation of antiwar protests in the U.S.

However, as noted, the U.S. administration learned the lessons of Vietnam and later restricted media's access to battle zones. In this regard, the administration ensured American public support of the 1991 Gulf War, which was "packaged" for television, with the US military and government supervising the images of this war as tightly as they supervised images from the wars in Grenada and Panama and the 1999 Kosovo War.

Nevertheless, images have not always been in favour of the American administration's side. An example of this can be seen in 1983 Lebanon, where pictures of a truck bomb which killed 241 marines in Beirut, and the wreckage of the Marine barracks in Beirut, prompted the eventual US pullout. In another incidence, in 1979 and 1980, the image of 50 American hostages that had been taken by Iranian captors, raised questions in America regarding the government of Khomeini - against the interest of the American government's policy. Even during the aftermath of what is probably considered the most-controlled television war – the Gulf war – TV and still images of Kurdish refugees moved US audiences and influenced the American government to assist these refugees.

Perhaps the most notable example of the ability of images to mobilise public opinion against the administration's policy took place in Somalia in 1993. On October 3, 1993, Somali militia fighters ambushed U.S. Army Rangers and Special Forces troops in bloody street battles that left 18 American soldiers dead. Some of their corpses were dragged through the streets of Mogadishu by jubilant mobs; these images were broadcast on American TV. Further, a day later, videotape of a dishevelled and bloodied U.S. helicopter pilot held in captivity was broadcast by CNN. The videotape, which CNN said was taken by a freelance Somali cameraman, showed Chief Warrant Officer Michael Durant identifying himself as the pilot of a U.S. Blackhawk helicopter. Reporting on the impact of these images on the US, the *Guardian's* Tisdall (1993) wrote,

> Ever since the Iranian crisis, hostage-taking has had the potential to outrage and mobilise the American public like no other foreign issue. No American has forgotten the yellow ribbons which were displayed throughout the country during the captivity of US hostages in Lebanon. (Tisdall 1993)

Arguably, as a consequence of the resistance these images created in the US, Clinton pulled American forces out of Somalia shortly thereafter.

In turn, the question should be asked: what determines the influence of images on American public opinion? Here, it has been widely argued that it is the *contextualisation* of the images, as presented by the administration and by the media, which influences public interpretation of the images most. Neuman (1996) believes that political leaders can dictate and help "define images", thus "trumping" media power and giving audiences "the captions".

Zelizer (2002), on the other hand, asserts that it is the media's (rather than the administration's) contextualisation of events that influence public opinion. For Zelizer, then, the power of images "depends on mediated forms of representation, by which the media help people encounter the events" (Zelizer 2002, p. 52).

Presidential historian Michael Beschloss (1999) argues in an interview to the Public Broadcasting Service that images can only influence American public opinion if American audiences are ambivalent about a foreign policy, or if they do not know very much about the government's policy. In this way, images can help to "fill the vacuum", and affect the way they think about the world but only in cases where the administration does not explain "what they are trying to do and how we [Americans] should think" (Beschloss 1999). Referring to the 1993 images from Somalia, Beschloss argues that the images had the power to influence public opinion only because President Clinton did not make a case for American presence in Somalia. Specifically, he asserts that while President Bush initially sent forces to Somalia as part of a humanitarian mission (famine), Clinton changed the policy to a manhunt of the Somali leader without the public's consent.

In Carruthers (2000) view, to measure the power of war images is not as clear-cut as described in the above accounts, but rather a much more complex task. Carruthers argued:

> Still and moving photography lends itself to interpretation in different – sometimes utterly incompatible – ways. By some viewers, images of war are read in a straightforwardly anti-war fashion, as necessary testimony to war's inhumanity. But others will regard war footage as evidence of the enemy's barbarity and affirmation of the necessity of fighting the good fight…The impact of film on the audience is consequently immensely hard to predict…Consequently film, despite – and conversely because of – its recognized potency and reach, is also the most double-edged of propaganda weapons. (Carruthers 2000, p. 71)

As all this indicates, the question regarding the way that the public interprets war images is still under heated debate. Researchers are in agreement, though, that the administration works hard to bring forth to the public through media the images of military success and at the same time prevent access to images of military failures and cruelty to civilian casualty. Further, researchers also agree that when such images are presented, the administration tries to undermine them through promoting its own interpretation of the images (the captions).

REFERENCES

Abdul-Mageed, M. (2008). Online News Sites and Journalism 2.0: Reader Comments on Al Jazeera Arabic. *TripleC* 6(2): 59–76.

AKI News Agency (2005, November 22). Qatar: Bush proposed bombing Al-Jazeera, says memo. In: *ADNKRONOS International*. Retrieved from: http://www.adnki.com/index_2Level.php?cat=CultureAndMedia&loid=8.0.231468005&par=0

Al Jazeera documentary Channel. (2009). Retrieved from: http://www.facebook.com/pages/Al-Jazeera-Documentary-Channel/22974490138?v=info&ref=mf.

Albert, M. (1997, October). What makes alternative media alternative? Toward a federation of alternative media activists and supporters — FAMAS. *Z Magazine*. Retrieved from: http://subsol.c3.hu/subsol_2/contributors3/albertTextInd.html

Alexa Global Statistics, 2009. Retrieved from: http://www.alexa.com/siteinfo/aljazeera.net

Allan, S. (2004). The culture of distance: online reporting of the Iraq war. In S. Allan & B.Zelizer (Eds.), *Reporting war: journalism in wartime*. London and New York : Routledge.

Allen, R., (Ed.). (1995). *To be continued…soap opera around the world*. New York: Routledge.

Alt, R. (2004, April 21). The Al-Jazeera Effect: How the Arab TV network's coverage of the coalition is influencing opinion in Iraq. *The Weekly Standard online.* Retrieved from: http://www.weeklystandard.com/Content/Public/Articles/000/000/003/992hodmd.asp

Amin, H. (2003, Spring-Summer). Watching the war in the Arab world. In: *Transnational Broadcasting Studies* 10. Retrieved from: http://www.tbsjournal.com/amin.html.

Amin, S. (1997). *Capitalism in the age of globalisation*. London: Zed Books.

Ammon R. (2001). *Global television and the shaping of world politics: CNN, telediplomacy, and foreign policy*. Jefferson, NC: McFarland.

Anderson, R. & Carpignano, P. (1991). Iraqi Dupes or Pentagon Promoters? CNN Covers the Gulf War. Fairness and Accuracy in Reporting report. Retrieved from: http://www.fair.org/extra/best-of-extra/gulf-war-cnn.html

Anderson, W. T. (2004). *All connected now: Life in the first global civilization*. Boulder, Colorado: Westview Press.

Ang, I. (1985). *Watching Dallas: Soap opera and the melodramatic imagination*. London: Methuen.

Antola, L. & Rogers, E.M. (1984). Television flows in Latin America. *Communication Research*, 11 (2), 183–202.

Appadurai, A. (1990). Disjuncture and difference in the global cultural economy. *Public Culture*, 2 (2), 1–24.

Appadurai, A. (1996). *Modernity at large: cultural dimensions of globalisation*. Minneapolis: University of Minnesota Press.

Archibugi, D., Held D. & Köhler M. (1998). *Re-imagining political community: studies in cosmopolitan democracy*. Stanford, California: Stanford University Press

Associated Press (2003, September 2). Al-Jazeera launches English website. Retrived from: http://www.theage.com.au/articles/2003/09/01/1062403457471.html

Ayish M.I. (2002). Political communication on Arab world television: Evolving patterns. In: *Political Communication*, 19 (2): April-June, pp. 137–154.

Ayish, M.I. (2008). *The new Arab public sphere*. Berlin: Frank and Timme.

Aysha, E. (2005). Globalisation contra Americanisation in the 'New' US Century September 11 and the Middle East Failure of US 'Soft Power'. *International Relations* 19 (2), pp. 193–210.

Azran, T. (2004). Resisting peripheral exports: Al-Jazeera's war images on US television. *Media International Australia*, 113, 75–86.

Azran, T. (2006). From Osama Bin-Laden's mouthpiece to the darling of the alternative media websites': The representation of English.Aljazeera.Net in the West". In R. Berenger, (Ed.) Cybermedia Go to War: Role of Converging Media During and After the 2003 Iraq War (pp. 103–14). Spokane, WA: Marquette books.

Babak, B. (2007). CNN Effect in action: How the news media pushed the West toward war in Kosovo. New York: Palgrave Macmillan.

Bagdikian, B. (2000). *The media monopoly*. Boston: Beacon Press.

Bahry, L.Y. (2001). The new Arab media phenomenon: Qatar's Al-Jazeera. *Middle East Policy*, 8 (2), 88.

Baker, J. III (1995). *The politics of diplomacy*. New York: G. P. Putnam's Sons.

Barber, B.R. (1996). *Jihad versus McWorld*. New York: Times Books.

Barkho, L. (2006). The Arabic Al-Jazeera vs. Britain's BBC and America's CNN: Who Does Journalism Right'. *American Communication Journal*, 8: 1.

Barthes, R. (1957). *Mythologies*. (Lavers, A., Trans). New York : Hill and Wang.

Baudrillard, J. (1995) *The Gulf War Did Not Take Place*. (Patton, P., Trans.). Bloomington and Indianapolis: Indiana University Press.

Bennett, W.L. (1990). Toward a theory of press-state relation in the United States. *Journal of Communication*, 40, 103–25.

Bennett, W.L. & Paletz, D.L. (1994). *Taken by storm: the media, public opinion, and US foreign policy in the Gulf War*. Chicago: University of Chicago Press.

Bennett, W.L. & Manheim, J. (1993). Taking the public by storm: information, cueing and the democratic process in the Gulf conflict.*Political Communication* 10, 331–51.

Bennett, W.L. (2003). Operation Perfect Storm: The press and the *Iraq war. International Communication Association & American Political Science Association, 13 (3)*. Retrieved from: http://www.ou.edu/policom/1303_2003_fall/bennett.htm

Bennett, W.L., Lawrence, R.G. & Lingston, S. (2007). *When the press fails*. Chicago: University of Chicago Press.

Beschloss, M. (1999). PBS' *Online Hour*. Retrieved from: http://www.pbs.org/newshour/bb/media/jan-june99/pictures_4–14.html

Boyd, D. (1993). Broadcasting in the Arab world: A survey of the electronic media in the Middle East. Ames: Iowa State University Press.

Boyd-Barrett, O. (1977). Media imperialism: Towards an international framework for an analysis of media systems. In J. Curran, M. Gurevitch & J. Woollacott (Eds.) *Mass communication and society*, (pp. 116–135). London: Edward Arnold.

Boyd-Barrett, O. & Thussu, D.K. (1992). *Contra-flow in global news: international and regional news exchange mechanisms*. London: John Libbey.

Boyd-Barrett, O. (1998). Media imperialism reformulated. In D.K Thussu (Ed.) *Electronic Empires. Global media and local resistance (pp. 157–176).* London, Arnold.
Boud-Barrett, O. & Xie, S. (2008). Al-Jazeera, Phoenix Satellite Television and the return of the state: Case studies in market liberalization, public sphere and media imperialism. International Journal of Communication 2, 206–222.
Carey, J. (2002). American journalism on, before, and after September 11. In B .Zelizer & S. Allan (Eds.) *Journalism After September 11* (pp. 71–90). London and New York: Routledge.
Carruthers, S. L. (2000). *The Media at War.* New York: St. Martin's Press.
Cassara, C. & Lengel L. (2004). Move Over CNN: Al-Jazeera's View of the World Takes on the West. In R.D. Berenger (Ed.) *Global Media Go To War* (pp. 229–34). Spokane, WA: Marquette Books.
Castells, M. (1996). *The information age: economy, society and culture' (Vol. 1): the rise of network society.* Oxford: Blackwell.
Chafetz, Z. (2001, October 14). Al-Jazeera Unmasked: An Arab Propaganda Machine in the guise of real journalism. *New York Daily News,* Retrieved from: http://www.nydailynews.com/archives/opinions/2001/10/14/2001-10-14_al_jazeera_unmasked_an_ara.html
Cherribi, S. (2006). From Baghdad to Paris: Al-Jazeera and the Veil. The Harvard International Journal of Press/Politics, 11, 121–138.
Chomsky, N. (1986). All the News that Fits. *Utne reader,* 56–65.
Chomsky, N. (1997, October). What Makes Mainstream Media Mainstream. *Z Magazine.*
Chomsky, N. (2001). *September 11.* New York: Seven Stories Press.
Clayman, S. & Heritage, J. (2002). *The News Interview: Journalists and Public Figures on the Air.* Cambridge, UK: Cambridge University Press.
Clausen, L. (2004). Localizing the Global: 'Domestication' Processes in International News Production. Media, Culture and Society, 26(1), 25–44.
Clutterbuck, R. (1981). *The media and political violence.* London: MacMillan.
CNN. (1997). *CNN International: The CNN News Group.* London.
Cohen, A., Gurevitch, M., Levy M. & Roeh, I. (1996). *Global newsrooms, local audiences: A Study of the Eurovision news exchange.* London: John Libbey.
Cohen, B. (1994). A view from the academy. In W.L. Bennett & D. Paletz (Eds.) *Taken by storm: The media, public opinion, and U.S. foreign policy in the Gulf War* (pp. 8–11). Chicago: University of Chicago Press.
Collins, R. (1994). *Broadcasting and Audio-Visual Policy in the European Single Market.* London: John Libbey.
Compaine, B. (2002). Global media. *Foreign Policy,* 133, 20–28. Retrieved from: http://compaine.bcompany.com/articles/globalmedia.html.
Cornwell, R. (2005, Fenruary 13). US: Nation accused of plan to Muzzle Al-Jazeera through privatization. *The Independent Online.* Retrieved from: http://www.corpwatch.org/article.php?id=11847
Cottle, S. (1998). Analysing Visuals: Still and Moving Images. In: A. Hansen, S, Cottle, R. Negrine, & C. Newbold, (Eds.) *Mass Communication Research Methods* (pp. 189–224). Houndmills, Basingstoke, Hampshire and London: Macmillan Press.
Cunningham, B. (2008, april 4). Dave Marash: Why I quit. Columbia Journalism Review. Retrieved from: ttp://www.cjr.org/the_water_cooler/dave_marash_why_i_quit.php?page=all
Currie, D.W. (2002). Hatred on the Web: It's Not Over 'Til It's Over. *NetNacs.com.* Retrieved from: http://www.netnacs.com/news/archive/nn-0207.htm
Da Lage, O. (2005). The Politics of Al-Jazeera or the Diplomacy of Doha. In M. Zayani (Ed.) *The Al-Jazeera Phenomenon.*(pp. 49–56). Boulder: Paradigm Publishers, pp xxx.

Deacon, D., Pickering, M., Golding, P., & Murdock, G. (2000). *Researching Communications*. London: Arnold and New York; Oxford University Press.

Deacon, D. & Golding, P. (1994). *Taxation and Representation*, London: John Libbey.

Denzin, N.K. (1989). *The research act*. New Jersey: Prentice-Hall.

Dirlik, A. (1996). The global in the local. In: R. Wilson & W. Dissanayake, (Eds.) *Global/local: Cultural production and the transnational imaginary*. Durham NC: Duke University Press.

Dorfman, A. & Mattelart, A. (1975). *How to read Donald Duck: imperialist ideology in the Disney comic*. New York: International General Editions.

Dube, J. (2003). Al-Jazeera Launches English Channel. *Pointer Online* http://www.poynteronline.org/dg.lts/id.32/aid.46709/column.htm

Dun & Bradstreet, (2005). Retrieved from: http://www.dnb.com

El-Nawawy, M. & Iskandar, A. (2002). The Minotaur of '*ConTextIndual Objectivity*': War coverage and the pursuit of accuracy with appeal. *Transnational Broadcasting Journal*, fall/winter 2002. Retrieved from: http://www.tbsjournal.com/Archives/Fall02/Iskandar.html

El-Nawawy, M. & Iskandar, A., (2002). *Al-Jazeera: How the free Arab news network scooped the world and changed the Middle East*. Cambridge, Mass.: Westview.

El-Nawawy, M. & Iskandar, A. (2003). *Al-Jazeera : the story of the network that is rattling governments and redefining modern journalism*. Boulder, Colorado and Oxford: Westview.

El Oifi, M. (2005). Influence Without Power: Al Jazeera and the Arab Public Sphere. In M.Zayani (Ed.) *The Al Jazeera Phenomenon: Critical perspectives on new Arab* media (pp. 66–79). London; Pluto Press.

Entman, R.M. & Page, B.I. (1994). The news before the storm: the Iraq war debate and the limits to media independence. In: W.L. Bennett, & D. Paletz (Eds.) *Taken by Storm: the media, Public Opinions and U.S. Foreign Policy in the Gulf War* (pp. 82–101). Chicago: University of Chicago Press.

Entman, R.M. (2004). *Projections of Power*. London: The University of Chicago Press.

Ewan, S. (1976). *The captains of consciousness*. New York: McGraw-Hill.

Facts on File. (1991). 51, 2621. New York: Facts on File Inc.

Fluorney, D.M. (1992). *CNN World Report. Ted Turner's International News Group*. London: John Libbey (Academia Research Monograph 9).

Fluorney, D.M. & Stewart, R.K. (1997). *CNN. Making News in the Global News Market*. London: University of Luton Press.

Foster, K. (1992). The Falklands War: A Critical View of Information policy. In: P. Young (Ed.) *Defence and the media in time of Limited War* (pp. 155–167). London: Cassell.

Fraser, N. (1992). Rethinking the public sphere. In C.Callhoun, (Ed.). *Habermas and the public sphere* (pp. 113–18). Cambridge, Mass.: The MIT Press.

Friedman, T. (2005). *The world is flat*. New York: Farrar, Straus and Giroux.

Garnham, N. (1979). Contribution to a political economy of mass communication. In P. Golding & G. Murdock (Eds.). *The Political economy of the Media*, 1 (2), 123–146. London: Academic Press.

Garnham, N., (1990). *Capitalism and communication: global culture and the economics of information*. London: Sage.

Gibbs, D. (2000). *Realpolitik* and humanitarian intervention: The case of Somalia. *International Politics*, 37, 41–55.

Gilboa, E. (2005). The CNN Effect: The Search for a communication theory of international relations. *Political Communication* (22), 27–44.

Gitlin, T. (2003). The whole world is watching : mass media in the making & unmaking of the New Left. (2nd edition). Berkeley, CA : University of California Press, 2003.

Glasgow University Media Group. (1985). *War and Peace News*. Milton Keynes: Open University Press.

Goldberg, V. (1993). *Power of photography: how photographs changed our lives*. New York: Abbeville.

Golding, P. & Murdock, G. (1991). Culture, Communications, and Political economy. In J. Curran & M. Gurevitch (Eds.) *Mass Media and Society* (pp. 18–19). London: Edward Arnold.

Gowing, N. (2002, 8 April). Don't get in our way. *The Guardian*. Retrieved from: http://www.guardian.co.uk/media/2002/apr/08/mondaymediasection8

Gurevitch M., Levy, M. & Roeh, I., (1991). The Global Newsroom: Convergences and Diversities in the Globalisation of Television News. In: P. Dahlgren and C. Sparks (Eds.) *Communications and Citizenship: Journalism and the Public Sphere in the New Media Age* (pp. 195 – 216). London: Routledge.

Habermas, J. (1989). *The structural transformation of the public sphere : an inquiry into a category of bourgeois society*. (Burger, T. trans. with the assistance of Frederick Lawrence). Cambridge, Mass.: MIT Press.

Habermas, J., (1992). Further Reflections on the Public Sphere' in Calhoun, C., ed. *Habermas and the Public Sphere* (pp. 421–461). Cambridge, Mass.: MIT Press.

Hafez, K. (2007). *The Myth of Media Globalization*. Cambridge, UK: polity Press.

Hallin, D. (1983, July/August). The Media Goes to War - From Vietnam to Central America. *NACLA report on the Americas*.

Hallin, D. (1986). *The 'Uncensored War': The media and Vienam*. New York and Oxford: Oxford University Press.

Hallin, D. (1994). *We keep America on top of the world: television journalism and the public sphere*. London and New York: Routledge.

Hallin, D. (1997). The media and war. In J.Corner, P. Schlesinger, & R. Silverstone (Eds.) *International Media Research: A critical survey* (pp. 206–31). London and New York: Routledge.

Hallin, D. & Mancini, P. (2004). *Comparing Media Systems: Three Models of Media and Politics*. Cambridge, UK: Cambridge University Press.

Hamelink, C. (1983). *Cultural autonomy in global communications*. New York: Longman.

Harman, D. (2003). For news, S. Africa may shun the West. *The Christian Science Monitor*, Retrieved from:http://www.csmonitor.com/2003/0109/p01s04-woaf.html

Heritage, J. & Greatbatch, D. (1991). On the institutional character of institutional talk: the case of news interviews. In D. Boden & D.H. Zimmerman (Eds.) *Talk and social structure* (pp. 93–197). Cambridge; Polity Press.

Held, D. (1995). *Democracy and the Global Order: From the modern state to cosmopolitan governance*. Cambridge: Polity Press.

Held, D, McGrew, A. Goldblatt, D. & Perraton, J. (1999). *Global transformations: politics, economics and culture*. Cambridge: Polity.

Helman, C. (2009, July 13). Will Americans Tune To Al Jazeera?. Forbes Online. Retrived from: http://www.forbes.com/forbes/2009/0713/comcast-al-qaeda-will-americans-tune-to-al-jazeera.html.

Herman, E.S. & Chomsky, N. (1988). *Manufacturing Consent : The political economy of the mass media*. New York: Pantheon Books.

Herman, E.S. & McChesney, R.W. (1997). *The global media: the new missionaries of corporate capitalism*. London and Washington, D.C.: Cassell.

Herman, E.S. (2003, December 9). The Propaganda Model: A retrospective'. *Against All Reason*. Retrieved from: http://www.chomsky.info/onchomsky/20031209.htm

Hickey, N. (1998). Is Fox news fair?. *Columbia Journalism Review*, 36(6).
Hine, C. (2000). *Virtual ethnography*. London, UK and Thousand Oaks, California: Sage.
Hjarvard, S. (2001). *News in a globalized society*. Sweden: Grafikerna Livrena I Kungalv.
Hosenball, M. (2002, November 25). Al-Jazeera is expanding it's Washington bureau. *Focal Point Publications*. Retrieved from: http://www.fpp.co.uk/online/02/11/Jazeera181102.html
Hoskins, C. & Mirus, R. (1988). Reasons for U.S. dominance of the international trade in television programmes. *Media, Culture and Society*, 10, 499–515.
Hoskins, A. (2004). *Televising war: from Vietnam to Iraq*. London: Continuum.
Humane ociety International, 2009. Retrieved from: http://www.hsus.org/protectseals.html
Huntington, S., (1975). The United States. In M.J.Crozier, S.P. Huntington & J. Watanuki (Eds.) *The Crisis of Democracy* (pp. 59–113). New York: New York University Press.
Huntington, S. (1998). *The Clash of Civilizations and the Remaking of World Order*. New York: Simon & Schuster.
Ibarra, S. (March 31, 2009). "CNN Ratings Down; Fox, MSNBC Grow". TVWeek. Retrived from: http://www.tvweek.com/news/2009/03/cnn_ratings_down_fox_msnbc_gro.php
Jaafar, A. (2006, November 13). Yanked by yanks. Variety. Retrieved from: http://www.variety.com/article/VR1117953878.html?categoryid=10&cs=1
Jakobsen, P. (1996). National interest, humanitarianism or CNN: What triggers UN peace enforcement after the Cold War?. *Journal of Peace Research*, 33, 205–215.
Jasperson, A.E. & El-Kikhia M.O. (2002, 25/8/2002). U.S. and Middle Eastern Media Perspectives on the Aftermath of the Sept. 11 Terrorist Attacks, a Harvard Symposium *Restless Searchlight: The Media and Terrorism*,. Retrieved from: http://www.apsanet.org/~polcomm/APSA%20Papers/JaspersonEl-Kikhia.pdf
Jasperson, A. E. and El-Kikhia, M.O. (2003). CNN and Al-Jazeera's Media Coverage of America's War in Afghanistan. In P. Norris, M. Kern & M. Just (Eds.) *Framing terrorism: The news media, the government and the public* (pp. 113–132). New York and London: Routledge.
Jensen, K.B. (Ed.). (1998). *News of the World. World Cultures Look at Television News*. London: Routledge.
Johnson, T. & Fahmy, S. (2008). The CNN of the Arab world or a shill for terrorists? How support for press freedom and political ideology predict credibility of Al-Jazeera among its Audience. *International Communication Gazette* 2008, 70, 338
Jowett, G.S. (1993). Propaganda and the Gulf War. *Critical Studies in Mass Communication* 10(3), 287–300.
Karim, K. (2000). Making Sense of the 'Islamic Peril'. In B. Zelizer & A. Stuart (Eds.) *Journalism After September 11* (pp. 101–115). London: Routledge.
Kaplan, A. (1964). *The Conduct of Inquiry*. San Francisco: Chandler.
Katz, E. & Liebes, T. (1984). 'Once Upon a Time in *Dallas*'. *Intermedia* 12(3), 28–32.
Kellner, D. (2001). *9/11, Spectacles of terror, and media manipulation: A critique of Jihadist and Bush media politics*. Retrieved from: http://www.gseis.ucla.edu/courses/ed253a/911terrorwarmedia.htm
Kennan, G. (1993, September 30). Somalia, Through a Glass Darkly. *The New York Times*. Retrieved from: http://www.nytimes.com/1993/09/30/opinion/somalia-through-a-glass-darkly.html
Knightley, P. (2000). *The first casualty - from the Crimea to the Falklands: The aar correspondent as hero, propagandist and myth maker*. London: Prion.
Kohler, M. (1998). From the national to the cosmopolitan public sphere. In D. Archibugi, D. Held & M. Kohler (Eds.). *Re-imagining Political Community. Studies in Cosmopolitan Democracy* (pp. 231–251). Cambridge: Polity Press.

La Jornada, (2005, Mar 02). Telesur: A counter-hegemonic project to compete with CNN and Univisión. *Venezuela analysis.* Retrieved from: http://www.venezuelanalysis.com/analysis/976

Laqueur, W. (1976, March). The futility of terrorism. *Harper's*, 99–105.

Latouche S. (1996). *The Westernization of the world: the significance, scope and limits of the drive toward global uniformity.* (Mooris, R., trans.). Cambridge: Polity Press.

Liebes, T. (1990). *The Export of Meaning: Cross-Cultural Readings of 'Dallas'.* New York: Oxford University Press.

Liebes, T & Kampf, Z. (2004). The PR of terror: How new-style wars give voice torrorists. In S. Allan & B. Zelizer (Eds.) Reporting war: Journalism in wartime. Milton Park, UK; Routledge.

Lipset, S.M. & Schneider, W. (1983). *The confidence gap.* New York: Free Press.

Livingston S. (1997). *Clarifying the CNN Effect: An examination of media effects according to type of military intervention.* John F. Kennedy School of Government's Joan Shorenstein Center on the Press, Politics and Public Policy at Harvard University. Retrieved from: http://www.hks.harvard.edu/presspol/publications/papers/research_papers/r18_livingston.pdf

Lopez, A. (1995). Our welcomed guests: *telenovelas* in Latin America. In: R. Allen (Ed.) *To be continued…* (pp. 256–275). New York: Routledge.

Lull, J. (2000). *Media, communication, culture: A global approach.* Cambridge: Polity Press.

Lynch, M, (2006). *Voices of the New Arab Public: Iraq, Al-Jazeera and Middle East Politics Today.* New York: Columbia University Press.

Macgregor, B, (1994).International television coverage of the bombing of the Baghdad 'bunker,' 13 February 1991. Historical Journal of Film, 14 (3), 241–268.

Madden, N. (1999, 1 December). Media Powers in Asia take offerings to net. In: *Advertising Age International supplement.*

Martin-Barbero, J. (1993). *Communication, culture and hegemony: from media tomediations.* (Fox, E, trans.). London: Sage.

Mason, R. (2009, March 23). Al Jazeera English focused on its American dream. Daily Telegraph. Retrieved from: http://www.telegraph.co.uk/finance/newsbysector/mediatechnologyandtelecoms/5039921/Al-Jazeera-English-focused-on-its-American-dream.html

Mattelart, A. (1979). *Multinational Corporations and the Control of Culture.* England: Harvester Press and New Jersey: Humanities Press.

Mattelart A. (1991). *Advertising international: the privatization of public space.* (Chanan, m. trans.). London:Routledge. Originally published in 1989 as L'Internationale publicitaire, Paris: Editions La Dwecouverte.

Mattelart, A. (2000). *Networking the world, 1794–2000.* (Carey-Libbrecht, L. and Cohen, J.A.Minneapolis, trans.). Minnesota: University of Minnesota Press,

McChesney, R., 2002. September 11 and the Structural Limitations of US Journalism. In: B. Zelizer & S. Allan (Eds.) *Journalism After September 11* (pp. 91–100). London and New York: Routledge,

McNair, B. (2005). The emerging Chaos of Global News Culture. In: A. Stuart (Ed.) *Journalism: critical issues* (pp. 151–164). Maidenhead : Open University Press,

McPhail, T.L. (1987). *Electronic colonialism: The future of international broadcasting and communication.* Newbury Park, CA: Sage.

Meinhoff, U.H. (1994). Double talk in news broadcasts. In D.Graddol & O. Boyd-Barrett (Eds.) *Media TextInds; Authors and readers* (pp. 168–178). Cleveldon: Multilingual Matters, in Association with the Open University.

Mermin, J. (1996). Conflict in the sphere of consensus? Critical reporting on the Panama invasion and the Gulf War. *Political Communication*, 13, 181–194.

Mermin, J. (1997). Television news and American intervention in Somalia: The myth of a media-driven foreign policy. *Political Science Quarterly*, 112, 385–403.

Mermin, J. (1999). *Debating war and peace: Media coverage of U.S. intervention in the post-Vietnam era*. Princeton, NJ: Princeton University Press.

Michalsky, M. & Preston, A. (2002). *After September 11: TV News and Transnational Audiences*. A report for an international symposium held in the UK, September 11, 2002. Retrieved from: http://www.afterseptember11.tv/download/11%20September%20Research.pdf

Miladi, N. (2003). Mapping the Al-Jazeera phenomenon. In D.K. Thussu & D. Friedman (Eds.) *War and the Media* (pp. 149–160). London: Sage.

Miles, H. (2005). *Al-Jazeera: The inside story of the Arab news channel that is challenging the West*. US: Grove Press.

Miller, A.H. (1974). Political issues and trust in government, 1964–1970. *American Political Science Review*, 1974, 68,. 951–972.

Miller, A.H., Erbring, L., & Goldenberg, E.N. (1979). Type-set politics: impact of newspapers on issue salience and public confidence. *American Political Science Review*, 73, 67–84.

Morgan, D.L. (1997). *Practical strategies for combining qualitative and quantitative methods*. Portland, OR: Portland State University.

Morley, D. (1976). Industrial conflict and the mass media. *Sociological Review*, 24(2), 245–68.

Morrison, D. & Tumber, H. (1988). *Journalists at war: the dynamics of news reporting during the Falklands conflict*. London; Sage.

Moss, L. (2007). Tempest brews over Al Jazeera English. Multichannel. Retrieved from: http://www.multichannel.com/article/128891 Tempest_Brews_Over_Al_Jazeera_English.php

Mueller, J. (1989). *Retreat from doomsday: The obsolescence of major war*. New York: Basic Books

Murdock, G. & Golding, P. (1997). For a political economy of Mass Communications. In P. Golding and G. Murdock (Eds.) *The Political economy of the Media*, Volumer 1 (3rd edition) (pp. 3–32).

Nahmias, R. (2005, August 24). Arabs slam pullout coverage. Ynet News. Retrived from: http://www.ynetnews.com/articles/0,7340,L-3132511,00.html

Navasky, V. (2002). Foreword. In: B. Zelizer & S. Allan (Eds.) *Journalism After September 11* (p. xv). London and New York: Routledge.

Neuman, J. (1996). *Lights, camera, war: is media technology driving international politics*. New York: St. Martin's Press.

Nisbet, E.C, Nisbet, M.C., Dietram, Scheufele, D.A. & Shanahan, J. (2004). Public diplomacy, television news, and Muslim opinion. **The Harvard International Journal of Press/Politics**; 9, 11–37

Oliviera, O. (1993). Brazilian soaps outshine Hollywood: is cultural imperialism fading out?. In K Nordestreng, K. ans Schiller, H. (Eds.) *Beyond national sovereignty* (p. 116–131). Norwood, NJ: Ablex Publishing.

O'neill, B. E. (1996). The United States and the Middle East: Continuity and Change. In H.J. Wiarda (Ed.) *U.S. foreign and strategic policy in the post-Cold War Era* (pp. 107–130). Westport, CT: Greenwood Press,

Oren, M.B. (2002). *Six Days of War: June 1967 and the Making of the Modern Middle East*. New York: Oxford University Press.

Paletz, D.L. & Entman, R.M. (1981). *Media power politics*. New York: Free Press.

Pedelty, M. (1995). *War Stories; The Culture of foreign correspondents*. London; Routledge.

Preston, P. (2001). *Reshaping communications: technology, information and social change*. London: Sage.

Rainie, L., Fox, S., &Fallows, D. (2003). The Internet and the Iraqi War: How online Americans have used the Internet to learn war news, understand events, and promote their views. *Pew Internet & American life project*. Retrieved from: http://xinwen.cass.cn/mediadmin/pdf/file/%E4%BC%8A%E6%8B%89%E5%85%8B%E6%88%98%E4%BA%89.pdf

Rath, T. (2002, February 7). Al-Jazeera in English? CNN in Arabic?. The Daily Star (Beirut). Retrieved from: http://www.medea.be/index.html?page=&lang=&doc=1056

Reese, S. (2009, May 25). Globalized journalism in the public sphere. *Paper presented at the annual meeting of the International Communication Association, Sheraton New York, New York City, NY Online*. Retrieved from: http://www.allacademic.com/meta/p12985_index.html

Reuters, (2004, July 14). Al Jazeera Adopts a New Code of Accuracy and Good Taste. In *The New York Times Online*. Retrived from: http://www.nytimes.com/2004/07/14/international/middleeast/14jaze.html

Roman, M. (2003, September 11). Spanish judge orders Al-Jazeera reporter to jail. San Francisco Gate. Retrieved from: http://web.archive.org/web/20060212173348/http://www.sfgate.com/cgi-bin/article.cgi?f=/news/archive/2003/09/11/international0805EDT0515.DTL)

Robertson, R. (1987). Globalisation and societal modernization: a note on Japan and Japanese religion. *Sociological Analysis*, 47 (5), 35–42.

Robertson, R. (1992). *Globalisation: social theory and global culture*. London: Sage.

Robinson, P. (2002). *The CNN effect: The myth of news, foreign policy and intervention*. New York: Routledge.

Rushing, J, (2007). *Mission Al-Jazeera: Build a bridge, seek the truth, change the world*. New York: Palgrave Macmillan.

Sakr, N. (2007). Challenger or lackey? The Politics of news on Al-Jazeera. In D. Thussu (Ed.) *Media on the Move: Global Flow and Contra-Flow* (pp. 116–132), London: Routledge.

Schaffer, A. (2003). Embeds and Unilaterals The press dun good in Iraq. But they could have dun better. *MSN Online*. Retrieved from: http://slate.msn.com/id/2082412

Schrumm, W. (1964). Mass Media and National Development. Stanford: Stanford University Press.

Schiesel, S. (2001, October 15). Stopping Signals From Satellite TV Prove Difficult. In *The New York Times Online*,. Retrieved from: http://www.nytimes.com/2001/10/15/business/media-stopping-signals-from-satellite-tv-proves-difficult.html

Schiller, H. (1976). *Communication and Cultural Duration*. White Plains: International Arts and Sciences Press.

Schiller, H. (1991). Not Yet the Post-Imperialist Era. *Critical Studies in Mass Communication* vol 8 (1), pp. 13–28.

Schiller, H. (1993). Transnational Media: Creating Consumers Worldwide. *International Affairs*, 47,1, pp. 47–58.

Schudson, M., 1992. Was There Ever a Public Sphere? If So, When? Reflections on the American Case. In: C. Calhoun, (Ed.) *Habermas and the Public Sphere* (pp. 143–63). Cambridge, Mass.: MIT Press.

Schlesinger, P. (1999). Changing Spaces of Political Communication: The Case of the European Union. *Political Communication*, 16, pp. 263–279.

Schorr D, (1991, July–August). Ten days that shook the White House. *Columbia Journalism Review*. pp. 21–23.

Seib, P. (2009). *The Al-Jazeera Effect; How the New Global Media Are Reshaping World Politics*. Virginia: Potomac Books.

Serra, S. (2000). The Killing of Brazilian Street Children and the *Rise of the* International Public Sphere. In: J. Curran, J. (Ed.) *Media Organisations in Society (pp. 151–171)*. London: Arnold.

Shaw, M, (1996). *Civil society and media in global crises: Representing distant violence*. London: Pinter.
Schechter, D. (2003). *Media wars: News at a time of terror.* Lanham, MD: Rowman & Littlefield Publishers, Inc.
Sinclair, J., Jacka, E. and Cunningham, S., (Eds.) (1996). *New patterns in global television: peripheral vision*. Oxford: Oxford University Press.
Solnick, A. (2002). Based on Koranic Verses, Interpretations, and Traditions, Muslim clerics state: The Jews are the descendants of apes, pigs, and other animals. *Memri*. Retrieved from: http://memri.org/bin/articles.cgi?Area=sr&ID=SR01102
Solomon, W.S. (1992). News frames and media packages: covering El Salvador. *Critical Studies in Mass Communication*, 9, pp. 56–74.
Somfalvi, A. (2005, September 15). Israel-Qatar relations warming. *Ynet News*. Retrieved from: http://www.ynetnews.com/articles/0,7340,L-3142774,00.htm.
Sparks, C., (1998). Is There a Global Public Sphere?. In: D.K Thussu, (Ed.) *Electrpnic Empires. Global media and local resistance* (pp. 108–24). London: Arnold.
Sontag, S. (1977). *On Photography. Penguin, London*
Sontag, S. (2003). *Regarding the pain of others*, New York: Farrar, Straus and Giroux.
Sreberny, A. (2003). The Global and the Local in international Communications. In: J. Curran & M. Gurevitch (Eds.) *Mass Media and Society*, (pp. 93–119); reprinted in Kelly Askew and Richard Wilk, (Eds.), *An Anthropology of Media*, Blackwell, 2002/3.
Sreberny-Mohammadi, A. (1984). *Foreign news in the media: International reporting in twenty-nine countries*, Vol. 93. Paris: UNESCO.
Stanley, A. (2006, November 16). Not coming soon to a channel near you. *Spiegel online*. Retrieved from: http://www.spiegel.de/international/0,1518,448850,00.html
Strobel, W. (1997). *Late-breaking foreign policy: The news media's influence on peace operations*. Washington, DC: United States Institute of Peace Press.
Sudweeks, F, Hrachovec, H. & Ess, C. (2008, June 24–27). *Proceedings of Cultural Attitudes Towards Technology and Communication*, Nîmes, France.
Sullivan, S. (2002, February 20). Courting Al-Jazeera, the Sequel: Estrangement and Signs of Reconciliation. *Transnational Broadcasting Studies Journal Online*,. http://www.tbsjournal.com/Archives/Fall01/Jazeera_special.htm.
Taylor, P.M. (1992). *Munitions of the Mind: War Propaganda from the ancient world to the Nuclear Age*. Wellingborough: Patrick Stephens.
Tisdall, S. (1993, October 5). *Mogadishu outrage puts Clinton in firing line. The Guardian*, Retrieved from: http://www.guardian.co.uk/world/1993/oct/05/usa.simontisdall1
Tischler, L. (2007, December 19). Al Jazeera's (global) mission. *Fast Company*. Retrieved from: http://www.fastcompany.com/magazine/104/open_aljazeera.html?page=0%2C2
Thompson, J. (1995). *The media and modernity*. Cambridge: Polity Press.
Thomson, A. (1992). *Smokescreen*. London: Laburnham and Spellmount.
Thussu, D.K. (1998). Localising the Global: Zee TV in India. In: D.K. Thussu (Ed.) *Electronic Empires - Global Media and Local Resistance* (pp. 273–294). London and New York: Arnold.
Thussu, D.K. (2006). *International Communication: continuity and change* (2nd edition). London: Arnold.
Tomlinson, J. (1991). *Cultural imperialism: a critical introduction*. London: Pinter.
Tuchman, G. (1976). Objectivity as Strategic Ritual: An Examination of Newsmen's Notions of Objectivity. *American Journall of Sociology* vol. 77, No. 4, p. 1066.
Tuchman, G. (1978). *Making News*. New York: Free Press

Tufte, T. (2000). *Living with the rubbish queen: telenovelas, culture and modernity in Brazil*. Luton: University of Luton Press.

Tumber, H. & Webster, F. (2008). Information War: encountering a Chaotic information environment. In . S. Maltby & C. Keeble (Eds.) *Comunicating War* (pp. 62–74). Suffolk, UK: Amira.

Tunstall, J. & Palmer, M. (1991). *Media Moguls*. London: Routledge.

Twentieth Century Fund, (1985). *Battle Lines: Report of the Twentieth Century Fund Task Force on the Military and the Media*. New York: Priority Press Publications.

UNESCO (1998). *World Culture Report 1998: culture, creativity and markets*. Paris: United Nations Educational, Scientific and Cultural Organization.

Usher, S. (2004, May 27). Al-Jazeera film storms US box office. *BBC Online*. Retrieved from: http://news.bbc.co.uk/2/hi/middle_east/3755553.stm

Volkmer, I., (1999). *News in the global sphere: a study of CNN and its impact on global communication*. Luton: University of Luton Press.

Volkmer, I., (2002). Journalism and Political Crises in the Global Network Society. In: B. Zelizer, & S. Allan (Eds.) *Journalism After September 11* (pp. 235–246). London and New York: Routledge.

Wells. A. (1973) *Picture tube imperialism? The impact of US television in Latin America*. New York: Orbis.

Williams, F, Rice, R. & Rogers, E. (1988). *Research methods and the new media*, London and New York: The Free Press.

Woods, I. (2008, March 25). Europe Move May End Seal Slaughter. Sky News. Retrived from: http://news.sky.com/skynews/Home/Sky-News-Archive/Article/20080641310427

Woodward, B. (2003). Bush at War. New York: Simon & Schuster.

Yin, R.K., (2003). *Case study research : design and methods*. Thousand Oaks, California: Sage Publications.

Yin, R.K., (2003). *Application of case study research*. Thousand Oaks, California: Sage Publications.

Zayani, M. (Ed.) (2005). The Al-Jazeera Phenomenon: Critical. Perspectives on New Arab Media. Paradigm Publishers.

Zednik, R., (2002). Perspectives on war: inside Al-Jazeera. In: Columbia Journalism review, 40(6), 44–47. Retrived from: http://www.allied-media.com/aljazeera/articles/inside_al_ja.htm

Zelizer, B. (1992). CNN, the Gulf War and Journalistic Practice. *Journal of Communication*, Vol. 42 (1), pp. 66–71.

Zelizer, B. (2002). Photography, Journalism and Trauma. In: B. Zelizer, B. and S. Allan, S. (Eds.) *Journalism After September 11* (pp. 48–67). London and New York: Routledge.

INDEX

ABC news
  on Bin Laden's Sept. 16, 2001 message, 56
  coverage of Al-Amiriya disaster, 51
  indexing hypothesis and, 129
  selection of, 120
  views on Al-Jazeera, 58, 62–63, 67
Abizaid, General John, 86–87
Abu-Gaith, Sulaiman, 71
Abu Ghraib Prison photos, 89–91
Accuracy in Media, 107–9, 110
Administration. *See* US Administration
Afghanistan war, media coverage
  civilian casualties, 47–51
  overview, 41–43
  US military actions, 43–47
Africans Together Vision (ATV), 19
Agence France-Presse (AFP-France), 14
Aidid, Muhammad, 28, 79
air superiority images, 43, 45
Akamai Technologies, 82
Al-Ali, Mohammed Jasim, 34–35, 85, 108
Al-Amiriya disaster, 27, 50–51
Al Aqsa Intifada, 32, 33, 37, 135, 136
Al Arabiya, 12, 86–87, 90
Alexa (2009), 2
Alexa Global Statistics (2009), 99
Al Hajj, Sami, 35, 108
Al-Hurra, 90–91
Al Ittijah Al Mo'akis (The Opposite Direction), 36–37
Al-Jazeera effect
  analysis of, 117–20
  description of, 3–4
  frame magnitude of, 45
  globalization and, 7, 11, 77
The Al-Jazeera Effect: How the New Global Media Are Reshaping World Politics (Seib), 3
Al-Jazeera English, in US
  Accuracy in Media's opposition, 107–9
  Al-Jazeera Arabic and, 102

cable providers for, 106–7
continued opposition to, 109–11
internet viewing of, 111
public relations for, 104
recruitment strategy, 102–3
US media response to, 104–6
Washington broadcasting center, 103–4
world-wide viewing of, 101–2
Al-Jazeera facilities, attack on, 83, 91, ix
Al-Jazeera: How the Free Arab News Network Scooped the World and Changed the Middle East (El-Nawawy & Iskandar), 3
Al-Jazeera: The Inside Story of the Arab News Channel That is Challenging the West (Miles), 3, 106
Al-Khofous border dispute (1992), 32
Al-Kuwari, Hamad, 35
Allouni, Tayseer
in Afghanistan, 41
arrest of, 35, 39, 108
Bin Laden interview with, 68
on civilian casualties, 48–49
on successful air operations, 44
Al-Mirazi, Hafez, 70–71
Al-Nasiriyah images, 74–77
Al-Qaeda messages, re-presentation of
Bin Laden videos, 56–67
CNN exposé, 67–72
overview, 53–54
US Administration's position, 54–55
Al-Qaradawi, 105
Al Sayliyah base, 32, 34–35
Al-Sheik, Ahmed, 87–88
Al-Shouli, Youssef, 41, 46, 48
alternative media websites, 94–95, 96
Al Thani, Sheikh Hamad Bin Khalifa
Colin Powell requests of, 54, 55, 60
political aims, Al-Jazeera and, 31–32
relations with Israel, 134–36
relations with US, 133–34
Alt, Robert, 86–87
American Morning with Paula Zahn (CNN), 70–71, 85
American National Election Study (1974), 127
anti-hegemonic media. *See* counter-hegemonic media
anti-ideology filter, 115
"Arab media is biased" frame, 80–86
Arnett, Peter, 50
Associated Press International (API-USA), 14
ATV (Africans Together Vision), 19
Atwan, Abd Al-Bari, 37
Ayoub, Tareq, 83, 91, 114, ix
Aysha (2005), 11
Aziz, Tariq, 10
Aznar, Prime Minister Jose Maria, 39

Babak (2007), 9–10
Baker, James, III, 10
Balout, Jihad, 74
Barak, Ehud, 37, 136
Barnes, Fred, 62
Baudrillard (1995), 43
BBC World News
in Afghanistan, 41
on Al-Jazeera office bombing, 46
Arab viewing of, 36
competition with, 18–20
low US ratings struggle, 104
Ben Gana, Khadija, 33
Ben Moussa, Mohamed, 110
Bennett, Lance, 42, 117, 126, 128–29
Bergen, Peter, 56, 68
Beschloss (1999), 139
Bin Jeddo, Ghassan, 34
Bin Laden, Osama
interview, CNN exposé, 67–72
messages, Administration's position, 54–55
September 16, 2001 message, 55
videos, credibility of, 56–67
See also Taliban; terrorist organizations
Black Hawk Down: A Story of Modern War, 28
Blair, Prime Minister Tony, 46
blogs, response to Al-Jazeera website, 94–95, 96–97
Boghossian, Dr. Boghos, 51
Bollywood, 16–17
The Boston Globe, 105
Boyd-Barrett (1997), 14
Boyd-Barrett and Xie (2008), 35

Bradley, Ed, 60–61
Brandchannel.com, 2
Brandi, Dianne, 43
Brokaw, Tom, 42, 58–59, 129
Brown, Aaron, 77
Brown Lloyd James (BLJ) PR agency, 104
BSkyB news, 102
Buckeye Captains, 104, 107, 110
Burlington Telecom, 104, 107, 109
Burman, Tony, 111
Burns, Chris, 109
Bush, President George H. W., 10, 28, 79
Bush, President George W., 46, 47, 56, 60
Byrnes, James, 137

Caribbean News Agency (CANA), 18
Carruthers (2000), 139
Carter, President Jimmy, 25
cascading activation model, 130
CBS news
  Al-Nasiriyah images on, 74–76
  on Bin Laden's message, 56
  bombing images, 43, 44
  coverage of Al-Amiriya disaster, 51
  praising Al-Jazeera, 58
  selection of, 120
  views on Al-Jazeera, 58, 60, 65–66
censorship. *See* media censorship
Center for Research on Globalization
    (CRG), 96
Chavez, Hugo, 19
Cherribi (2006), 33–34
China Central Television (CCTV), 20
Chomsky, Noam, 114, 126, 131
civilian casualties
  at Al-Amiriya, 27, 50–51
  at Fallujah, 86–89
  self-censorship of, 47–51
Clayson, Jane, 60
Clinton, President Bill, 139
CNN
  Afghanistan war coverage, 41–42, 43, 44
  Al-Amiriya disaster coverage, 50
  Al-Nasiriyah images, 74–76
  Arab viewing of, 36
  on Bin Laden's message, 56
  competition with, 18–20
  coverage of Tareq Ayoub's death, 83
  exposé of Bin Laden interview, 67–72
  global news perspective, 47–48
  Gulf War coverage, 27
  pan-Asian study of, 17
  response to Al-Jazeera English, 105–6
  selection of, 120
  use of Al-Jazeera reports, 44–46
  views on Al-Jazeera, 58, 62–64
CNN Live Event/Special, 77, 78, 87
CNN: Q&A with Riz Khan, 103
coalition of alternatives, 99
Cold War, 13, 24, 114
Cole, Stephen, 103
Columbia Journalism Review, 111
Comcast, 106
Communist perspectives, 81, 114
comparative analysis, 118
conflict mediation, 10–11
consensus, sphere of, 128
conservative perspective, 33–35
contextual objectivity, 38
contra-flows of news, 16–17, x
Control Room (documentary), 2, 103
Corry, John, 25
counter-hegemonic media
  Al-Jazeera and, x–xi
  beginnings of, 13–14
  information war and, 17–21, 113
  media imperialism and, 14–17
  war images and censorship, 27–29
credibility, of Al-Jazeera
  Bin Laden videos, 56–67
  conservative perspective, 33–35
  liberal perspective, 35–39
  loss, Al-Nasiriyah images and, 80–86
  political perspective, 31–32
critical perspective, in war coverage, 24
cross-cultural understanding, 11–12, 35–39
Crossfire (CNN), 36
cultural imperialism, 14–17
Curran (1991), 122–23

dailykos.com, 99
Daily Mirror, 46
Da Lage (2005), 32
Davis, Elmer, 24
Dawn News (Pakistan), 19
Dawson, Tom, 110

Defenders Council of Vermont, 109
Defrank, Tom, 42
deviance, sphere of, 128
Disney, 16
Dobbs, Lou, 88–89
dominating center, 3, 13
double standard, in media censorship,
  77–80, 113, 118
Duke, David, 34
Durant, Michael, 28, 79–80, 138

Early Show (CBS), 60
El-Nasser, Nasser, 135
El-Nawawy and Iskandar (2002, 2003),
  34, 38
El Oifi (2005), 32
El-Thani, Prime Minister Emir Hamad bin-
  Jassim, 135
embed strategy, Iraq invasion and, 73–77
*The Emerging Chaos of the Global News
  Culture* (McNair), 12
Emir of Qatar. *See* Al Thani, Sheikh Hamad
  Bin Khalifa
enemy's voice frame
  Al-Qaeda messages, Administration and,
    54–55
  Bin Laden videos, credibility of, 56–67
  CNN exposé of Bin Laden interview,
    67–72
  overview, 53–54
english.aljazeera.net
  implications of, 99–100
  overview, 93–94
  re-presentation of reports, 94–95
  Western internet users and, 96–99
Entman (2004), 125, 130
Entman and Page (1994), 130
Evening News (NBC), 78
Ezra, Gideon, 37, 136

Face the Nation (CBS), 65–66
Fahmy and Johnson (2007), 38
Fakhri, Ghida, 59
Falklands/Malvinas War coverage, 25–26
Fallujah battle, 86–89
Fandy, Dr. Mamoun, 85
Fast Company magazine, 110
FDD (Foundation for the Defense of
  Democracies), 62
Federal Communications Commission (FCC)
  guidelines, on Fairness Doctrine,
  81, 114, 128
Federal Republic of Yogulavia (FRY), 10
First World War media coverage, 23–24
Fisk, Robert, 83
flak response, to media reports, 45, 54, 115,
  131, ix
Fleischer, Ari, 57
Flournoy (1992, 1997), 10–11
foreign policy, media and, 8–10
Fouda, Yosri, 60
Foundation for the Defense of Democracies
  (FDD), 62
Fox News, 38, 39
  on Al-Jazeera and NYSE, 82
  on Al-Jazeera office bombing, 46–47
  bombing images, 43
  on censoring Bin Laden's message, 57
  discrediting Al-Jazeera news, 84
  response to Al-Jazeera English, 106
  selection of, 120
  views on Al-Jazeera, 58, 61–62, 65–67
Fox Special Report with Brit Hume show,
  61–62, 84
frame magnitude, 45
frames
  "Arab media is biased", 80–86,
    113–14
  defined, 45
  enemy's voice. *See* enemy's voice frame
  humanitarian, 5, 47–51, 119
  military, 5, 43–47, 119
  qualitative analysis of, 118–19
France 24, 19, 20
Fraser (1992), 123–24
Fratangelo, Dawn, 59
Frost/Nixon, 103
The Frost Report, 103
Frost, Sir David, 102–3
FRY (Federal Republic of Yogulavia), 10

Garnham (1992), 124
Genelius, Sandra, 44
Geneva Conventions, selective invoking of,
  76–80

Ghali, Boutrus, 10
Gibson, John, 62, 65, 66
Gillerman, Danny, 135
Gitlin, (1980), 45
global information order, revolution in
 counter-hegemonic global media, 17–21
 media imperialism and, 14–17
 overview, 13–14
global public sphere. *See* public sphere
global spread, of Al-Jazeera, 18
Globecast satellite carrier, 107
Goldberg, Jeffrey, 73
The Golden Age of War Correspondents, 23
government-controlled media, in Middle East, 35–36
GovTeen.com, 97–98
Gowing, Nik, 9, 46
Grenada invasion (1983), 26
Guardian newspaper, 38–39
Gulf War (1991)
 anti-hegemonic images during, 27–28
 civilian casualties, 50
 CNN advantage during, 62
 coverage, 130
 impact of war images, 138
 media censorship during, 26–27
 relations with Qatar during, 134

Habermas, Jurgen, 121–24
Haddad, Sami, 37, 59
Hallin (1984, 2000)
 on media professionalism, 123, 131–32
 study of war reporting, 80–81, 114, 126–28
Hamas, 34, 105, 108
Hannity, Sean, 103
Hastings, Max, 25
hate websites, 94–95, 98–99
Hawkins, David, 103
hegemony paradigm, 130–32
Herman (2003), 131, 132
Herman and Chomsky (1988, 1997)
 on censorship of East Timor massacre, 9, 114
 on corporate media manipulation, 122
 hegemony theories of, 125, 126
 propaganda model, 130–32
Hezbollah, 34, 105–6, 109
Hickey (1998), 131
historical background
 to anti-hegemonic war images, 27–29
 to attacking Al-Jazeera credibility, 56–67
 to international media flow, 14–17
 to Israel-Qatar relations, 134–36
 to US-Qatar relations, 133–34
 to war coverage and censorship, 23–27
Hoskins (2004), 73, 76
Howard, Ron, 103
Hudson (2005), 83
humanitarian frame, 5, 47–51, 119
Hume, Brit, 47, 84, 106
Huntington (1975), 25, 127
Hussein, Saddam
 Al-Amiriya casualties and, 27, 29, 51
 Al-Jazeera and, 34–35, 59, 85
 Al-Qaeda terrorist and, 71
Hussein, Uday, 108

indexing theory, 126–30
Indymedia, 96–97
information war
 Abu Ghraib Prison photos and, 89–91
 counter-hegemonic media and, 17–21
 first Al-Qaeda messages and, 55
 networks' views on, 58
International Commission for the Study of Communication Problems, 14–15
Internet, for global perspective, 99–100, 115
Inter Press Service (IPS), 13
interviews, with US media, 119–20
Intifada
 Al-Jazeera and, 32, 33, 37
 Israel-Qatar relations during, 135, 136
Iraq war, media coverage
 Abu Ghraib photos, 89–91
 "Al-Jazeera is biased" frame, 80–86
 Al-Nasiriyah images, 73–77
 Battle of Fallujah casualties, 86–89
 image censoring, 77–80
Islam, 33–35, 56
Israel-Qatar relations, 134–36
ITAR-TASS news, 13
"I want Al-Jazeera English" website, 104
Izarra, Andres, 19

Jakobsen (1996), 118
Jasperson and El-Kikhia (2002, 2003), 12, 45
Jennings, Peter, 51, 56
Johnson, Larry, 67
Johnson, Shoshanna, 74
Jordan, Easton, 68, 69
journalistic professionalism, 35–39, 123, 131–32

Kagan, Daryn, 70, 87–88, 89
Kandahar bombing (October 23, 2001), 49–51
Kedar, Professor Mordekhai, 37
Kennedy, Senator Ted, 90, 91
Kerry, John, 90
Khan, Riz, 103, 105–6
Kholeifi, Ahmed, 35
Kimmitt, Mark, 87
King, John, 44–45
Kiss, Bob, 107, 109
Knightley (2000, 2003), 23, 83
Kondracke, Mort, 61
Kosovo Liberation Army (KLA), 10
Kosovo War, 9–10, 138
Kristol, Bill, 65
Kuntar, Samir, 34
Kurdish refugees (1991), 9
Kurtz, Howard, 41–42, 63–64, 69
Kuttab, Ramallah Daoud, 37

La Nueva Televisora Del Sur (The New Television Station of the South), 19
Lauer, Matt, 59
Lebanon (1983), 138
legitimate controversy, sphere of, 128
Lexis Nexis news database, 1, 80, 120
Liasson, Mara, 61
liberal perspective, 35–39
Liebes and Kampf (2004), 53
Life magazine, 137
Livingston (1997), 9
Livni, Zipi, 37, 135
local governmental policy, media and, 8
Lou Dobbs Tonight (CNN), 88–89
Lupinacci, Ernest, 110–11

MacBride, Sean, 15
mainstream media websites, 94–95, 98
Manufacturing Consent (Chomsky), 114
Marash, Dave, 102, 111
martyrs (shahids), 20, 33, 109, 136
massacre, of Afghan civilians, 49–51
Maupin, Matthew, 78–79
MBC (Middle East Broadcasting Center), 32
McChesney (2002), 64
McCullin, Donald, 25
McGinnis, Susan, 76
McGregor, Brent, 50
McIntyre, Jamie, 45
McMahon, Collin, 69
McNair (2008), 12
media censorship
  in Afghanistan war, 42
  of Bin Laden's messages, 57–58
  of civilian casualties, 47–51
  double standard in, 77–80, 113
  in line with Administration, 67–72
  of military actions, 43–47
  war coverage and, 23–28
media frames. *See* frames
media globalization argument
  Al-Jazeera and, 11–12, x–xi
  contribution to conflict mediation, 8, 10–11
  influence on foreign policy, 8–10
  influence on local policy, 7, 8
  naivety of, 12
  overview, 7–8
media imperialism, 14–17
media, Middle East, 35–36
mediators, journalists as, 11
Mermin (1996,1997,1999), 118
Merryman, Russell, 111–12
methodology. *See* research methodology
MHZ networks, 111
Michalsky and Preston (2002), 100
Middle East Broadcasting Center (MBC), 32
Miklaszewski, Jim, 78
Miles, Hugh, 106
military failings, media coverage of, 44–46
military frame, 5, 43–47, 119
Miller, Erbring and Goldenberg (1974), 25, 127
Miller, John, 56

Mission Al-Jazeera: Build a Bridge, Seek the Truth, Change the World (Rushing), 3
Mitchell, Andrea, 56
Mitchell, Major Peter, 94
More than One Opinion, 37
Murdoch, Rupert, 102, 131
Musharraf, Pervez, 19

Naco (1990), 130
NBC news
on Al-Jazeera's NYSE expulsion, 82
on Bin Laden's message, 56
censorship of Iraqi event, 69
coverage of Al-Amiriya disaster, 51
selection of, 120
views on Al-Jazeera, 58, 59, 65, 66, 81
Neuman (1996), 139
news filters, 131
news visuals analysis, 119
The New Television Station of the South (La Nueva Televisora Del Sur), 19
New World Information and Communication Order (NWICO), 15
New York Stock Exchange (NYSE), Al-Jazeera and, 81–82, 114
New York Times, 104–5
Nicaragua incident, 128–29
Nightline (ABC), 102
Nightly News (NBC), 65, 66, 84

objectivity, 35–39
O'Brien, Miles, 66
O'Donnell, Kelly, 77
Office of Global Communications (OGC), 20, 55, 114
Oliver, Lidsay, 102
Olmert, Ehud, 135
Omaar, Rageh, 103
Operation Cast Lead (2009), 37–38
Opinionjournal.com, 98
oppositional media theory, 127
O'Reilly, Bill, 47, 62
The O'Reilly Factor (Fox News), 62, 85
Organization of the Islamic Conference (OIC) Summit Meeting, 135
Osgood, Charles, 66, 67

Palestine Hotel incident (2003), 83
Pan-African News Agency (PANA), 18
Panama war (1989), 26
Parsons, Nigel, 102, 106
Pearl, Daniel, 41, 53, 105
Pearl, Judea, 105
Pedelty (1995), 26
Pedrosa, Veronica, 103
Peer, Shahar, 136
Pellecchia, Ray, 81
Peres, Shimon, 37, 134, 135, 136
Peretz, Prime Minister Amir, 135
Peters (1995), 122
Phares, Dr. Walid, 62
Phillips, Kyra, 45
The Picture Which Shames US Army (Ridley), 93–94
pluralization, of ideas, 7, x
political communication, war reporting and
hegemony paradigm, 130–32
indexing theory, 126–30
overview, 125–26
politically unaffiliated websites, 94–95, 97–98
political perspective, of Al-Jazeera's credibility, 31–32
political science, view of media globalization, 12
pool system, of media control
adoption by US Government, 26–27
in Afghanistan war, 42
during Falklands/Malvinas War, 25–26
Powell, Colin, 38, 54–55, 60
precision bombing, 27, 47, 50–51
Press TV (Iran), 19
principle of good taste, in media coverage, 74–77
private commercial networks, 36
professionalised media, 35–39, 123, 131–32
propaganda model, 130–32
public sphere
criticisms of refeudalisation, 122–24
emergence of globalization, 124
refeudalisation argument (Habermas), 121–22

Qatar interests, Al-Jazeera and, 31–32
Qatar-Israel relations, 134–36

Qatar-US relations, 133–34
qualitative frame analysis, 118–19
Quetta bombing (October 23, 2001), 49–51

Racine, John William, 82, 93
Rantburg.com, 98
Rather, Dan, 51, 60
Readers' Choice Award, 2
Reagan Administration, 128–29
real-time satellite feed, 27
recruitment strategy, of Al-Jazeera English, 102–3
refeudalisation argument, 121–23
reformist government-controlled networks, 36
Regarding the Pain of Others (Sontag), 43
Reliable Sources (CNN), 63–64
religious network, Al-Jazeera as, 33–35
re-nationalization, 117
research methodology
  comparative analysis, 118
  inherent difficulties, 117
  media and title selection, 120
  news visuals analysis, 119
  qualitative frame analysis, 118–19
Reuters (UK), 14, 17
reverse colonization, 16
Rice, Condoleeza, 38, 55, 57
Ridley, Yvonne, 93–94, 98
Robertson (1992), 13
Robinson (2002), 9, 118
Rodgers, Walt, 41–42
Roll Call magazine, 61
Ross, Christopher, 65
Rumsfeld, Donald
  Al-Jazeera interview with, 38, 55
  allegations against Al-Jazeera, 34, 49, 85, 86
  on civilian casualties, 88
  pool system under, 42
  self-censorship endorsement, 78
Rushing, Josh, 102, 103
Russel, William Howard, 23
Russia Today, 19, 20

SABC International (South Africa), 19
Schorr, Daniel, 9
Schram, Wilbur, 14
Schudson (1989, 1992), 122–23, 131
Schwarzkopf, General Norman, 27
Second World War media coverage, 24, 137
Serra (1999, 2000), 8
Sesno, Frank, 105
Shalom, Silvan, 135
Shocking Images Shame US Forces (Ridley & Smallman), 94
Simon, Bob, 27
Six-Day War with Israel (1967), 84
60 Minutes (CBS), 56, 58, 60, 89, 132
skeptic zappers, 100
Sky News, 38, 76
Smallman, Lawrence, 94
Solomon (1992), 130
Somalia (1993) media coverage, 28, 79–80, 138–39
Sontag, Susan, 43, 53, 74
sphere of deviance, 80
Spitting Image, 103
Stenley, Alessandra, 105
Stephanopoulos (2001), 63
"stop Al-Jazeera.com" website, 108
Strobel (1997), 118
Strock, George, 137
The Structural Transformation of the Public Sphere (Habermas), 121
Sultan, Wafa, 37
supra-national perspective, 7

Taguba, Major General Antonio, 89
Taliban
  Al-Jazeera and, 39
  Bush administration and, 47
  in Kabul (Buddha statues), 58
  media coverage of, 44–45
  Western media and, 41
  See also Bin Laden, Osama
Taranto, James, 98
telenovelas, 16
terrorist organizations, 34, 38–39, 49
  See also Taliban
Tet Offensive, 24–25, 75, 127
That Was the Week That Was, 103
Thompson (1995), 122, 123
Tischler, Linda, 110
Tisdall, Simon, 28, 138

Today (NBC), 59, 70, 77, 81
Tomlinson (1999), 124
torture, US military and, 89–91
triangulation of sources, 117–19
Turner, Ted, 10–11, 62
Twitter, 112

unilaterals, 41
United Nations Educational, Scientific, and Cultural Organization (UNESCO), 15, 17
United Press International (UPI-USA), 14
The Unresolved Problem (Fox News), 62
US Administration
  media re-presentation of Al-Qaeda messages and, 67–72, x–xi
  position on Al-Qaeda messages, 54–55, 65, 114–15
  wartime news reporting and. *See* political communication, war reporting and
USA Today, 105
US cable and satellite carriers, 115
US Continues to Humiliate Iraqis (Smallman), 94
US military actions, Afghanistan war, 43–47
US-Qatar relations, 133–34
US war coverage
  anti-hegemonic images and, 27–29
  development of censorship and, 23–27

Vietnam Syndrome, 90
Vietnam War, 24–25, 138
The Village Voice, 103
Volkmer (2002), 11

Wadah, Khanfar, 34, 35
war images
  anti-hegemonic, 27–29
  development of censorship and, 23–27
  humanitarian framing of, 47–51
  impact on public opinion, 137–40
  Iraq war and. *See* Iraq war, media coverage
  military framing of, 43–47
wartime news reporting. *See* political communication, war reporting and
Watson, Paul, 79–80
Web and New Media, 112
Webby Awards, 2
websites
  Al-Jazeera English. *See* english.aljazeera.net
  attack on Al-Jazeera, 82, 93
  political affiliations of, 95
  re-presenting Al-Jazeera reports, 94–95
Weekly Standard journal, 86–87
Western global media hegemony
  background of, 14–17
  information war and, 17–21
Western internet users, 96–99
The Will of the Martyrs of New York and Washington Conquest, 70
Wolf Blitzer Reports (CNN), 67–69, 87
Wolfowitz, Paul, 86
Woodruff, Judy, 64
Woolsey, Lynn, 88–89
World Report, 10

yes satellite television provider, 102
Young, Jeff, 82
YouTube, 112

Zahn, Paula, 48–49, 70–71
Zayani (2005), 33
Zelizer (2000), 137
Zelizer (2000, 2002), 139